# ONLY TRENDS MATTER

## MATTER

A Step Change in Management Accounting

DAVID WILLCOX

Order this book online at www.trafford.com
or email orders@trafford.com

Most Trafford titles are also available at major online book retailers.

Printed in the United States of America.

ISBN: 978-1-4669-7296-4 (sc)
ISBN: 978-1-4669-7295-7 (hc)
ISBN: 978-1-4669-7297-1 (e)

Library of Congress Control Number: 2012923810

*Trafford rev. 01/10/2013*

 www.trafford.com

North America & international
toll-free: 1 888 232 4444 (USA & Canada)
phone: 250 383 6864 ♦ fax: 812 355 4082

# CONTENTS

# FOREWORD

## by Professor David Dugdale
## Bristol University UK

It is a real pleasure to write this foreword and a privilege to have been invited to do so. I met David Willcox, the author, when he studied for his Masters in Business Accounting, he was already dissatisfied with management accounts and his research showed that other managers were too. Nothing new there, you will say. However, David not only identified the problem, he had the skills, the drive and the power to do something about it. He wasn't just another student seeking an MSc to add to his CIMA qualification, he was also responsible for managing a multi-million pound business.

In this book David recounts his journey from diagnosing the problems in management accounts to their transformation into a document that became crucial to the management of his business. Some of the problems are well known. Management accounts often slavishly follow the financial reporting cycle and include comparison to a budget cast in stone many months ago. Other researchers and consultants have noted the absurdity of treating business results in this way and recommended the increased use of rolling forecasts and even the abandonment of budgets. David's analysis acknowledges these contributions but he has different focus: a new *presentation* of information based on graphical trends.

David's hands-on, practical experience permeates the book. His description of the dominance of financial year reporting, the pointless comparisons with out of date budgets, the obsessing with historical figures and the nonsense of "wiping-the-slate-clean" each financial year is obviously born out of long experience (and frustration).

He recognises that now it is more important than ever to make management accounting really relevant. Businesses are becoming more dynamic yet management accounts often provide impenetrable columns of numbers and irrelevant comparisons, despite the incredible advances in IT of the past twenty years. Something must be done!

This book provides a systematic approach that, if implemented, will transform information so that managers can actually use it to analyse business issues and track their efforts to make improvements. The key is graphical presentation of rolling twelve month totals so eliminating seasonal effects and revealing revenue and cost trends.

Simply adopting this approach would probably bring enormous benefits, but, working with the format over a prolonged period, David introduced further, new ideas and he shares these with the reader. If understanding trends is vital these trends must not be distorted and he shows how costs should be separated into those that are intrinsic to ongoing operations and those one-off and optional expenses that, if not identified, would distort trends and understanding. He approaches the issue not from a dry academic standpoint but from the point of view of a practical manager. What are the one-off expenses resulting from management decisions and unanticipated events? These are the "exceptional" expenses that would distort trend analysis and must therefore be separately identified.

When trend graphs are produced covering both historical and forecast data and cost trends are presented in the same format, managers have an extremely powerful, easily understood tool in their hands and David goes on to show how the presentation can be used in practice. He recognises the overwhelming importance of the net profit target and, despite their well-documented deficiencies, the importance and resilience of budgets in many organisations. The power of percentages is demonstrated to good effect as David emphasises the importance of cost structure trends and the need to take action when the net profit/revenue percentage is threatened. Empowering managers to act is more important than fixed/variable cost analysis and line by line interrogation of budget variances. And David shows how budgets can easily be incorporated into the graphical presentations. Budgets have many deficiencies but these can be mitigated when they are placed in context by easy comparison with actual and forecast results.

In the final chapters of the book David discusses forecasting and the use of non-financial performance indicators (NFPIs). Throughout there is a refreshing emphasis on practical applications. His examples show that forecasting should not be (just) about extrapolating trends but about identification of changes in the environment and concrete plans to deal with these. Only definitely agreed and authorised policies and plans should be reflected in the forecast and optional, exceptional items should be identified separately. On NFPIs he is clear that *both* financial and non-financial information is vital and he provides good examples of the importance of "getting the level right". Senior managers should be interested in (a few) top-level measures, not in the multiplicity of measures that are needed lower down the organisation. Throughout the book David's management style shines through: empowering managers to run their operations but within a well-disciplined and well-informed organisation.

Although this book has wise advice on budgeting, forecasting and non-financial performance measures these topics are, to some extent, incidental. The main thrust of the book is to persuade the reader that the presentation of key financial trends, in an understandable manner can make a vital difference to a business. This is a practical response to making sense of those tabulations of month, year-to-date and variance columns. It avoids discarding last year's data, overcomes the financial year fixation of traditional reporting and budgeting and switches attention from bickering over past variances to planning what should be done. This is a book aimed at managers and the ideas will have greatest impact where a CEO is persuaded and throws his or her weight behind the new presentation. However, *any* manager can ask for information in this format and accountants can start reporting trends. The technology is there. It just needs to be used and this book shows how.

# PREFACE

When I researched and developed the system for remodeling our management accounts it was not with the intention of writing a book about it, that decision came much later. It all started in 2001 when out of pure frustration with the time we wasted discussing *history* at our board and executive meetings I became resolved to find a better way of reporting financial results to our managers. We had to find a way of promoting discussions about the future, not the past and the management accounts appeared to be a good vehicle for this purpose. I had the germ of an idea but concluded the best way forward was to carry out some research; someone somewhere must have found an answer to this problem, there was no point in *"reinventing the wheel."*

At about this time I received a circular from Bristol Business School based at the University of the West of England, they were seeking applications for masters degrees in accounting and I decided to attend their recruitment night, I felt that this was a possible avenue to carry out the research required to solve our problem. The degree included a research methods module, alongside a dissertation. My existing accounting qualification meant the course could be completed in 12 months, part time, and to cut a long story short I was awarded the masters degree a year later. The resources of the University and in particular the support I received from Professor David Dugdale, my tutor, were of major help in completing the research. I learned a great deal over that 12 months, particularly about the widespread nature of the problems with current day management accounting, but I could find no direct solution to my dilemma; it appeared that if anyone had solved the problem of finding a way of transforming the management accounts it had not been widely publicized. It appeared that management accounts have hardly changed in content and format for 40 years or more despite the technological revolution that has taken place over that time.

My research questions were set out as follows:

- Can the management accounts help the board focus their attention on the key issues effecting future performance rather than focusing just on historic variances?
- Can the management accounts provide more help to managers by widening their time frame? Cut offs at the end of every financial year meant much valuable historic data was lost. An organization's affairs don't start and begin again at the end of a financial year.
- Can the management accounts improve the budgetary control process to provide up to date, realistic and meaningful comparative data and provide durable cost control over the life of the budget?
- Can the management accounts contain regular forecasts of future financial performance that consider current trends?
- Can the management accounts help the empowerment process of managers by providing them with a broader view of the business on which to base their decisions through more understandable presentation?

Although my research failed to identify answers to all these questions it did aid my thought process, my early ideas had developed and it was time to try them out. All in all it took another 12 months of trial and a further period of training our managers before I was content with the system. It became known by our managers as GAPP, Graphical Accounting Performance Presentation, and this term became common language throughout the company.

The system cured my frustration and addressed all of the questions mentioned above; our board meetings became forward looking, our forecasting regular and more accurate and our budgets relevant for longer. It was not long before we adopted the same system for our non-financial performance indicators and our sales analysis. To what extent GAPP contributed to our future success is hard to quantify but we did increase our profits every year following its introduction and there is no question that it improved our management processes; our decision making was faster and our strategic management planning reformed. In addition the manager's understanding of the management accounts was transformed, they could now tell, at a glance, whether their performance was improving or deteriorating and see their future challenges in the full context of the business. We soon learned that last month's performance, the main focus before we introduced the system, shrank in importance, *it was the TREND in our performance, historic and future, that mattered. This took priority.*

The business was sold a few years later and I decided it was time to move on. It was also an opportunity to fill the gap in available literature that I had identified during my research: a book on how to transform management accounts into a forward looking, easily understood financial report that would add value to the work of management accountants and, more importantly, instigate faster, more informed management decisions and better strategic development.

*Don't jump to the conclusion that this book is just for accountants. It is a practical book that avoids technical jargon and it details how to implement and use the system; most managers of any discipline and from any type of organization, public, private, social or charitable will find the content understandable and associate with the thoughts it contains. It is my hope that it might lead to ending a management accounting paradigm that has existed for several decades.*

# INTRODUCTION

Management accounts, interim accounts, financial statements, or by whatever other name they are known, are periodic profit and loss accounts and balance sheets produced during an organization's financial year. They are specifically adapted for the use of management in their day-to-day activities, and are used by all types of organizations—commercial, charitable, social, and public—in all parts of the world. They are the most ubiquitous financial reports in use today by millions of organizations.

They are not regulated or considered a statutory requirement, and they are not subject to compulsory audit, as may be the case with annual financial accounts that have to adhere to certain accounting standards. Nor do they have a prescribed regularity; they can cover a day, a week, four weeks, a month, and even quarterly as determined by the internal management. Neither do they adhere to any standard format; their design is entirely down to management.

The term "management accounts," as we will refer to them in this book, must be differentiated from that of "management accounting." There may only be one syllable added but there is a wealth of difference. The latter is a much wider term described by the UK's leading management accounting body and one of the largest accounting institutes in the world, the Chartered Institute of Management Accountants, as:

- advising managers about the financial implications of projects
- explaining the financial consequences of business decisions
- formulating business strategy
- monitoring spending and financial control
- conducting internal business audits
- explaining the impact of the competitive landscape

Management accounts are an important part of this spread of functions and responsibilities and they play a role in most of them. The regular production of management accounts is therefore an important and vital responsibility of an organization's accountant.

It is interesting that the term used for the most common financial report has no historic definition; key the words into Wikipedia and you receive the response *"The page 'management accounts' does not exist,"* yet the words are used commonly within organizations when they are referring to their regular profit-and-loss accounts.

The term *management accounts* has been used for many years. It is not clear when it was first adopted. It may have been created some time after the formation of the Institute of Cost and Works Accountants in 1919 in the UK. This was later changed to the Institute of Cost and Management Accountants in 1972 and later to the Chartered Institute of Management Accountants in 1986 (CIMA). The inclusion of the word "management" was therefore a later addition to the institute's name, which was perhaps a response to the growing use in the Western world of the term "management accounting," so it is possible that the term "management accounts" is around thirty to forty years old.

This book examines why current-day management accounts now fail to fully achieve their objective, and it explores how they can be updated to address the current dynamic, commercial, and economic environment that we find ourselves in today.

*It is staggering that management accounts are still presented in largely the same way as they were when the term was first adopted despite monumental advances in information technology and other accounting techniques.*

Criticism of management accounting techniques has been around for decades. These are the words of Johnson and Kaplan in their renowned book "Relevance Lost: The Rise and Fall of Management Accounting," first published in 1987:

> *"Today's management accounting information, driven by the procedures and cycle of the organization's financial reporting system, is too late, too aggregated, and too distorted to be relevant for managers' planning and control decisions."*

They go on to describe why modern corporations must make major changes in the way they measure and manage costs and how the advent of IT can assist in the cost-analysis process. Despite this book's acclaim, the key financial report in an accountant's toolkit has not changed.

*What are the most important criteria for management accounts?*

Accuracy, timeliness, informative, relevant, understandable, and prompt early corrective or improving actions—all these are important requirements; yet apart from perhaps the first in the list, there are serious concerns about the others.

In CIMA's list of functions, quoted above, the words "explaining" and "advising" appear in three out of the six functions, so communication of financial information, in an understandable and effective way, is a vital ingredient of an accountant's responsibilities; and the correct presentation and communication of financial results is as important as the information itself. Even the most valuable financial information can be useless to management if it is badly presented and fails to be understood by its target audience. In view of this critical fact, the style of presentation of management accounts and of accounting information in general is a subject that has received very little, if any, serious attention in management publications.

The research carried out for this book among line managers and board members identified much dissatisfaction with their management accounts. It was clear that if these were accounts for "managers" then they are lacking in a number of significant and important ways. In fact there is a strong argument that they are hindering and misleading managers rather than helping them. Consider these facts about management accounts:

- When presented, they are already out of date.
- They erroneously compare actual performance with a budget that as the financial year progresses becomes increasingly out of date; a budget fails to consider unforeseen events such as unexpected competitor activity, loss of key personnel, major product failure, disruptive plant breakdown, economic downturns, competitor innovation, and a host of other unforeseen happenings.
- They cumulatively cover a different time period every time they are presented, so there is no consistency from month to month.
- They usually fail to consider differing numbers of days in each accounting period (calendar months, bank holidays, etc.).
- They fail to consider seasonal factors.
- They disregard any valuable data from previous financial years.
- They give no indication of what might happen in the future.

To attach the word "management" to them implies they help managers do a better job but the evidence from the research combined with common sense and the facts above indicate otherwise. It can only be concluded that the inclusion of the word "management" is a *misnomer*; they would be better named "interim profit and loss accounts," and frankly these are of very limited use to managers.

Accountants often credit managers with having the same natural numeric skills and perceptions they possess themselves. This is a dangerous assumption. Managers suffer the same human inhibitions as most of us, they are naturally reticent to admit that they don't understand something, even when asked if they do and in many cases they don't realize that they have not grasped the key elements hidden in the figures; this can mean that the full implications of the information being presented are not appreciated by those that are meant to use it. Faced with a wall of columns and numbers, some managers, even the best ones, become bewildered.

There has also been much justifiable criticism from managers about timings; management accounts are produced at the end of an accounting period, or more accurately, a number of weeks after the accounting period finishes. At this point many managers regard them as about as useful as last week's newspaper. They are history and not helping them anticipate their future challenges.

Faced with these deficiencies many managers and academics have developed alternative ways of reporting essential results, measures that can be used on a daily basis to help them manage their department's operations. These are often non-financial measures that do not require the specialist attention of the accountant. These performance indicators have considerable value in managing the drivers of the business but they shouldn't stand alone; in the final reckoning it is the financial measures that stakeholders use to measure the organization, so these have to be high on the priority list of managers too. Current-day management accounts are slipping further down this performance-measure priority list as every year passes, and this disturbs the balance of measures necessary in modern organizations.

When looking back over a career in accounting and general management, it is hard to believe that it took me about twenty years to appreciate that there had to be a better way for accountants to communicate financial results to their managers. I was stuck in a time warp. Unfortunately most management accountants are still trapped in this paradigm. As a result the managers and board members relying on these accounts are stuck in the same paradigm.

A change in current practice is long overdue.

This revelation to me was finally prompted by a frustration over the time devoted to discussing history at board meetings, and the erroneous comparisons with budget that wasted so much time. This detracted directors and managers from focusing on the really important issue: the future.

Perhaps it is easier to talk about the past because the facts are less disputable. It is harder to talk about the future; it is more speculative, requires more imagination, and entails a combination of foresight, judgment, and business acumen. But more importantly it means managers have to commit to something almost intangible, and this contains the risk of getting it wrong with the consequent damage to reputations. Many shy away from taking risk despite the fact it is fundamental to managing any kind of organization; modern-day management accounts promote a backward-looking style of management. This book promotes management accounts that look forward as well as back, but the systems proposed provide the tools to do this more accurately and therefore reduce the risks.

The realization of this problem initiated research for a better way of reformulating and presenting the most common financial report, and this led to the development of a system to address it. The system and improvements that evolved have been tested over many years, so the ideas are not theoretical, the practicalities and problems have been worked out, improvements made, and the positive results achieved are real.

The system outlined is also aimed to complement, not replace, the use of non-financial performance indicators (NFPIs), balanced scorecards, and dashboards that are now commonly advocated so it will strengthen any existing management reporting systems. It is not suggested that it replaces these other new techniques. I admit, however, that this new approach targets the promotion of management accounts into the vanguard of performance measurement tools and so tackle this growing weakness that has been ignored for many decades.

*Management accounts should be a relative measure, not an absolute one.*

A monthly financial revenue result, a profit-and-loss account that we refer to as management accounts, should not be just an absolute measure of the moment, it should be a relative measure too. Unfortunately today's management accounts stop short of this relativity.

Accountants are often asked to produce absolute numbers; for example, "Can you give me a cost for this new product so that we can price it." That's an absolute value but management accounts should not be treated in this way. For example, "Last month we made $200,000 profit, that's $1,700,000 this year, so we are just ahead of our budget of $1,600,000."

Some might say that comparing actual with budget makes it a relative number, but this argument is flawed. These numbers are just the tip of the iceberg; they are "absolute" numbers, they don't tell us whether we are getting better or worse, or if we will beat our budget by the end of the year, or how this result will affect our performance next year, or which areas of our business are going to let us down if current trends subsist. A "relative" number would provide the answers to these vital management questions. "Relative" means how the absolute measure at this time is related to what has happened in the past and what is likely to happen in the future—what history tells us about the way we are headed and whether our forecasts are feasible.

A conventional set of management accounts usually breaks down the income and costs to date for the current financial year and this is where most of them stop, yet much of the critical information needed to convert them into "relative" numbers has already been produced, forgotten about, and discarded by most management accountants; they make the false assumption that it's history and no longer relevant. Such "absolute" financial results at a specific point in time in the current financial year are "relative" to this important but discarded historic financial data. When this history is considered, it can help to provide answers to the probing questions mentioned above. To achieve this, management accounts must utilize this historic data in a certain way. They will then be converted to a relative measure, and this adds considerable extra value.

The disappointing aspect of this simple fact is that this step change in the value of the same information managers are presented with can easily be made available if an accountant were to just *present* management accounts differently. The solution is as straightforward as that. Accountants are not required to create any new numbers or make any dramatic changes, just use numbers they have already created but in a different way.

If this applies to your organization don't think for a moment that you are alone. Recent research confirmed the scale of this problem: a survey carried out by Oracle in 2011 that questioned business managers from 1,500 organizations around the globe revealed that 82 percent suffer from a lack of visibility into their own organization's management accounts, which impaired their financial performance and the success of their businesses; they felt that this was due to large amounts of data presented in confusing ways. The survey revealed that half of the respondents believed that the situation created potentially erroneous business decisions. Professor Andy Neal, deputy director of AIM Research, which carried out the study for Oracle, said "Organizations today face significant challenges in extracting accurate information on profit and performance."

Another recent survey carried out by the Access Group, "Directors' Guide, Time to Reduce Your Profit Leaks," found that 88 percent of respondents acknowledged they had profit leaks, 32 percent didn't know where they were occurring, and 63 percent said that better reporting tools alongside greater visibility across the organization were the top two measures that could help to prevent profit leaks. These two examples are typical of other similar surveys carried out on the same subject. The simple techniques described in this book tackle both these issues (and much more) head on; it will supply greater visibility across your organization. You can also take assurance that it is a tested and proven tool, not a dream or an untested theory.

My own direct research also confirmed the findings of the research mentioned above, managers do indeed have trouble in extracting the information they need from conventional, *numeric* management accounts and tracking the changes to the cost/income structure of their organizations, which are key to finding the profit leaks. (NB the word "income" in this book covers all revenue on the top line/s of the profit and loss account)

The likely solution did not actually take long to find; in fact, during the research carried out it was the managers themselves that came up with the answer. The vast majority found graphs easier to understand than rows of tabulated numbers. The huge majority also said that the conventional management accounts they received were "history" in every sense of the word and they were of little use in managing their day-to-day challenges.

However, what appeared to be an easy solution at first sight turned out to be a harder nut to crack. This book will help those who choose to embark on this transformation in their financial reporting to avoid some of the same pitfalls experienced by me. It proposes concepts for the conversion of your numeric management accounts into a management report that will act as a catalyst for action that will make an important contribution to improving business success. The system could be described as illustrative management accounting and it has been described as a "crystal ball" on an organization's future financial performance. It illuminates management accounts in a way that conventional presentation is unable to achieve. The management accounts become a business reporting tool, as well as a financial reporting system, because they prompt questions into all aspects of an organization's operations. Imagine your vision through a window, constricted by condensation, when it is suddenly and dramatically improved with one sweep of the hand across the window surface. Suddenly there is a clarity and depth of vision not perceived before.

The system can operate effectively in isolation from other management systems, or the concepts can compliment, integrate, and enhance the potency of balanced scorecards, dashboards, and non-financial indicators, as well as reduce reliance on highly criticized traditional budgetary control systems.

Furthermore, your organization does not need to be large with a sizeable IT department to take advantage of the techniques outlined. Medium and small businesses, public bodies, charities—in fact any organization can implement the proposed ideas. All organizations, whatever their size, can benefit. Some extra investment of time from the accountants and the imaginative use of the IT skills they already possess will be required, and some time from other managers too, but the cost of this is money wisely invested.

There is nothing complex about the system proposed. It doesn't contain advanced mathematical techniques or radical accounting breakthroughs, it utilizes and applies straightforward statistical methods that all readers will be familiar with. All that is required is a break with a convention that has been in use, with little change, for several decades despite the dramatic breakthroughs in IT that have revolutionized business in so many other ways. But it also needs courage to change this age-old way management accounts have been presented. It is hoped that this book will provide the confidence to make this change. The pioneering work has been completed. The testing and trials of the system have been done. And it requires no adaptation; it can be applied to all organizations without tailoring. Some thought may be needed to the way costs are recorded and grouped, but little more than this. Nor does the proposed system entail risk, unlike some other new performance-measurement techniques that promote,for example, the abandonment of budgets with all its attendant dangers.

It is still a mystery to me why, in view of the simplicity of the systems described, it has not been adopted on a universal basis, because the ideas outlined not only help management better understand what the management accounts are telling them, they will also simultaneously provide a window on the future financial consequences of present and past performance that instigates prompt and early action to counter adverse indications. The statistical approaches proposed will raise questions about an organization that would likely not have arisen until much later had the management accounts been presented in their traditional numeric format. The system will certainly raise questions about the feasibility of any business forecasts or future budgets, and this new approach will also help managers to better appreciate how their individual cost performance is affecting the business; it also provides an alternative aspect on the question of so-called fixed cost.

All this will help managers to act faster, be realistic, and when used to full effect, the system will help them to develop better strategic management. It is, however, not purported to be a substitute for good management practice, innovation, or effective leadership; the ideas outlined in this book are not presented as a panacea.

But it will help your organization be more effective, and remember that in business efficiency is doing things right but effectiveness is doing the right things; this system helps to highlight those areas that need these "right things."

I reiterate that this book does not propose the replacement of nonfinancial performance measures (NFPIs) or denigrate the importance of measuring issues such as quality of service or product reworking, delivery performance, stock-outs, etc. In fact, the system will not only work alongside NFPIs that may be used to measure these critical business issues, but can also be applied just as effectively to them, with significant benefits deriving from a uniformity in presentation. In fact, ironically, NFPIs are already sometimes presented in a similar manner to the proposed system in many organizations.

As mentioned above, the suggested system will also complement scorecard systems, e.g. the balanced scorecard and dashboards; in Kaplan and Norton's legendary book 'The Balanced Scorecard," they make the point that building a balanced scorecard should encourage organizations to link their financial objectives to corporate strategy. I quote: "the financial objectives serve as the focus for the objectives and measures in all the other scorecard perspectives. Every measure selected should be part of a link of cause-and-effect relationships that culminate in improving financial performance." The approach to the presentation of management accounts presented in this book enhances the monitoring of performance measures selected under a balanced scorecard system; it will assist the association and integration of corporate strategy with financial measurement.

*But management accounts are still produced too late to be of help, so what difference will presenting them graphically make?*

How often have you heard criticism of the management accounts for being presented too late to be of any real value? Management accounts for any accounting period often take two to three weeks following the end of the period to which they refer. There have been thousands of initiatives by senior management across all types of organizations to shorten this period. Accountants have invested much time and money trying to achieve a reduction in management account delivery times and some have succeeded in reducing the period significantly. The problem is that the accounting "books" can't be accurately finalized until after the last day of the accounting period and it is not until then that most accountants want to begin the process of producing the management accounts; any earlier and they must contain guesswork, so by using conventional approaches, the faster that management accounts are produced at the end of any accounting period, the less accurate they may be.

The fact is that even if it were possible to accurately produce them the day after the accounting period ended many would still say that they are too late. They are still history. How can this be addressed?

Changing the management accounts to include a *trend* of performance is a massive step forward in improving their value and solving the "too late" criticism. Extending a predictable trend in the management accounts, especially for the following couple of accounting periods, can be a very accurate prediction of what is going to happen over the following few months; an examination of such extended trends within management accounts is therefore not so much examining history but telling management in advance what is going to happen at the end of the next accounting period and the one after that. *Management accounts become early rather than late.*

In addition, by utilizing additional data that will be examined later, a period in excess of twelve months can be predicted in advance. Of course, just extrapolating a graph well into the future without considering all the other known factors that might affect future performance is not recommended, but examining these extrapolations for the next month or two can be surprisingly accurate.

It is important to recognize however that while an accountant has sole responsibility for the recording and communication of historic results, this is not the case with budgets and forecasts, which are reliant upon the input of other managers. The accountant may have responsibility for collating and presenting these numbers but the responsibility for creating and deciding upon them lies elsewhere.

This is a major opportunity, however, for an accountant to apply his analytical skills to assist managers in this function; a process that has the benefit of involving accountants in all aspects of the business; it is an opportunity not to be missed for increasing the value of the accountancy function.

Using trends in this way not only removes criticism of the historic nature of management accounts, it also means they can no longer be accused of being too late. Even if it takes two to three weeks to produce them, following the period end, management can now examine what is likely to happen in the next couple of months with considerable accuracy.

Leading companies have already recognized the need for their financial reports to look forward, often managing their organizations using conventional and rolling forecasts as well as the actual historic results reported alongside the traditional budget presented in their numeric management accounts. This makes good sense but the additional benefit of using a graphical trend analysis approach to presenting management accounts enhances this forward-looking approach by combining it with historic trends. The ideas outlined in the following pages combine history, rolling forecast, and current profit-and-loss accounts within the same presentation. It will be seen that this tests the feasibility of the forecast and budget and emphasizes the urgency of any action that may be needed. This is a major advance on examining rolling forecasts in isolation of previous trends.

Ask yourself this question: do the current management accounts in your own organization lead or follow the key discussion in your organization's future? You will not be alone if you conclude that they have been of limited value. The managers interviewed during my research revealed that the management accounts were "down the list" when they were asked to prioritize the performance reports they receive.

These days the accounting press regularly highlights deficiencies in the value and contribution of the accounting function in modern-day business. How often have you read in the business press over the last few years the term "improving the value added of the accounts department," or the derogatory and insulting title "spreadsheet jockeys" when referring to management accountants. The phrase "only there to produce the numbers" has also been bandied around to describe "backroom" management accountants that fail to get involved in the depths and strategic direction of the business. Finally, the ultimate insult: "they're just an overhead."

A survey by PricewaterhouseCoopers almost supports these derogatory comments, finding that on average management accountants spend 60 percent of their time "gathering data" when investigation, analysis, and effectively communicating their findings—the value-adding functions—should be their main priority. We know from CIMAs research that many leading companies are already transforming their accounting functions to be more effective and provide better decision-making support. There have been strong recommendations that accountants should actively seek to reduce the time spent on gathering information and increase their "value-adding" time.

Too often the management accountant's role stops at costing, recordkeeping, reporting history through the management accounts, and other *ad hoc* financial reports when so much more could be achieved through analysis that uses the information, often buried in their accounting records, to look forward and effectively communicate this to management. This would lead to knowledge, currently only available to accountants, to be gathered, collated, and shared.

The system outlined in the following pages is a key to unlocking the secrets contained within the accounting records and management accounting system; these are a significant, underutilized asset to any organization.

Unfortunately one can only conclude that many accountants have not grasped the dynamics and accounting needs of fast-moving, modern-day business; their actions and financial reports are of limited value to the forward management of an organization. Radical change is urgently needed. Accountants have at their fingertips the opportunity of transforming the impact and value of the financial information they present to management, furthermore it does not require the development of new accounting techniques—we have more than enough of these—it is achieved by simply changing the way information is *presented*. The adoption of this approach provides a significant leap forward in improving communication between accountants and management. It can also open the door for management accountants to investigate every corner of a business, questioning the logic, the strategy, the assumptions, and the forecasts of their colleagues; and it will not only turn an accountant into a "business partner," it will also add to the satisfaction an accountant gains from the job. He may even start calling customers by that name instead of debtors, and start to understand that it's customers, new and existing, that drive growth, and that it is research and investment in new products and services plus intelligent marketing that can expand sales. This deeper involvement by management accountants in their organizations will generate a deeper passion for their business; the change in their *modus operandi* can be the catalyst that's needed.

If you are a management accountant wrestling with the problem of adding value to your role, then this book will provide a structure that can begin to transform your contribution, but you will still have to grasp the opportunities that it will provide, you will need to take the initiative. It will provide a tool to convert you from a historian to a foreseer, but like all new tools and systems it will only succeed if you take action by investigating, analyzing, and confidently feeding back what you find. Failure to act on your findings would be like having a bike for your birthday then complaining you're not any fitter when you don't actually ride it every day! I warn you it won't be easy, not all will immediately recognize the benefits that will ensue if the system is adopted. Some may just regard it as the next accounting or management gimmick, so you will need to persist. I was CEO when I introduced this system, and even though I had the power to impose it, I had to work hard to persuade the managers of the benefits it would bring.

It is always good practice for management accountants to have periodic meetings with managers to agree what they are looking for from the finance function—how else are they to understand a manager's problems and needs? It pays to remember the qualities of a good accountant:

> *To win the confidence of the management team, contribute to the strategic discussion, provide a balance of argument among the decision makers, be skeptical of ideas that have not been thought through in detail, drill down into the figures and operations and understand what makes them tick, analyze data and report effectively, objectively, succinctly, and fast; tell management what it may not want to hear without losing its confidence, have the courage to act on one's own initiative without instruction from the top, and use your function to warn or guide management about the financial consequences of the direction the business is heading—all guided by the strategic objectives of your organization.*

Accountants must see the writing on the wall; their future as valued members of senior management teams is not secure unless they start to add value, moving away from being considered an "overhead," the label unfortunately used too often to describe the accounting function, sometimes justifiably.

*Presenting financial information*

How much time do accountants currently devote to considering the best format for the information they *present*, a method that elicits the best use of that data and its comprehension by the non-accounting managers that read it? Probably not enough. Some don't even consider the matter at all. Before issuing a report, most accountants devote their time to finding and verifying that the figures themselves are correct, but this stops far short from fulfilling the responsibility of an accountant.

How much effort is wasted and opportunities lost because managers have not fully appreciated or understood situations and consequences that are buried in the numbers displayed in the management accounts and other financial reports. Remember that managers are not quick to own up to the fact that they don't fully understand the figures; on their own admission some very bright and intelligent managers admit they are "blinded" by columns of numbers. This doesn't make them weak managers but it does point to a weakness in the accounting department that allows valuable information to be squandered and fails to recognize when managers are not fully cognizant of the information they are studying. It is as if the accountant is using this mystery to demonstrate their skill and superior knowledge, even allowing them to exhibit a certain power over their peers.

Your organization's databanks and records contain priceless information that properly illustrated can be a driver to your organization's success, but unfortunately it is so often ignored.

Management accounts are the vital interface between the accounting records and management; the design of the report itself is therefore critical to management's interpretation of the financial measurement of business performance and no report should be issued before this issue has been considered. Over the last few decades, within the plethora of published material available to accountants and managers much attention has been paid to *what* information should be communicated but very little attention to the *way* it is presented.

Although this book will focus on the key financial report in any organization, it will also illustrate how the proposed technique can be applied to other financial reports and non-financial indicators too. The nature of the book also dictates a critique on the process of budgeting, a much-maligned business practice, and demonstrates how the system can assist more responsive, adaptable, and accurate budgeting. In addition it takes a new view on the nature and behavior of costs and dispels the myth of "fixed cost." The book will also investigate the absolute need for regularly forecasting business performance and how this process can be improved by integrating it with the management accounts and trend analysis.

The ideas I share with you were prompted by recognition, gained from my own experience, that the management accounts review at board meetings often led to long discussions about history rather than where the organization was going. While the management accounts are a key item on most board meeting agendas the ensuing discussions often degenerated into cross-questioning over historic adverse variances from budget, and these discussions often become a witch hunt (much to the suppressed pleasure of those not under the spotlight). Such discussions were also skewed and confused by the accuracy and appropriateness of the budget, but more of that later.

This is not to say that historic variances from budget should not be explained or corrections made where history indicates action is needed, but this is not the most important subject at a board meeting, where discussion should focus on the future, not the past. Present-day conventional management accounts do not facilitate such discussion, often to the frustration of all board members. It is why perhaps so many enlightened board members, tired of postmortems, have switched their attention to alternative reports that better address their business prospects and strategy.

The findings of the research among managers were surprising. The high level of dissatisfaction and the inferior importance rating given to management accounts was much worse than expected.

This research evidence was an indictment of present-day management accounts.

## The real value of historic information

Let's not denigrate the value of history too much. As we shall see, it has an important role to play. Not only can it tell you where you have gone wrong in the past and therefore guide and prompt corrective action, but properly presented, it can also help tell you where you are going—most would agree this is of equal, if not greater, importance.

While history should not dominate a board agenda, it can reveal historic trends, and with that comes an exposure of the rate of improvement or deterioration together with the widening of performance gaps. The management accounts can reveal all this when presented graphically, but it is virtually impossible to include this amount of information in conventional numeric format management accounts.

*When did you last hear about the vital role management accounts have in the formation of strategy, long-term planning, identifying key issues, and empowerment?*

In the last two decades the focus has changed. It has moved away from financial measures. On this subject, books and business publications have been dominated by the value of the balanced scorecard, lean accounting, enterprise resource management, enterprise performance management, KPIs and non-financial performance indicators, quality improvement, improving customer service, eliminating non-value-adding activities, and many other techniques.

These advances clearly have a place in modern business; each has something to say in their favor. The basic principle of many is that improvements in strategic management, value added, quality and service, etc., will improve market share and growth, and implemented successfully, the profits should follow. In principle this may be true, although financial control must be an essential factor in these various techniques; there is usually a very small difference between the sum of all costs when it is deducted from income received. It is very easy indeed to get the balance wrong however good the non-financial factors. Only financial measures can be relied upon when the balance is so fine. Dickens had it right when he wrote in David Copperfield:

> "'My other piece of advice, Copperfield,' said Mr. Micawber, 'you know. Annual income, twenty pounds; annual expenditure, nineteen pounds, nineteen shillings, and six pence; result, happiness. Annual income, twenty pounds; annual expenditure, twenty pounds ought and six pence; result, misery. The blossom is blighted, the leaf is withered, the god of day goes down upon the dreary scene, and in short, you are forever floored. As I am!'"

Who could have said it better than Dickens? And note the very small difference between success and failure, just 5 percent of income. For those unfamiliar with the old British currency of shillings and pence, it was legal tender before currency decimalization in the UK in 1971.

Many businesses actually operate at even lower margins than this, and only financial measures are capable of this level of control.

It must be right to say, however, that improvements in strategic management, service and quality should increase turnover, reduce costs, improve efficiency, and if properly researched and managed, increase profit too.

But beware, everything has a cost and paramount is management time. Some of the newer management and performance-measuring techniques require the introduction of new cultures and systems that can consume management time at an alarming rate, sometimes to the overall detriment of the business. In these circumstances it is easy for management to take its eye off the ball.

It is not unusual, either, for these new management techniques to be later abandoned, particularly when new management is introduced to an organization that wants to place its own stamp on the strategic control systems formerly adopted; this starts the whole process of change again, often to the dismay of the staff. There have been many cases where improper introduction or inadequate management of new business techniques has almost resulted in a company's failure.

Some organizations have adopted a generic scorecard approach, abandoning their budgetary control systems and ignoring the fact that each organization must design a tailored system that suits its own circumstances and strategic objectives. When approached generically it is often unsuccessful, again leading to disenchantment of the staff and eventually ending the project.

But these new scorecard techniques should not be judged by the failures, they can be valuable tools if used wisely and many have implemented them successfully. Their introduction, however, must not be underestimated. They require objective analysis and very careful planning, followed by close management; they also have to be "sold" to the staff operating them, and this step, too, must not be overlooked.

While some of these new techniques acknowledge the need to monitor the financial results of the strategic measures they promote, they fail to get down to the basics of how this financial measurement is *presented* effectively.

There appears to be a dearth of research or published material on the subject of management accounts presentation. This deficiency may well have contributed to conventional monthly management accounts slipping in rank among business reports. to the extent that they now play a diminished role in modern-day performance management. This is a failure on the part of the accounting profession. It has not identified the importance of updating the old-fashioned approach when preparing management accounts and ensured a modernization of practice within the industry.

In the final analysis, a board has to be primarily interested in the company's profit and financial stability than its non-financial performance indicators, its ERM system, or even its balanced scorecard; these are, after all, just the tools utilized to improve an organization's *financial* performance. Without good financial reporting, how can management know the value accruing from improvements reported in the NFPIs etc and whether the actions these measures have prompted have been worthwhile? A board has to concede that failure to produce satisfactory growth and healthy financial results can mean an uncertain future. Financial measures, and in particular the management accounts, must therefore play an important role in the performance measurement systems used by lower-tier managers, who are also ultimately judged by the company's profits/capital growth and/or viability; managers must ultimately use management accounts to evaluate their own performance. In view of lower-tier management's opinion of current-day management accounts this is all the more reason to improve their design and value.

Because the final accounts are therefore the concluding accounting measurement of an organization's performance, top management are obliged to cascade these financial reports down to lower management. This should promote financial measures to a driving force at all levels.

But my research indicates that lower levels of management do not place them at the top of their priority list, it confirms that management accounts have not adapted to fit new business needs or been integrated with strategic control measures; nor have they always improved to provide data of more relevance to the increasing dynamism of business and the markets. Fast-moving organizations need financial information that tells them where they are headed, especially in a world where instant communication and rapid change is the order of the day.

Of course there will always be a need for reporting past results; directors, managers, owners/shareholders, other stakeholders, and the Revenue must be aware of the historical financial results of the business. The interim financial statements in quoted companies are often needed by owners and the end-of-year financial accounts/statements are mandatory. This must continue, and much has been written about the form and information that these contain. This book is not purporting to change or comment on this practice but the guidance on the structure of presentation of this public information does not apply to management accounts. A management accountant's responsibility must differentiate these reports from the management accounts, which have to go much further than this.

Over the last two decades significant strides have been made in the development of new methods of costing associated IT and other accounting techniques, but the same cannot be said for the way financial information is presented to management. It is reiterated that in most cases companies present their management accounts in essentially the same format as they did thirty to forty years ago; a numeric table that lists actual financial performance of the last accounting period and the year to date compared to budget. These accounts may calculate variances and sometimes show last year's results; occasionally they may even show some percentages. Now and again they will include a forecast till the financial year-end, but all data is in a numeric tabular format, and as we have established this is not always understandable or of value to managers

Have your managers ever said to you "I'm just confused by all these numbers"? "Can you tell me what all these numbers mean?"

If you are an accountant reading this, what have you done to address these remarks? Have you just taken them as a justifiable criticism or treated them as a weakness in the manager? Evidence seems to indicate the latter and this is a mistake when by admission many good managers have a weakness with numbers.

### Historic information contains gems of information

Hidden among the mass of figures produced every month (or whatever accounting period you operate) can be found gems of information that pinpoint which direction the company is really heading, which managers are really (or not) performing, which costs are becoming out of proportion to income, and the feasibility of a forecast. Conventional management accounts fail dismally to pick out these numbers; they are simply not apparent in sets of numeric tables. This may have been good enough twenty to thirty years ago before the electronic and communication revolution when businesses were much slower to change, but it surely isn't good enough now.

The research indicates that this old numeric format, only depicting past results, is still utilized by the vast majority of organizations.

Some have argued that they compensate for this by producing separate forecasts and other reports, but when their practices are examined in more detail it is usually found that these additional reports are flawed; their forecasts often fail to consider the existing trends in a business and how they relate to the future trends they are forecasting. For example, when current financial year-end forecasts are produced they are too often guided by the budget for the remaining part of the financial year without considering the other critical factors. This indicates a lack of thoroughness. Present-day forecasting practice also seems to be infrequent and sometimes only prompted by poor financial results; often they do not follow recommended best practice, process, or frequency. It will be found that when professionally-prepared forecasts are integrated with graphical management accounts they become more accurate, and only then is maximum benefit achieved. This is covered in detail later in the book.

While spreadsheets and new IT packages for accounting and budgetary control reporting systems that first became commonly available in the nineties have taken the drudgery from the preparation of financial reports, vastly improved the manipulation of data, and facilitated a neat, slick presentation, they haven't changed the numeric format of management accounts. Latterly some software houses have developed new methods of computerized forecasting and budgeting systems that better communicate through company computer networks, but few, if any, have developed an integrated management accounts presentation that fully meets the financial reporting needs of today's businesses in a single report—at least my research has yet to find one.

The fact is that traditional management accounts have failed to take full advantage of these new information technologies and apply them to the growing needs of modern businesses.

Another factor integral to the management accounts is the budgetary control process. Over the last twenty years, we have entered a new era in business and commerce. Organizations can no longer rely on their markets and competitors changing gradually or remaining static and so allowing years to adapt to changes. The rapid growth of the economies and industries of the Far East, globalization, the Internet, the transformation of business through IT, and advanced methods of communication, all act as catalysts to change. Business environments are now fully dynamic but conventional management accounting practice has not moved to respond to these new demands. Organizations can no longer rely solely on the twelve-month budget to control and guide their operations and control their costs. Budgets fail to offer the financial controls for which they were originally designed; circumstances now change so rapidly that budgets are out of date very soon after their completion. Nor do organizations continually re-budget throughout the year; it is claimed that the management time devoted to this activity is just too long to make it a practical possibility, but where is the sense in comparing actual to budget every month when the budget is hopelessly out of date? Much has been written about the inadequacy of modern-day budgeting, yet most organizations still stick to the original age-old system of the annual budget. This practice is discussed in more detail later but in tackling the deficiencies of management accounts it is also necessary to tackle the presentation of the budget and its failings while accepting that the reason why so many organizations still persist with the annual budget is not because they are unaware of its weaknesses, it is because as yet no generally acceptable alternative has been found. It will be revealed how the implementation of graphical management accounting counters many of the problems with current-day budgeting.

We have now established that management accounts must progress from being just a record of history. Through the use of trends and assisted forecasting they can also become predictions of the future, revealing the feasibility of meeting a budget and the likely results beyond the financial yearend.

*The easy way to improve the standing of the accounts department*

The criticisms leveled at the value of the accounting function have already been discussed but it is worth reminding readers that there is no simpler way to begin to address the criticism leveled at the decreasing value of the accounting function than to improve the way in which management accounts are constructed and presented. What's more, these changes can be achieved relatively easily—no fancy expensive software, no massive companywide training initiatives, and no formidable and risky culture changes.

This book will introduce a template that will help management accountants down the value-added path, but it is a book for managing directors, CEOs, chairman, presidents, vice presidents, general managers, and many other managers too. It is a practical book that aims to be thought-provoking. It will help accountants and managers to either implement the ideas expounded or hopefully inspire them to find other similar solutions that achieve like objectives. The book is aimed at changing a paradigm, to get accountants out of the rut of numeric tabular management accounts, and transform their financial reporting into an essential tool that management will come to rely upon and value.

The content of the book requires no technical or accounting skills to read, and implementation is well within the experience and knowledge of a trained accountant with good spreadsheet skills. The ideas are capable of conversion into more expensive bespoke IT packages if that is the preferred route, as is often the case in larger organizations with multiple sites, subsidiaries, and international operations who may have the IT resources to design the software needed.

Although the ideas expounded have been tried and proven over many years by the writer in a medium-sized organization employing around 350 personnel, it is a template capable of adaptation to suit all needs. Naturally it can be improved—everything is capable of improvement—and I would welcome the further ideas of those who implement such a system where these may enhance the concept's effectiveness

A management accountant's role is to help his colleagues make better decisions through the provision of relevant and timely financial data. The concepts outlined in this book will considerably aid the accountant achieve this goal, and in turn be good for the organization by improving the value gained from the accounting function.

This could not have been expressed better than the words written by an ex-president of CIMA, Aubrey Joachim, following the completion of his term of office in 2010 and printed in the institute's monthly journal, *Financial Management*:

> "... the need for finance (is) to assume a broader role, not only supporting a business but also professional objectivity to ensure that risk and performance are managed in the long-term interests of all stakeholders.

*As the world emerges from recession, businesses need management accountants that can combine financial expertise with commercial knowledge. Why management accountants? Because they are the only professionals with a complete financial toolkit and the business understanding to use it. This kit includes the ability to provide a longer-term planning framework to ensure strong governance at board level . . . The toolkit also enables CIMA members to help their firms strike a balance between improving operational efficiency and developing their competitive positions. We can also play a key role in assessing the data available and filtering the information to inform all stakeholders . . . the real challenge is for us to get engaged by business to play such a role. This would advance the science of management accounting, perhaps not in terms of new quantitative techniques, but in terms of influence, which is more important."*

By changing the way financial information is presented to management, an accountant is afforded the opportunity to challenge and delve deeper into their organization's business. It will be a valuable addition to the "financial toolkit" mentioned in Aubrey Joachim's article.

However, the implementation of the systems outlined will demand a few changes that will affect all managers. Such changes can be achieved more easily if they have the full support of the chief executive and the board. The prize is large: forward-looking, predictive management accounts will restore their rightful position on the board agenda, and drive board members to address the future financial implications of the decisions and plans they are making today. This complements, not detracts from, any other modern performance measuring or strategic management philosophy already adopted.

The benefits of graphical presentation of management accounts and its advantages over the current practice of using a conventional numeric/tabular approach can be summarized as:

- Presenting past performance in a manner that provides a complete picture, a reminder of results compared to budget and previous forecasts, over a useful timeframe, *at a glance*. This clearly highlights which areas of the operations require focus and/or attention.
- Allows management to view how optimistic (or pessimistic) the budgeting and forecasting process has been and act to improve future predictions.
- The adoption of trend analysis adjusts for seasonal variations, smooth and put in perspective the impact of anomalies/abnormal, income and expenditure, which can otherwise distort month-by-month results, and provide a trend of historic performance that helps to foresee future results, and so furnishing an early warning of year-end and following-year financial performance.
- Provides a platform for more accurate forecasting and clearly indicates where forecasts are inconsistent with current trends.
- Prompt questions, many more questions than with the current practice of numeric presentation, about the direction the organization is headed, where costs are becoming out of kilter to varying income levels and over optimistic/pessimistic budgets and forecasts.
- Be more understandable to those managers and directors that often do not find it easy to interpret management accounts; some admit to being blinded by columns of numbers.
- Facilitate the correlation of non-financial performance indicators with their associated income and costs.
- Complement and enhance the effectiveness of all forms of balanced scorecards and dashboards.

- Reduce reliance on outdated traditional budgetary control systems, and if wished, act as a stepping stone to "beyond budgeting" principles.
- Can be used in any type of enterprise, public or private, anywhere in the world.

The ideas contained in this book are not complex. They are easy to understand and it is surprising that they have not already been widely adopted.

They will become a significant tool in the manager's armory but they do not pretend to be a cure-all. They do not replace inventiveness, strategic thought/planning, entrepreneurialism, lateral thinking, or innovation; nor do they eliminate the use of other non-financial indicators as you will see in chapter 6, but they will help to focus manager's minds on adverse trends and their future consequences, and this will prompt earlier action and better results.

The writer is not an academic; his career began as a management accountant but soon turned to general management. As managing director he has successfully led multimillion-turnover, international businesses in both the manufacturing and service sectors. He has therefore been on the delivering and receiving end of management accounts. It is from these experiences spanning three decades that the ideas were formulated, developed, tested, used, and finally succeeded in improving business results. This book describes the research and conclusions of that journey.

His research and the practical application of the resulting system was conclusive. It was time to treat conventional numeric management accounts as "history" in the colloquial sense. A new era in the presentation of management accounts is long overdue.

# CHAPTER 1

# How the Presentation of History Can Help You Predict the Future

As outlined in the introduction to this book the conventional numeric, tabular approach to the presentation of management accounts that has been prevalent for many decades is stuck in a time warp, no longer adequate for the dynamic environment that business and other organizations find themselves operating in today. Comments from managers gathered during the research for a better way of presenting these financial reports reinforced this. Some of these comments are repeated verbatim below:

- "What I really need to know is are we getting better or worse."
- "Management accounts are a sea of numbers and I don't have time to decipher them."
- "These columns of figures don't tell me whether I shall hit my target this year."
- "Management accounts are history, what we really want to know is how the future is looking."
- "They show a result of what I have done, rather than pointing me to the future."

- "They're too narrow a view, too historical and backward thinking. Not enough trends."
- "They don't show the consequences of anything you want to implement."
- "Looks mainly at how well costs have been controlled against the budget."

When the managers were asked in which format reports were easier to understand (graphical or numeric), the overwhelming majority said "Graphical."

These manager's comments were supported by my own experience; board meeting after board meeting was dominated by discussions about history prompted by traditional numeric management accounts with too much emphasis on examining variances from budget and intensive, time absorbing quizzing of the director responsible for any adverse comparisons with the budget. This occurred despite the fact that all knew the budget was several months old and that times and circumstances had changed; it was out of date and the "fixed" budget clearly didn't reflect this.

What boards and managers really need to know is what impact the implications contained in the accounts have on future performance and in what direction the company is headed, which parts are getting better and which are deteriorating. They want management accounts that not only tell them what their latest results are, but also point to the forthcoming critical areas that need attention; accounts that attempt to forecast what would happen if they failed to act and what could happen if they did.

This does not denigrate the value of historical or variance analysis. Carried out correctly, this is a necessary diagnostic tool, so long as actual results are being compared to a relevant budget. However, if management accounts could look forward and track the trends in income and cost then preventative measures and earlier action could be taken when adverse conditions are forecast. Trend analysis combined with reliable forecasting *foresees* shortfalls, rather than discovering them after they have happened. The early action this prompts can be critical to an organization's success

Transforming the management accounts to include these crucial factors is a major step forward in management accounting and the new routine encourages a forward-thinking approach that becomes embedded both in the minds of the accountant and the management. But it also leads to better cost control, monitoring of margins, quotation conversion rates, product and service sales cycles, optional cost decisions, and much more. When achieved this is *a step change.*

Led by the research, the development of a new convention for the presentation of management accounts identified a number of objectives:

- Any presentation of columns of figures to managers must be supplemented, if not substituted, with the same information presented graphically. This included comparisons with budgets.
- The addition of trend lines was vital.
- New-style management accounts must indicate what is likely to happen in the future as well as show the history. The inclusion of forecasts was critical.
- It was necessary to find an improved way of monitoring and controlling costs supplementing that offered by a budget.

These were simple objectives, but how could a complex financial document that contains thousands of numbers be converted into a set of simple graphs that would not only report historic financial results in the current year compared to budget, but also show trends in current performance *and* forecast what is likely to happen to the results in the future, as well as contain much more information about cost movements and structure than already shown in traditional management accounts? It was evident that this extra information had the potential of further complicating the report and making it even more difficult to understand than the numeric, tabular version it was replacing. Furthermore, this change had to be achieved without dramatically increasing the workload of the accounting department or incurring significant extra costs. All new ideas have to be sold to the receiving audience and this would be even more difficult if it raised costs.

The advantages offered by graphical presentations soon became clear; trend analysis enables a virtually instant view of whether a present situation is getting better or worse and at what rate the change is occurring. An added benefit from utilizing graphs is that two or more sets of numeric data relating to the same timeframe could be compared simply by using more than one data line on a graph. Including all this extra information in a set of numeric, tabular management accounts was just not feasible, but when presented graphically it actually became easier to read despite all the extra data it contained.

In addition it was possible, by using the same format, to better compare internal departments, products, salesmen, non-financial indicators, quotation conversion rates, and much more; the addition of trends to these comparisons revealed a whole new dimension. So much more information was revealed, it was difficult to believe we were looking at the same numbers as those in the numeric version.

During this process certain critical questions had to be answered: the time span of the graphs, how far forward and back the graphs should reveal, how the continuity of business from one year to the next was to be represented, how trends were to be calculated, how many graphs to produce, how to deal with extraordinary items of cost and income, whether inflation would distort the trends and critically how to monitor and evaluate costs when income was not as predicted or budgeted. The initial research, evaluating answers to these questions, putting the system on trial, coming up with the best solutions, and training the managers took around two years to complete, but it was all worthwhile. The results achieved were much better than anticipated and the whole team was *talking trends;* crucially our net results year by year following the introduction of the system improved significantly.

This book summarizes the research and describes the final system adopted. It will tell you how we got there.

## *Time Span of the graphs*

Consider the simple graph in Fig. 1.1 showing actual sales month by month for a current financial year that runs from January to December, a period currently in use by many organizations, but it could be any financial year whatever the start and end dates.

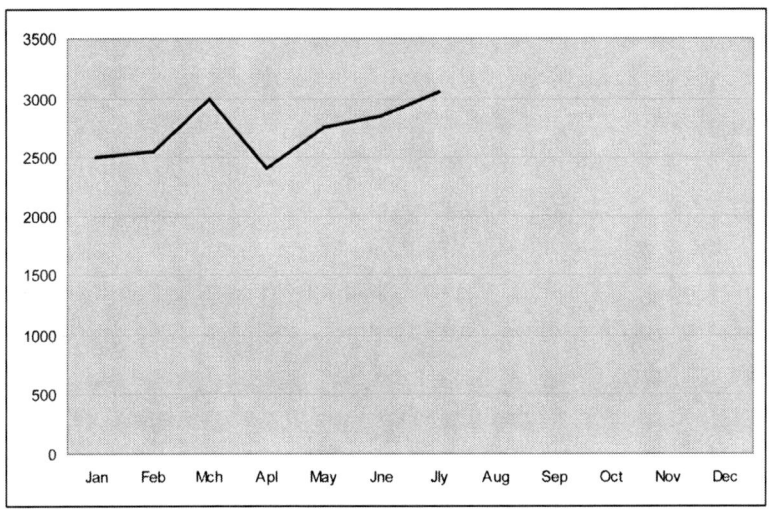

*Actual sales month by month in current financial year*

*Fig. 1.1*

This graph assumes that the organization concerned produces management accounts every month. However, the accounting periods could equally be four weekly or quarterly. It will not alter the theory, but for the purposes of consistency throughout this book the financial years will run from January to December, and the accounting periods are monthly.

Such graphs are probably in general use in many organizations for a miscellany of reports, although not usually as part of the management accounts.

The time span in the horizontal axis shown in Fig. 1.1 only shows the current financial year, and the figures it contains would be the same as would appear in conventional, numeric management accounts. They begin at the start of the financial year and report monthly and cumulatively each month until the financial year-end.

This financial year time-span convention omits any information contained in last year's accounts, thereby treating all previous results as history and no longer relevant. This means that there is therefore no consistency in cumulative timeframe within each set of management accounts; i.e., each management account covers a different time period from one month to twelve months. This lack of consistency in each report appears not to be questioned, yet consistency of presentation is considered an important criterion for performance measures—a contradictory situation that will be discussed in more detail later.

What can be concluded from the above graph from a manager's point of view? It shows the result month by month in the current year but not the result to date. Does this presentation allow management to see a trend? Does it help anyone visualize what may happen throughout the rest of the financial year or into the next?

Sales appear to be rising, but with only seven months of the year visible it is unlikely that such a short period can be enough for establishing a meaningful trend. Are there any factors such as bank holidays or seasons that need to be taken into account? Clearly more information is needed before any conclusions can be made.

In conventional numeric management accounts the only visible results are those for last month and the cumulative to-date total, each individual month is not visible. Any judgment of performance, therefore, can only be based on a comparison with budget and reliance on this is, at the very least, uncertain. The defects of budgets will be examined in some detail later together with their application to the trend charts.

But there are also defects in the graphical presentation in Fig.1.1. It is well known that when viewing a graph for the purpose of estimating a trend people are sometimes led to see what they want to see; there has been much research into this and we know from these studies that seasonal variations and exceptional or abnormal events can skew the figures; that gradual trends are hard to detect by eye and that people can be drawn to "outliers" and miss subtle changes. Outliers are those points on a graph outside the usual operating areas, usually caused by some abnormal event.

Any graph developed for the presentation of management accounts would need to address these known defects. Any subjective influences need to be eliminated because the consequences of misreading the graphs could be serious if they lead to wrong decisions by managers.

As a first step toward improving the picture, the graph could be extended in the time range so that a period of at least twelve months is visible. This would be the first step toward seeing a trend because it would include all seasonality.

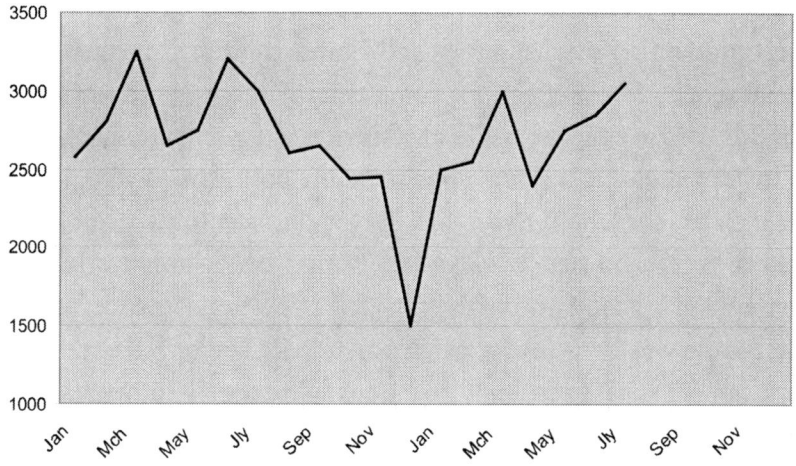

*Actual sales for the current financial year to date*
*and the whole of the previous financial year*
*Fig. 1.2*

The monthly sales values, to the beginning of the previous financial year, have been added in Fig 1.2.

It is evident from this additional information that the business portrayed by this expanded graph may have some seasonal factors; for example, Christmas appears to be a time of poor income/sales. However, it's not immediately apparent if any other seasonality exists. There appears to be higher sales during the summer months but there also appears to be a reduction in the sales trend last year followed by a rise in the trend after Christmas, even if the Christmas dip is excluded. It is not clear whether this post-Christmas rise is a recovery or a seasonal rise. Are sales really improving or is the rise simply one that would be expected following a seasonal dip? Could this just be an illusion? Was there indeed a downward trend in the first place? It is clear that the graph is actually raising more questions than it answers.

Within any organization it is usually well known whether seasonality exists; Christmas can be the best month in some retail businesses or the worst month for the building trade, which effectively closes down over Christmas and the New Year. Staff holidays can limit production over summer and Easter in many businesses, and the absence of customers, for some enterprises, over school holiday periods can be a factor, while for others, e.g. organizations operating in holiday areas, it is relied upon to be the best time of year. In some businesses, seasonality can be a factor on more than one occasion over a year; summer holidays and spring bank holidays lead to a consequent loss of working days, which affect performance; and then there is the weather, which can have an impact, prolonged winter snow for example. These seasonal variations will be well known to you for the circumstances in which you operate, but whatever knowledge you may have regarding the seasonality in your organization, it is plain to see from the seasonal variation in the graph in Fig. 1.2 that it is still difficult to visualize a trend using monthly figures only. If your organization has no seasonality this may not apply but there aren't many types of organizations like this, even the insurance industry, which may be able to spread its premiums equally throughout the year, may find that claims can be seasonally effected. Car insurance companies, for example, find that snow and ice in winter pushes up claims even though their income remains steady. Even many public operations that have "even" incomes through the year can find that costs vary during the year depending on the seasons: more flu in winter pushes up costs in the Health Service; treating road ice in the winter adds to the costs of local authorities.

## Establishing Trends

It is clear that if we are to establish a trend from the month-by-month graphs such as that in Fig. 1.2, it is necessary to find a statistical method of creating a trend that will eliminate any impact of the seasons and smooth the slight variations experienced month to month.

To consider seasonal factors when depicting trends, it is necessary to consider what happened in the same period in the previous year; building a trend from data taken only from the current financial year within any seasonal business cannot be calculated without complex mathematics and other compensating factors, so it is simpler and more understandable to use data from the corresponding months of the previous year.

This conclusion prompts another associated question that must be addressed before examining the most suitable trend-calculation method.

## The irrationality of current financial year only reporting for managers

Why, when businesses are continuous processes, do accountants persist in dividing their results into discreet financial accounting years and only presenting the current year in their management accounts? At the end of each financial year a line is drawn under its results and it all starts again from zero as if the previous year had not existed. The process has been simply mirrored to reflect the *financial* accounts (the end-of-year accounts for the auditors, shareholders, and the Revenue) without regard for the different needs of managers. Perhaps when management accounts were first created the needs of managers were much less. This could be true because these were the days without computers, the Internet, emails, mobile/cell phones or even fax machines, when Telex machines reigned and the excitement of the day was one of the new, exciting electric adding machines (if you were lucky) or an NCR accounting machine, which was the envy of many, akin to an enormous typewriter with rows and rows of numerical buttons and a long carriage that chattered from side to side and into which an account card was inserted and updated. Business was largely completed by post or phone and the pace of change was very slow by comparison with today. Management accounts then were largely drafted by hand and possibly copied by a typist for final presentation. Today's business life would have been impossible to forecast forty years ago and very little current technology could have been imagined, but management accounts now are *not* much different from the way they were presented then.

Once a year financial accounts prepared for the Revenue, companies' house, shareholders, and other stakeholders, which have to adhere to the financial year are fine, but a manager's accounting report needs go much further. What do current numeric tabular management accounts actually provide for managers? A comparison with the current month's budget, plus an accumulative comparison of a varying number of months as the year progresses. All know that the budget is out of date, probably soon after the financial year has started, and then will decline in accuracy as the year progresses. All this is then complicated by seasonality, thus the cumulative result does not accumulate evenly or in proportion to the number of months out of twelve. It is very difficult for managers to draw conclusions about where the results are going from such management accounts and it's impossible for them to forecast with any accuracy how the financial year result will turn out.

It's accepted that for some purposes a line has to be drawn in the financial results somewhere; virtually all organizations have a financial year-end and have to prepare financial accounts for all the other interested parties, but for day-to-day management purposes, adopting a proportional approach dictated by the financial year does not make sense. An organization's affairs don't end and start again at the crossover of financial years, so why should the management accounts portray it this way? Only including the current year obscures information and misleads managers about the direction a business is headed.

Management accounts were first established to help managers run the business better. They were a step in the right direction but little development of them has taken place since. Dismissing history can also introduce a false sense of relief that can be damaging; I have witnessed managers expressing thanks for the fact that a poor year has ended, expecting that a new financial year will bring a change of fortune. It is not a new year that brings a change of fortune, it is management action that brings about change, and being released from the truth of a profit-and-loss result by having the "slate wiped clean" at a year-end does not encourage fresh thinking. Managers and accountants should not be psychologically released in this way but current practice encourages it and this can be damaging to an organization. In reality the only important information for managers is which way the organization is headed. *Only the trend matters*, yet this is totally obscured when last year's result is discarded.

There is no legal obligation to produce management accounts that cover a varying number of months every month as an accumulative total or even show only the current year. It appears to be pure convention, a habit that has existed for decades, probably centuries, without change despite all the increasing demands on an organization that has relentlessly increased over this time.

Some may argue that management wants to see the result building up to that which their stakeholders are going to see at the year-end because that is what they will be judged on, but there is no logic in this argument. In conventional management accounts, at no time during the year is it possible to see a result remotely comparable to the year-end result until the last month of the year, when it is too late to do anything about it.

In fact where is the logic of producing accounts that show a progression of numbers where at no point in the year are managers able to numerically extrapolate the numbers to help them foresee what is likely to happen at the year-end because they fail to consider the seasonality and other factors that upset the uniformity of the numbers.

It is the duty of a management accountant to produce financial information that assists managers in doing a better job; confining a set of management accounts to reporting a purely periodic, one-month-at-a-time outcome for the current financial year when all know its shortcomings is not satisfying this duty, especially when the same information presented differently can provide a manager with considerably more.

Consider also how unhelpful traditional numeric management accounts are in the first few months of any financial year. Comparisons with budget are of limited value at this early stage of a financial year because it is common for management accountants to use the budget as the guide to what *actual* values to include in the management accounts. This arises because at this early time of a financial year the "end of financial year" workload combines with delays in receiving and processing new-year purchase invoices and end-of-previous-year adjustments. It is felt that the best guide to actual costs would come from the budget. At this time of the financial year, therefore, the budget-to-actual-cost comparisons are of very limited value. This is compounded by the fact that since the budget was probably completed at least two to three months earlier, it is probably already out of date; and if the business is affected by seasonal variations at that time of the financial year too then one has to ask whether any degree of accuracy can be relied upon, indeed whether such management accounts are worth producing at all!

As mentioned above, financial accounts for a defined financial year are necessary for the Revenue, the shareholders, the markets, and companies' house returns, etc. An end-of-year line has also to be drawn for auditors, allowing them to confirm that they represent a true and fair assessment of the results of the organization. These annual accounts, however, are of no day-to-day use to management; their frequency, format, and promptness (they usually take two to three months to produce) are all unsuited for management's consumption. Since they differ from management accounts in all these respects, there is no reason why the time period covered by financial accounts should influence that of the management accounts. It is also accounting practice that profit-and-loss accounts should assume business continuity, valuing assets and treating the business as a going concern; while widely adopted for the production of annual financial accounts it is also an important factor in the preparation of management accounts, this seems at odds with current management accounts time spans which assume last year didn't exist. Where is the continuity in this? All the facts point to the fact that it is bordering on absurd to consign the previous year's result to the bin when an organization simply moves from one financial year to the next. As shown in Fig.1.2 above, the month-to-month historic results from last year are still very relevant to the management of an ongoing business.

In a nutshell, *management* accounts have been led by the *financial* accounts, allowing the latter to define the period for which management accounts are prepared. This is in reality putting the "cart before the horse": the management accounts should lead the process and not blindly follow the convention for financial accounts. It is the needs of management, not those of shareholders and the Revenue, that must be paramount in management accounting; these outside stakeholders only need end-of-year totals, unlike management that needs financial results many times a year. The period for which management accounts are prepared should therefore be determined by this factor only; the financial accounts are merely a once-a-year summary of the management accounts, with the addition of end-of-year issues such as tax and annual reports, etc.

Accountants and managers need to escape from this mindset of month-to-month reporting for only part of a financial year. This paradigm that has persisted for as long as most of us can remember must be cast out

It is reiterated that business is continuous, so it should be measured continuously and a twelve-month rolling total system overcomes all the shortfalls of the present system.

## *Management accounts need a statistical approach*

My research among managers clearly indicated the need for management accounts to provide a glimpse of the future, and we have seen that this entails using a more statistical approach. The *Oxford English Dictionary* describes statistics as "the process of collecting and analyzing data, especially for large quantities of data . . ."

A nominal ledger collects large quantities of numbers but the conventional management accounts that are drawn from it are not statistical analysis. They are simply a summary of the credits and debits in a nominal ledger with a few adjustments. For example, the statement that our income this month is $1.76M and our income so far this year is $7.2M tells us very little about how the business is progressing or where it is going. This is merely a collection of the value of outgoing invoices or cash till receipts for the month and then the year to date. We make attempts to convert these numbers into a meaningful report by comparing them to the budget but we know that this can be an unreliable comparison to make, which becomes increasingly irrelevant as the financial year progresses. This isn't statistical analysis. Despite this, we appear to myopically continue the process; a practice still adopted, incidentally, by the majority of organizations in the world according to much research, which will be examined in more detail later. There is, however, one line on the budget that has more relevance than the rest and which usually retains its importance for the whole year. This line is the bottom line, the net result. Stakeholders may forgive any amount of variances from budget throughout the accounts if the bottom line meets or exceeds their expectations. Consequently it is this line on a budget that management are most interested in and perhaps there is a lesson to be learned from this, as we shall discover in the next chapter.

To achieve the aims set out at the beginning of this chapter there is a need for management accounts to be converted from being a financial statement to a more valuable "statistical" analysis.

## Twelve month rolling totals

It is clear that organizations are, in the final analysis, measured over a twelve-month period, their financial year, so this fact can be utilized by measuring *annual* financial performance continuously; i.e., twelve times a year. This effectively means that a twelve-month rolling total result is produced at the end of each accounting period

This does not mean, nor is it suggested, that management are precluded from or should not examine the result of the last month's accounting period and any variance analysis that springs from it; this will become more evident later in the book, but in the final analysis it is the gradual movement of the twelve-month rolling total that matters and whether this *trend* is moving toward the end of financial year targets. Under traditional methods of management accounts, no amount of analysis of the last month's result or even the cumulative result in a seasonal business/organization will reveal whether the end-of-year target is within grasp.

But the usefulness of trends goes much further than this. They can help tell you whether your forecast is feasible, whether your budgets are realistic, whether the changes you make to increase your returns are working, whether the timeframes for improvement are attainable, how your mutating cost structure is affecting your final result, and much more.

A twelve-month rolling annual total produced every month eliminates any seasonal effects, misleading "flashes in the pan," and human subjectivity that can lead to false optimism or pessimism;

when viewed on a graph, these twelve-month totals provide a window that shows a visual progression or diversion toward or away from the end-of-year goals. In other words, it helps to ensure that there are no surprises at the financial year-end. A trend will reveal which direction the result is heading and it becomes considerably easier to see whether this is toward the target or not, as well as revealing the *rate* of growth or decline.

There are methods other than twelve-month rolling totals that can be used to establish trends, but these can be complex and difficult to calculate. Some are also difficult to understand, which is a factor of considerable importance when dealing with management reports. The added benefit of twelve-month rolling totals is the direct relationship with the twelve-month financial year. It is therefore a natural choice, a simple measure that is understandable and easily explained to managers; one that accurately reflects seasonality and duplicates the financial-year period most organizations utilize. In addition, it is a method that can facilitate the usual management reporting cycle, whether this is monthly, every four weeks, or quarterly, etc. A twelve-month rolling total, when depicted in a graph alongside the previous twelve-month rolling total, also shows a trend stretching over thirteen to twenty-four months.

Rolling totals are not uncommon; they are probably the most widely used statistical method of evaluating stocks on the world's stock markets although in these cases they may be 200-month or fifty-month rolling totals that are designed to reflect election or market cycles rather than financial years. They are used because of their simplicity and their ability to smooth out short-term fluctuations with the aim of revealing the true underlining trend. They are probably the most widely used statistic in general use today and therefore a familiar statistic that most will have experienced.

Some argue that a twelve-month rolling total is slow to react to changes, and it is accepted that the twelve-month period of the total does dampen any monthly changes (from a visual point of view) but familiarity with this quality will soon allow a manager to spot the more subtle changes that occur and detect the changes in the trend of results using the steepness of the line. This dampening effect does have the advantage of smoothing trend lines and this assists comprehension.

The reason for this dampening effect is that in arriving at a twelve-month rolling total the latest month is added to the total and the same month from twelve months ago is subtracted. So the difference up or down can be quite small, in relative terms, to the annual total displayed in the graph; the value of the change is for only one month but it is being applied to the total for twelve months. There is a further benefit from this dampening effect, it lowers the impact of any temporary blips or extraordinary items in individual accounting period values (sales or cost) that might otherwise distort the trend and produce a misleading report. In other words, it significantly lessens the impact of the outliers that can deceive the eye.

As will be seen in practice, it requires a number of significant changes in the twelve-month rolling total to generate a significant change in the slope of a trend. In practice, more often than not it is small, consistent, month-to-month changes in the numbers and business circumstances, internally or externally, that are responsible for trend changes. Such changes can be difficult to spot in conventional numeric management accounts but are very clear in twelve-month rolling totals.

If felt necessary, it is possible to overcome this "slow to react" criticism by adopting a six-or three-month rolling total, but this should only be used where a business does not experience seasonal fluctuations. Also, while this approach will react to changes in performance more noticeably, it may not smooth any unusual fluctuations that can distort a result and otherwise be misleading. The other downside of shorter rolling totals is that their total can't be compared to the organization's twelve-month financial year, and as will be seen later this can be a disadvantage.

Whatever method of calculating a trend is used, however, the same principles outlined above can be applied. I found from years of experience following the introduction of this system and the application of twelve-month rolling totals that managers had no difficulty in seeing trend changes and that the benefits offered by using the full 12 months far outweighed any imperfections.

For purposes of this book, all trends are based on twelve-month rolling totals, which research indicates will suit most organizations.

Fig. 1.3 applies a twelve-month rolling total to the actual month by month sales performance shown in the graphs shown earlier in this chapter.

*N.B.: this shows the rolling total from January of the year previous to the financial year, which entails taking account of the month-by-month sales values for the year before that. These have not been shown in this graph.*

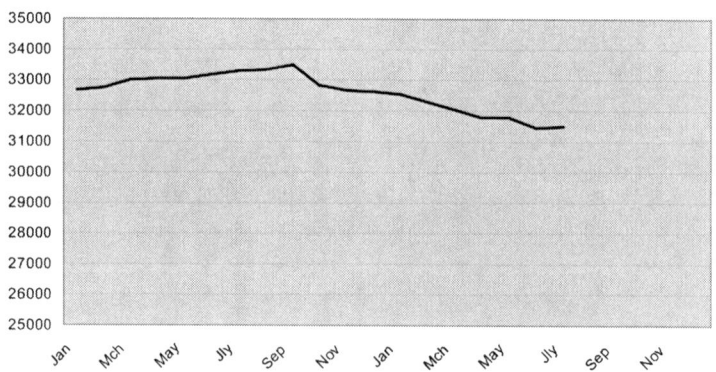

*Twelve-month rolling total of sales*

*Fig. 1.3*

*When examining the graph in Fig. 1.3, note that the vertical scale shows only the tip of the total value of annual sales (i.e., from £25-35,000) and this exaggerates the downward slope of the trend. It is common practice for vertical axes to be abbreviated in this manner and most managers will be familiar with the practice.*

This graph indicates a trend that, although it uses the same numbers, is not readily seen in the month-by-month graph considered in Fig. 1.2. In the earlier graph it might have been perceived that following a dip the sales income was improving. As can now be seen, this would have been an incorrect assumption; it is evident from Fig. 1.3 that since last October sales have been on a downward annual trend of around 7 percent (33500 down to 31500). It does prove the rule that the eye can deceive if looking for trends when plotting only monthly performances and this example clearly shows why a statistical method of reflecting a trend is essential. It is evident from figures 1.2 and 1.3 why it is likely that prompter action would have been taken by management to correct the position when viewing the trend than if only the traditional financial year-to-date figures had been presented.

## How far forward and back does a graph need to display?

The amount of history shown on a graph can go back as far as the manager needs. It is only limited by visual clarity, page space and what value the historical information has to managers. Generally the older the information shown, the less value it has.

In the examples shown above and throughout this book, graphs go back to the beginning of the previous financial year. This provides between twelve months' and twenty-four months' history in every monthly management account report, dependent upon the time of the year; clearly the later in the financial year, the more history will be visible. This time period is sufficient to facilitate a twelve-month rolling trend but also acts as a reminder of performance over the previous financial year and a better portrayal of peaks and troughs. For many this will provide as much useful history as needed, but if earlier history is required then this would be available once the system has been running for a few years by simply referring to previous-year editions of the management accounts. The period chosen, however, is optional and does not alter the principles outlined.

In this book, therefore, all graphs depicted will show only the previous year's history.

Graphs will extend forward on the horizontal axis to show the rest of the current year, and as we shall see later, the whole of the next financial year. It is evident that with conventional numeric management accounts the forward vision provided by the budget becomes shorter and shorter as the year progresses, and as the year-end approaches the forward vision virtually disappears. Budgets for the following year are not usually agreed until a month or two before the year-end, so the insight they may provide is not available until very late in the year. Even then the forward budget does not appear in the current year's management accounts when they are produced in numerical tabular form; this means they are never viewed in context with the current year's trends As mentioned above few organizations produce budgets for the following financial year until toward the end of each financial year, but these can be included in the graphs once they are completed. Forecasts however will have been visible on the graph through to the end of the next financial year, so overlaying the trend in the actual results. When forecasts to the year-end and beyond are included in the graphs, the absence of the budget for the following year becomes less important in terms of forward vision. The challenges and benefits arising from the creation of these forecasts will be covered in the later chapter on forecasting, but it is important to understand that the visualization of current trends, as depicted above, will help to substantiate or discredit budget and/or forecast trends for up to twenty-three months ahead. These forecasts will also be of considerable help when constructing any budget for the following year.

Using a three-year time span and overlaying forecasts and future budgets on the same graph, management never lose sight of the anticipated business result in the following financial year. This is a major weakness of conventional management accounts that give no indication of where the business is heading either later in the current year or into the following year.

*Should the graph attempt to forecast any further forward than the current year-end and the following year?*
Many organizations produce three-, five-, seven-, ten-year forward plans. And I have seen even thirty-year forward plans in housing associations that rely on long-term loans to finance their developments.

However, forecasts that look this far forward are usually sporadic, often accompanied by full business plans and generally created separately from the monthly management accounts. There is generally no attempt to integrate such forecasts with the management accounts on a month-to-month basis. Many deride such long-term forecasts as having little value and it is true that the further ahead an organization forecasts the less accurate it will be, but some types of business do need to plan much further forward than others. Much will depend upon the time it takes to develop new income streams; oil companies, for example, take many years to find and develop new oil fields; the nuclear industry several years to find a site, consult, obtain permission, and build a plant; some manufactured products can take many years to design and develop, take the aeronautical and pharmaceutical industries for example; and big infrastructure projects require lengthy consultation processes. Forecasts in these cases may have to be for many more years ahead and would not usually be integrated with the management accounts.

In view of the frequency of management accounts and the greater accuracy needed for shorter-term forecasts, a reduced period forward will prove more practical for the purposes of the graphical representation of management accounts whatever industry or purpose an organization is engaged in. The frequency of forecasts is a subject covered in the chapter on that subject.

From my experience, it was found that a period till the end of the following financial year was a practical and manageable timeframe that facilitated more regular forecasting.

When adding future budget and forecast trends to actual management account trends, the feasibility of the future plans and predictions becomes very clear. For example, if the current year's trend is going down and next year's budget or forecast is going up then an immediate red light is switched on. Any such change in the direction or sudden steepening of a trend line is a signal to examine more closely; such optimism is common, so this simple visual test is a valuable tool. There must be some consistency in the trends unless there are good reasons put forward for the optimism and firm plans or research to justify such trend changes.

Forward visibility of such trend changes viewed in the context of historic trends is an important characteristic of the graphical system and a major benefit of adopting this approach.

The vision of continuity and the future that a graphical approach provides is clearly missing in a conventional numeric, tabular approach. As mentioned above, graphs portray the capability to realize future budgets and greatly assist the production of forecasts into the following year.

It will now be evident how the inclusion of forecasts within the graphs will transform the value of management accounts.

To summarize, therefore, the graphs presented in this book will span a three-year period: the current year and the financial years either side. This will provide between twelve and twenty-three months' history and forecast. In my experience, this has proved manageable and adequate for establishing current trends and forecasts, providing timely early warnings of potential untoward happenings.

*How many graphs should be produced for a set of management accounts?*

It is likely to be impractical to produce a graph for every account in a nominal ledger or every line from the detailed pages of conventional numeric management accounts, which can contain hundreds of lines. This is not advised or necessary. There is, therefore, no standard number of graphs recommended. Every organization needs to establish its own requirements. The needs of a manufacturing company with hundreds of product lines are very different from a local authority, hospital, or retail operation.

In making the decision of how to group or divide income/costs when deciding upon what graphs to produce, there are a number of factors to consider:

- Differentiating costs by way of their behavior in relation to volume or income. This subject is covered in detail in the next chapter, but to give a simple example, it would not use the benefits of the system recommended in this book if a cost that varies in some way with volume sold was grouped with one that bears little or no relation to volume. For example, a direct material cost of a product included with the cost of refurbishing the factory. It will become evident and very clear in the next chapter why this is the case, and the principles of an alternative way of classifying costs
- Responsibility centers. As with any set of management accounts, it is important that some differentiation takes place that groups income/costs by an individual, branch, department, function, or product/service group etc.
- Manageability. There will be an optimum size for any final report (group of graphs). This will depend on how the reports are distributed and disseminated among managers. All this has to be weighed against practicality and usability.
- When it comes to income, graphs may be produced for each type of income or for each branch or each division or each sales person or any other profit/service center. It is important to choose sufficient graphs to highlight variations in income and gross margin type that may exist within a grand total. (It is easy to have individual product sales going down that are more than offset by those going up. This will not be revealed by only producing a graph for the grand total.)

- It may be wise to consider some graphical reports separate from the management accounts but whose values coincide so that they are directly comparable. This assists the "mining" process when examining variances and other performance issues. In my last organization, such separate reports were produced for each product range, about fifteen in total. These graphs covered the same timeframe and included trends for actual performance, budget, and forecast but also included the trend in values of quotations. This added trend line provided a useful guide in the trends of quotation conversion as well as an early indicator of a potential rise or fall in sales that assisted forecasting and impacts on production requirements. This may spark ideas on how the imaginative use of trends can provide you with a range of valuable additional management information as applied to the reader's own organizations.

## Dealing with extraordinary costs and income

It is important to examine the treatment of extraordinary or exceptional items of income or expenditure in calculating twelve-month rolling totals and trends. Such items may not only distort monthly figures, but if large enough may also distort a trend. Much will depend on the nature of the item and its value. There is an argument for taking "true one-off" extraordinary items below the line; i.e., shown after the net/operating profit has been struck to ensure that they are seen as out of the ordinary or one-off. This prevents them from interfering with the year's trading/operational result.

However, there will also be exceptional items that while unusual are not unique, just infrequent. In this case it is recommended that they be deemed to be part of normal trading and included in the result and the trends. Examples of such items might be the serious breakdown of a plant that requires major repair or an unexpected warranty cost that perhaps demands the recall of products. These may be unpredictable and only happen every few years, if at all, but their likelihood does need to be considered in any forecasts even if only included as a contingency factor in any budget. Discretion will be needed when considering the accounting treatment of these items and their inclusion in the charts, but then such consideration is probably already given even when including them in conventional numeric management accounts. It is a matter that needs to be left to the judgment of the accountant.

This subject will be examined in more detail in the chapter "Dealing with Costs."

## Dealing with inflation

Inflation takes care of itself in graphical presentation. In my experience over many years' use of this system, the need never arose to introduce any measures to adjust values to compensate for inflation. It is, after all, a fact of life and already fully reflected and accounted for within traditional management accounts and budgets. It is not extracted or treated differently. It would be expected for an income/cost trend to be gently upward to reflect inflationary price and cost rises and management will have a good idea of what adjustment to make for this when interpreting the trends. Price rises often occur at certain times of the year, and in the case of public organizations incomes are usually revised at a financial year-end. Such occasions would be reflected in the budget and forecasted trends.

In fact, the reflection of inflation in the graphs may assist the management with the timing of price increases. Such inflationary sporadic cost increases will become conspicuous in the graphs within the actual and forecast trends, and signal the need for compensating price adjustments. This can be of particular help where some costs rise and fall faster than others; this often arises in manufacturing industries where raw-material costs can be volatile, often dependent on world markets and its speculators.

The impact of these on variable costs is very quickly seen in graphical presentations, as we will see in the next chapter.

## Multilevel charts

Most organizations will be multi-product, branch, department, or service and one chart for sales income, for example, is unlikely to satisfy the needs of management. It will be evident to all that different products, services, etc., will grow at different rates; some will have reached market maturity while some will still be in the first flush of growth; some are likely to be shrinking while others are growing. In addition, many organizations will want to create mini profit statements for different product/service groups or divisions. Others may want to view sales and/or costs by salesman, department, operation, or branch.

This is simply achieved by producing separate graphs for each defined profit/cost center; these sub-charts are then amalgamated for the top-level chart, just as any such differentiation would be dealt with in a set of conventional management accounts.

When each of these second-or even third-level charts is produced showing the result against budget, complete with trend lines and a forecast of income and costs until the end of the following year, the benefit as a management tool increases dramatically.

Consider this analysis of the charts that may be found in a statistical analysis of management accounts. See Fig. 1.4. It identifies how net profit comprises charts showing trends in income and costs. Note how some boxes are shown in a multiple reports indication of the multilevel approach discussed above.

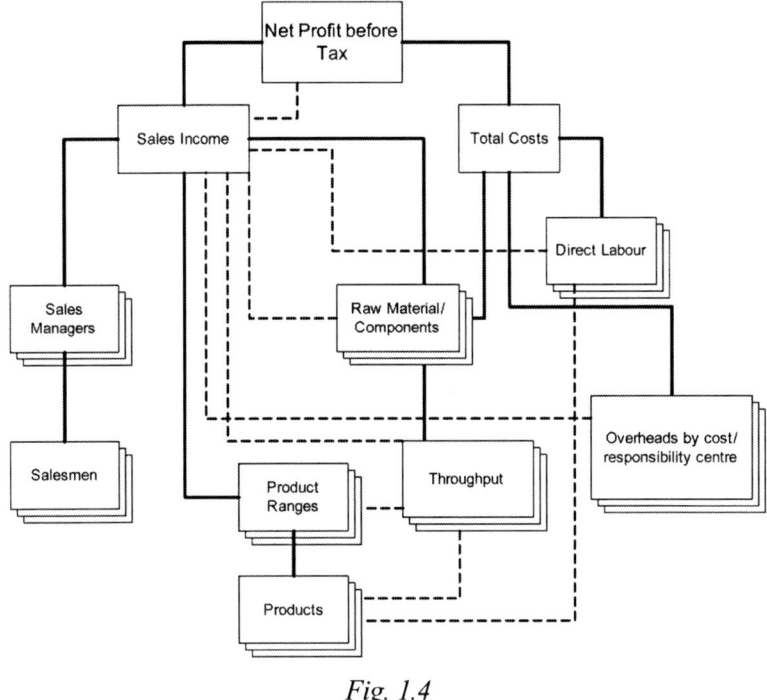

*Fig. 1.4*

The dotted lines on Fig. 1.4 indicate cost/income relationships, and as we shall see in the next chapter, this is a very important factor when interpreting the charts and tracking the constantly varying relationship between net profit, costs, and income.

In conclusion, it will now be clear that there are considerable benefits from the display of trends within the management accounts, forecasts, and budgets overlaid on the same three-year graph. By comparing past and expected performance, historic and forecast trends are immediately evident. Where trends have or are forecast to change, it will automatically raise the questions *why* and *how*. Not only do these trends test the feasibility of future budgets and forecasts, they also reveal the financial effects and timings of strategic changes and so assist in the integration and coordination of management accounts, budgets, and forecasts with an organization's strategic plans.

The simplicity of these graphical reports also makes it much easier for all managers, whether numerate or not, to understand almost at a glance whether a situation is improving or deteriorating.

The value to management, therefore, of graphical representation of the management accounts doesn't just improve its value, it also completely transforms it. The value of the early warnings given of likely performance gaps is invaluable.

Considering all the benefits of graphical presentation of management accounts and the simple use of twelve-month rolling totals that display illuminating trends in the organization's business, it is interesting to speculate why such systems have not been more widely adopted. After all, many non-financial indicators are presented graphically, ironically, because they are easier to read when presented this way. Some even indicate trends in performance. NFPIs presented graphically make it easier to monitor the process of continuous improvement, an essential aim of NFPIs. The same can easily be said about financial indicators such as the management accounts where continuous improvement in the results is also sought. With graphical presentation of financial trends, continuous improvement will also be visible in a better, more measured way. Indeed, if both financial and non-financial results are presented in a similar format there may even be possibilities of linking them.

So why are management accounts still presented in the same way as they have for many decades when such simple changes offer so many advantages?

Time is always at a premium for management accountants at the end of each accounting period and ever-increasing pressure has been applied to produce management accounts within a shortened deadline following the end of each accounting period. This is sometimes to the detriment of their accuracy and often leaves little time for the accountant to investigate anomalies and reasons for some of the irregularities that they contain, let alone also produce graphs. The conversion of numeric data to graphical format may have been just too formidable a task many years ago before modern IT systems and spreadsheets, but times have changed; IT has developed at a breathtaking rate over the last decade. All accountants now have spreadsheet technology at their fingertips and have become very skilled in its use; it is now almost an extension of their right arms. Spreadsheets will convert numeric data to graphs at the touch of a button. It is accepted that there is the time to set up the new system, insert all the formulae into a spreadsheet, but the return on that invested time can be significant.

If time is short at the month end there is no reason why the graphs should not follow on after the numeric version; there is also the option of limiting the number of graphs to the headline pages to begin with and the detailed pages later. Alternatively it may be acceptable for graphs to be produced every two months or even quarterly, although anything less than this will substantially reduce the benefit of the system and the reaction time to any predicted adverse trends.

The point made earlier in this chapter, however, is worth repeating: at the end of each accounting period the graphs for turnover, net profit, and the various costs will indicate improving, deteriorating, or flat trends in actual performance. In my experience, unless something weighty arises or any dramatic management action has taken place, these trends will take months to turn significantly. It is therefore not difficult to predict the likely twelve-month rolling result for the following two to three months with some degree of accuracy. This means that rather than waiting for two to three weeks for the result at the end of an accounting period, management is receiving advance notice of it with some degree of reliability. This releases pressure from the production of management accounts at the end of each accounting period and so releases time to convert them into graphical format.

Larger organizations may prefer to follow the route of bespoke software that integrates with their current accounting systems, and this can greatly shorten the end-of-month time requirements.

At the time of writing, no software packages that fulfill all the proposals outlined in this book have been located. However, the writer introduced a system very similar to that proposed in this book into a company with thousands of product lines and a staff of over 350 persons. This was completed using standard spreadsheet software by the existing management accountants, no additional staff was required. This is evidence of what can be achieved with standard software already available and in regular current use by existing accounting personnel. This involved no extra cost to the company but proved to be a massive advance. The benefits were found to be so considerable that within a very short space of time the numeric version of the management accounts was almost made redundant; it became a document referred to only when some detail was required and as prompted by the charts.

The value of the graphs at a board meeting is also significant, and all efforts should be made to ensure their availability for these policy-setting meetings. They turn a backward-looking meeting into a forward-planning meeting. The questions change radically from

"What caused this variance in our costs last month?" to "What are we going to do about changing this trend? If it continues, we will miss our targets this year."

This is a giant step forward, facilitated by a simple improvement in the way financial information is presented. There is no extra data here save for a forecast that you may be omitting at present. It is just better use of the data you already have.

# CHAPTER 2

# New Ways of Categorizing Costs

For thousands of years, probably since man first had paper and pen to write with, enterprises have recorded by type of expense the costs they incur during the course of their business. It is a natural thing for a businessman to do; all managers need to know how much has been spent on each cost type, and over a course of time, set these off against the income earned, so revealing their surplus or deficit.

This historic practice is no different today. Most organizations still accumulate costs by type as they are incurred, although for some time "like" costs have been recorded independently in a ledger, commonly termed *nominal* or *general ledger*. Following this, the same practice of extracting the costs and income to produce a profit-and-loss account is largely the same.

It is also likely that in history, just as now, attempts have been made to express costs in the form of a relationship with the income they refer to. In other words, how they vary with income and volume, although this is often completed outside the profit-and-loss account. This chapter examines these cost/income relationships in more detail and takes a fresh look at the division and type of cost. This analysis assists the production of meaningful trends, and it focuses on differentiating optional and unexpected costs from those that are necessary.

The term "ledger" probably conjures up a vision of a large leather-bound book, and until relatively recently, in historical terms, this is usually what it was. These days most organizations keep these records electronically and many IT packages exist for this purpose.

These ledgers contain all financial transactions carried out by an organization, whether these are subject to credit or cash payments or receipts, and they include revenue and capital items. It is still the base for the production of modern-day management accounts.

Although costs will have been recorded by type for a millennia or more, as far as we know it's only in the last 700-800 years that the concept of there being two sides to every transaction has been demonstrated within the nominal ledger, the system known as double-entry bookkeeping.

This system, which treats a business as a separate entity from its owner/s, was first described in a published book in the fifteenth century by a monk named Pacioli. Treating the enterprise as a separate entity facilitates the double-entry principle. For example, if the owner of an enterprise invests £100 then the enterprise has a creditor (the owner) and £100 in the bank, so a credit and debit in the nominal ledger respectively is recorded. Every transaction the enterprise completes is recorded twice in the same way, hence, double-entered.

If you don't know the history of double-entry bookkeeping, it can be found in the box below. What is remarkable is that the practice has subsisted for several hundred years without change. In accounting history there is evidence that many techniques have survived virtually unchanged for centuries. Some are more durable and just as applicable today. Profit-and-loss accounts in their present form, however, is not one of these; they have gone beyond their sell-by date.

*Frater Luca Bartolomes Pacioli is widely credited with the invention of double-entry bookkeeping, and indeed he wrote and published a book that explains the principle in 1494. However, pieces of a Florentine banker's account book dated 1211 show the earliest evidence of a system of double-entry bookkeeping.*

*It was therefore some 300 years later that Pacioli, an Italian monk, recognised that a double-entry system was commonly used in Venice and within his book, "Summa," he wrote, "we describe the system used in Venice," so it is clear he doesn't claim he actually invented it. In fact, we can only surmise that the system had actually been in increasing use over this 300-year period.*

*More recently a manuscript was unearthed; it's written in Italian and dated 1458, so preceding Pacioli's book, and is attributed to a man named Benedetto Cotrugli. He was actually born in Dubrovnik, Croatia, in 1416 and lived in Northern Italy; he was a merchant by profession. This manuscript documents a set of rules for keeping business records that are, in essense, still used today. The manuscript sets out a more detailed description of double-entry bookkeeping than was finally found in his book, "Book on the Art of Trade," published in 1573. His misfortune was that he did not publish the book himself in his lifetime, when he may have stolen the march on Pacioli.*

*Pacioli also talks of the trial balance (*summa summarium*). He says "debit amounts from the ledger are listed on the left side of the balance sheet and credits on the right. The two totals' equal, the old ledger is considered balanced." If not, he says, "that would indicate a mistake in your ledger, which mistake you will have to look for diligently with the industry and intelligence God gave you." This will ring true with the older generation accountants among you; many an hour has been spent, often well into the night, seeking errors in a trial balances.*

It can only be presumed that the practice of double-entry bookkeeping was devised, and caught on, because it acts as a useful check on the accuracy of the recording of the transactions it contains (Total debit balances equal total credit balances, unless a mistake has been made.). It would be expected that the format of the "ledgers" described in Pacioli's and Cotrugi's books have changed little since then. We may have moved from big books to electronic means of recording transactions but the principle of debits on the left and credits on the right still remains. No doubt the accounts within the ledger in Pacioli's time also grouped expenses and income by types with a separate account for each.

## *From recording costs to the use of costing systems*

It does not appear to be a big step from the system of double-entry bookkeeping to the creation of costing systems, but David Solomons in his often quoted and seminal article, 'The historical development of costing" (1952) contained within the book 'Studies in Costing," concludes that the last 500 years of accounting literature was mainly concerned with bookkeeping, not costing. ". . . (The) broader issue of making the accounting records mean something, of making them flexible and capable of providing information that would be significant, not for one purpose (say the measurement of profit and loss) or two (say, in addition the fixing of selling prices) but for any of the purposes which in modern business figures may be called upon to serve."

From this he means that the subject of "costing" is missing from these historic texts.

However, in a more recent article published in the *Accounting Historians Journal* in June, 2007 ("Early Cost Accounting Practices and Private Ownership 1745-1747: the Silk Factory Company of Portugal," Rodrigues, Lima, and Russell), it describes an example of cost-accounting practice in Portugal that explores the integration of cost and financial accounting systems within a double-entry accounting framework. It reveals that the company had used job-order product costing with allocations of overhead costs, allowances for wastage and shrinkage, and elements of rudimentary standard costing. Much of this practice is still used today. It is hard to believe that this is the only example of double-entry records leading to forms of costing over these centuries—we have just not yet found the evidence.

It is also interesting to note that despite the birth of the Industrial Revolution in Britain, which should have demanded an imaginative development of costing systems, very little was written on the subject in England up to the late 1870s; this paucity of material was amended with the publication of Garcke and Fells' "Factory Accounts" 1887, the first British textbook on the subject.

Solomon's research identified that much of the later initiatives in the development of costing techniques came from the USA and from engineering journals in the early part of the twentieth century; this would have been driven by the massive growth of industry in the US at that time, although notable that costing was driven by engineers not accountants. All this fits with the formation in the UK of the Institute of Cost and Works Accountants in 1919, now known as the Chartered Institute of Management Accountants.

Kaplan and Johnson (1987) tell us that by 1925 "virtually all management accounting practices in use today had been developed," although a list of accounting literature compiled by Boyne around 1996, covering the period 1887-1952, concludes that accountants had been active in the development of a wide range of costing and budgetary control matters over this period. Just how many were really "new" is clearly a moot point.

All these examples indicate that accounting developments have been slow to materialize and become common practice. Clearly a good proportion of accounting methods was developed 100 years ago and more.

Today we live in an environment where, within the practice of costing, costs are collected and recorded by type and then often selected types are further grouped in secondary or more ways to provide management with costing and accounting information.

Such cost groupings and methods are now prolific. Examine this daunting lexicon of costing terms that has been built up mainly over the last fifty years. It is a confusion of terminology:

> fixed, variable, semi-fixed, overhead, manufacturing, absorbed, activity based, opportunity, batch, incremental, sunk, contract, specific order, service, product, attributable, actual, non-manufacturing, burden, direct, indirect, standard, job, order, marginal, allowable, average, cost of goods sold, cost of sales, target, operating, replacement, past, historical, unit, process, value stream, back-flushed, etc.

And this list of terms is not exhaustive, so forgive omissions.

As an aside, many names are also given to margins; that is, what's left after costs have been deducted from income:

> throughput, gross profit, net margin, gross margin, contribution, net profit, return on sales, as well as other associated terms like above the line/below the line, profitability, return on capital employed (ROCE), income and expenditure, EBIT, EBITDA, etc.

It's little wonder that managers' minds can glaze over when confronted with management accounts that quote such costing and margin terms. And just to make matters more unintelligible, the terms are interpreted in different ways.

Even though some definitions in textbooks exist, there are no generally adopted standards, so under each heading accountants and managers will include income and/or costs that they believe suits and satisfies their needs as well as those of the business. I suppose this is to be expected. Different businesses have different priorities and needs, but it doesn't advance their general comprehension by the managers for whom financial reports are prepared.

The terms themselves have been created over many years as new ideas, technologies, thought processes, and other techniques have been developed to address fresh commercial challenges as they present themselves.

It is difficult to attach many of these cost-group classifications directly to an organization or business type (although some are clearly related to manufacturing), so this is not a factor in their choice. Often they were developed to better enable the true cost of products, processes, or services to be established for pricing decisions, or the division of costs over profit/cost centers, reasons that are just as relevant today.

Many, however, are quite general in nature so their utilization will depend on how the accountant or manager decides to portray results to provide a clearer picture of what is happening in an organization.

Although there are usually good reasons why these cost groups have been conceived, what cost is included in each grouping can be subjective; management may need the full cost of a particular process or contract, or they may require all the costs attributed to the sale and production of a particular product or service range and costs may, for management control purposes, be grouped together under responsibility, branch, division, cost, or profit centers. The reasons for cost groupings are wide, varied, and very numerous.

Costs, so recorded, are then usually grouped together in appropriate categories for purposes of presentation in management accounts.

Following is just an example of the composition of "cost groups" that may appear in a typical set of management accounts:

- *Manufacturing cost* may comprise raw materials, factory wages, and factory overhead (the latter may itself comprise of factory power, rent, rates, consumables, plant maintenance, plant depreciation, etc.).

- *Direct costs* may comprise raw materials and manufacturing labor and any other overhead that can be directly attributed to a product/service, etc., but exclude those overheads that can't be allocated directly.
- *Sales cost* may comprise sales office salaries, salesmen's salaries, commission, advertising, sales literature, marketing, etc., although marketing may well be shown under a different heading.
- *Customer services* may comprise salaries, stationery, telephone, etc., those interfacing directly with customers.
- *Various salary/remuneration headings; for example,* office, directors, managers, sales staff, etc. These will include gross salary employers' NHI, employers' pension contributions.
- *General overheads* may comprise managing director's salary, accounts department salaries, audit and legal fees, rent and rates, heating and lighting, buildings and maintenance, etc. And so on.

The opening pages to this chapter may appear to be fairly academic but they serve to illustrate the origins of cost recording and classification as well as the multifarious ways in which costs are presented within a set of management accounts. This illustrates the lack of consistency that can be found in the way in which different organizations collect and present their costs and then display them.

It's plain to see that there is much variety in how costs are categorized and grouped and hence the need for clarity in their presentation. This emphasizes the need for accountants to make clear, to those reading any financial report, which income or cost is included in each category or heading.

It is also evident that the only rule that managers need to know about how costs are grouped together is *there is no rule.* Vigilance is therefore vital. Misunderstanding which costs are included where can lead to making wrong decisions.

This diversity in approach also reflects the extreme variation in types of organizations in existence. It could not be of greater range, and each will usually determine the method that they believe suits them best.

However, there is not much evidence, either now or in the past, which recognizes how costs may be presented in a way that better reflects the relationships (or lack of relationship) they have with income/sales volume throughout the profit-and-loss account, and this subject is the focus of this chapter. It is this important aspect of the nature of cost that is fundamental to presenting accurate and meaningful trends and forecasts.

## *The problem with many cost groupings*

The problem with most of the cost groupings mentioned above is that they often mix costs together that can each behave differently when sales volumes, values, or mix vary from what is expected. This can prove confusing and misleading when comparing actual performance with budget/forecast or when monitoring the way cost proportions vary. It also conceals whether actual cost variations are reasonable, proportionate or will be sustained. The true nature of any calculated trend of a cost group may therefore not be accurately represented because some costs within the cost group will vary in proportion with sales volumes, some will vary out of proportion and some will hardly vary at all, yet all these types of costs are often grouped together within the same cost group within the management accounts. This introduces difficulty for managers attempting to evaluate and control what *has* happened and *will* happen in the future to the value of these costs when the organization's income differs from that which is expected.

To help combat this problem, some organizations adopt a "marginal cost" approach when presenting their management accounts.

For clarity, the term *marginal costing* has the following definition: *a fixed cost is one that does not vary with sales volume while a variable cost does; in this context, a marginal cost, sometimes called incremental cost, is the value by which a cost rises if one more product or unit of service is produced. "Contribution" is the term used to describe what is left after deducting variable costs from income.*

This approach was mainly devised and applied when pricing a product or service upon confronting a competitive situation. It works on the principle that if capacity has not been utilized it is better to take an order that offers a "contribution" even if this fails to cover its fair share of the "fixed" cost rather than not take the order at all. This practice rests on the basis that "fixed" cost will not increase as a result of taking the order and that the extra contribution earned will go straight to net profit. This is a questionable principle if used too often. Not only can it dilute margins, it can also be dangerous in practice unless it is strictly controlled because capacity is not always understood by those making the pricing decision. And when the capacity break point is reached, there can be a *step-up* in fixed cost. If a marginal cost approach to pricing becomes a general rule, a business will need to watch out. In addition, it must be remembered that some costs are semi-variable, and if classified as fixed within such a pricing decision may also rise if sales volume increases, albeit not in proportion to the volume increase.

Many organizations have adopted the principle of marginal costing within the management accounts even when there is potential for large variations in volume; that is, the layout follows the form: income less variable cost = contribution, rather than striking the traditional gross profit margin; the latter may include some "semi-fixed or fixed" costs in the calculation.

Taking a marginal cost approach to management accounts may be fine if there are only minor variations to actual volumes, but if the volumes start to vary significantly this approach has deficiencies. Comparisons with budget or attempting to monitor the way cost proportions change, particularly with the so called fixed costs, will be difficult and can be misleading. There will come the time when gradual growth in volume will result in steps up in fixed costs.

*N.B.: these steps will occur at different times depending upon the nature of each fixed cost.*

Management accounts presented in marginal cost format portray fixed costs that are differentiated from variable costs. This makes the assumption that the variable costs will vary with income/volume and fixed costs won't, although in the end analysis there are very few costs that are either fully fixed or fully variable when income varies.

Take a fairly extreme example to demonstrate the point. Say that income/volume is only half that which was budgeted. Would it be expected that total "variable costs" would have halved and total "fixed costs" remained the same? It is likely that "variable" costs, while perhaps dropping significantly, would not have halved. As far as fixed costs are concerned, it is likely that these would have fallen, although much would have depended on management action to cut these costs promptly to address the income shortfall; it is unlikely, however, that they would have stayed the same.

There is no escaping this fact. Few costs are truly fixed or truly variable, and no numerical system of presenting management accounts that I have seen fully account for this. This is a major weakness in traditional management accounts. In view of this fact, the pragmatic way forward is to ensure these variations in all costs are monitored. This is where graphical presentations that utilize trends score; all cost variations and their relationship to one another and the net result are closely observed.

While it is clear, therefore, that few, if any, costs are either truly fixed or variable, a marginal cost approach to presenting management accounts can be a step in the right direction but it needs to go much further. We need a better way of analyzing, structuring, and presenting costs in these important financial statements that will make them more informative and reliable to managers. Failure to recognize this will distort trends and will influence the accuracy of forecasts and future budgets. Attention is required, therefore, to change the structure/classification of costs within an organization, which will help to answer such questions as: "Why are our sales costs assuming a bigger proportion of our income?" "Why are our raw-material costs a lower percentage of our income than previously?" "Why is our marketing cost now taking twice the proportion of our income as it did six months ago?" And so on.

In the past, a technique known as flexible budgeting was sometimes used to assist with this. Flexible budgeting varied the budgeted costs to suit actual sales volumes/values/mix, and so making the comparison between budget and actual performance more logical. It's a technique that seems to have fallen from favor, and perhaps this is because varying the budget meant that the budgeted profit targets were also varied, and if this happened to be in a downward direction it detracted from a board's budgeted profit objectives and these were sacrosanct. This was often deemed unacceptable by boards because it changes the most important value, the net result of the budget through the backdoor.

The way costs are grouped together for management account purposes is therefore an important factor in understanding the nature and behavior of different costs. It is vital that managers have an appreciation of how each cost is likely to behave when income varies, and simply comparing costs with budget may not be sufficient because budgeted overheads are rarely, if ever, varied to reflect the actual income. As we have seen above this is further complicated by the fact that costs that behave differently when volume variations occur are actually mixed together within the same cost groups displayed in most management accounts.

Costs and income are generally recorded and accumulated in their appropriate account within the nominal ledger; these accounts are often further subdivided into separate sub-accounts when the cost/income concerned can be directly attributed to a particular branch, department, cost, or profit center. This division of costs and income, when extracted to form the management accounts, allows management to see the financial results by profit center or responsibility center, etc.

This is a common approach, which at least allows management to evaluate the profitability of a profit center but unfortunately still fails to consider the differing ways in which individual costs behave when income varies. Consequently even within a profit responsibility or cost center it is still common to find costs that behave inconsistently from each other when budgeted income/volume levels are not replicated in the actual results, so this approach to cost classification does not address the fundamental problem outlined above either. This is not to say that all costs relating to a particular cost/profit/responsibility center should not still be attributed. It simply means differentiating some costs from others within that center; i.e., categorizing costs in a different way.

*A new way of categorizing costs*

It is fundamental to better trend analysis and forecasting to find this better way and the suggested cost categories below (Fig.2.1) are probably different from any current way of analyzing costs with which you may be familiar, but it is essential to recognize the differences. This new approach of segregating cost types attempts to substantially reduce the problems outlined above:

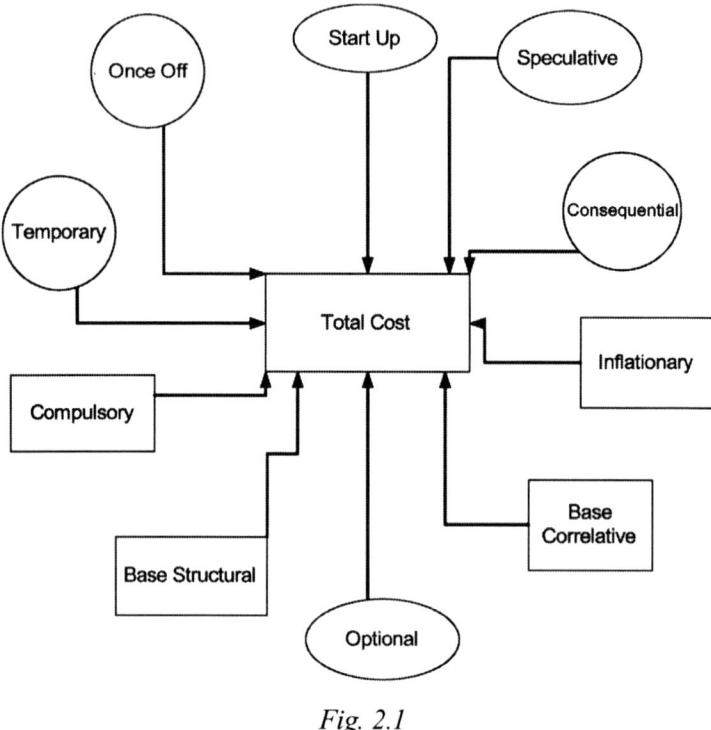

*Fig. 2.1*

For clarification, a description of each of these cost types follows:

- Start Up—This is the cost of initiating a new product, idea, research program, etc. It can be one-off or may be spread over a limited period. It will probably have been subject to a "business plan" that should have confirmed the feasibility of the investment. In day-to-day business it is a cost that will bear little relation to existing volume of business and may take some time to bear a true relationship to any income that derives from it. It may also have been part or fully capitalized and depreciated within the management accounts or it may just be written off in the year of the investment.

- Once off—This is not a capital cost but one that is written off in the P&L account during the year it is spent. It is not related to the sales or volume of business within the organization. It might be the costs of a reorganization, a refurbishment, redundancies, or other cost that was unexpected but necessary or unavoidable in the course of the business.

- Speculative—This is a cost for which the outcome cannot be predicted. It might be a one-off advertising campaign, a corporate brochure, or a PR campaign that promotes the values of the organization. It would be regarded as an optional cost but was probably directed at promoting the business or improving a business situation. However, the cost and any income that may derive from it are not directly related.

  *N.B.: where marketing and advertising are a day-to-day cost of securing the business and business volume directly linked to them, they would be classified as base correlative (see below).*

- Temporary—Typically a cost of short-term employed staff or short-term rental of plant or facilities for a particular project, usually entered into with a fairly definite exit point. It may or may not have any direct proportional link to the volume of the organization.

- Consequential—Not an optional cost but one which arises as a result of another unexpected happening. For example, a major product failure, out of the norm, that incurs rectification costs, perhaps under the company's warranty scheme. These would usually be of an extraordinary nature not general day-to-day warranty repairs.

- Optional—A cost that management could either incur or not which may or not have a significant effect on the performance of the organization. For example, a special staff party, replacing the office furniture, changing logos, etc.

- Compulsory—Could be tax, levy, fine, etc. or a cost which is forced upon an organization by external sources and where there is no alternative but to pay. It may bear no relation to income. Might be a VAT increase suffered by an organization that is unable to recover VAT.

- Base Correlative—This is a variable/semi variable cost that changes with the level of volume in a business. It may be close to or directly proportional to volume of sales. It could be raw material, sales commission, or production labor where this is paid on a piece work or similar basis.
- Base Structural—Might be termed overheads, or misleadingly fixed cost. In the US, it is sometimes known as burden when relating to production overhead. In essence they are all those costs other than the cost categories listed above that are usually essential to the running of the organization but not directly proportional to volume of business. For example, in a manufacturing business it would be essential to have premises where the product is assembled; e.g. rent or property depreciation, council tax, lighting and heating, accounting and audit, etc. They are sometimes, for pricing and net margin calculation purposes, shared across functions, products, departments, using some sort of overhead recovery system.
- Inflationary—Those increases in income/cost that arise due to inflationary pressure. They can sometimes be foreseen but only mitigated in the longer term through changing suppliers or putting up prices. They may well be included in one of the cost categories above and are usually not segregated.

*It should be noted that those costs within an oval shape are fully controlled and instigated by management, not linked to income/ volume levels. Those costs that are within a round shape are usually unexpected but essential costs, not directly determined by management but forced upon them owing to unforeseen happenings or circumstances. Those costs within a rectangular shape are the base costs of running the business. They can be largely foreseen and in the main are essential to the functioning of the business. They are predominantly controlled by management through efficiency, design, monitoring and wise procurement. This does not mean to say that base structural is strictly fixed and base correlative strictly variable.*

*We have already seen that no cost is strictly one or the other, but they do exclude all the costs shown above in the oval and round boxes that are in one way or another optional or unexpected.*

*This re-categorization of costs substantially improves the former fixed-variable only analysis.*

In a conventional set of management accounts all these categories of cost can be included within a single cost or profit center's total cost, and this can lead to misleading reports and to an ensuing complex analysis when investigating or determining a shift in performance or variance from budget, particularly when income/volume is different from that which is expected in a budget or plan.

The structure of a nominal ledger need not be changed significantly to reflect a new way of analyzing costs, as illustrated above, because these different costs may already be segregated by the use of different accounts within the ledger. If they aren't, then new accounts should be introduced, a simple enough matter; certain cost types, those depicted in oval and round boxes above, can then be extricated into separate lines/graphs of the management accounts so that they do not confuse those cost groups that relate to the day-to-day running of the business. These disproportionate costs demand different treatment and control, and if segregated, can be monitored separately from those costs that are directly related to the volume of business. Failure to do so can distort the trends of these latter costs.

In practice, some thought may be needed as to which classification a cost falls. For example, on occasions a cost that was not a regular occurrence may be treated as a base structural. It may be an irregular cost but nevertheless may be expected to occur, albeit infrequently and without prediction. Such a cost might be a major plant breakdown, for example, which it is known will happen sometime despite its unpredictability. In this case it could be considered part of running the business day to day and allowed for, even as a monthly reserve in the management accounts/budget.

It is important to recognize the difference between these irregular and somewhat infrequent costs from those extraordinary costs that are primarily included in the oval boxes above that are either truly exceptional or optional.

## *So is any cost fixed?*

In the final analysis the answer has to be no.

In the dynamic, liberated economies in which organizations and business now operate it must be accepted that nothing is fixed anymore; at least, nothing that is long-term. We know that some things are more fixed than others and that the various cost step effects that arise will have different timings from cost to cost, but they are nevertheless all variable albeit not incrementally with units of production. It just depends upon volume and management decisions.

Treating fixed, or to use the new terminology described above, "base structural" costs as variables doesn't mean regular redundancies, layoffs, short-term hiring, or buying and selling property when more or less capacity is needed, but it does mean that modern business has to open its mind to the way the fixed resources are managed and utilized. It may mean six-month contracts for certain services rather one-to two-year contracts. It may mean short-term leases rather than five-, ten-, or twenty-year leases, and it may mean short-term contracts for some staff or outsourcing services rather than employing staff. This move away from the mindset of fixed cost will allow greater maneuverability and agility when changes occur in the chaotic and opportunistic markets and rapid economic developments that occur these days.

Many still think that it is the variables that must be first to go down when sales fall and fixed cost only tackled when variable cost reductions are insufficient, but the fact is all costs have to be tackled simultaneously. The management and treatment of fixed costs will lead to much greater flexibility, particularly during unpredictable times. This change in attitude in management can only be achieved with a culture change across the whole organization—all managers must embrace this approach; they have to accept that no cost is sacrosanct. The concept of fixed cost needs to be buried. They mean fixed resources, and there aren't many of these anymore.

*Net profit is the "anchor point" to which all costs are related*

It was identified above why flexible budgeting failed to fulfill its promise. To the board and most other stakeholders, the net profit in a budget is its most important line.

In practice, the first item generally scrutinized in any set of management accounts is net profit/surplus. In almost every board meeting attended by the writer, when the management accounts come up on the agenda, everybody turns to the bottom of the page to look at net profit. It is a very human and normal first move, a natural reflex prompted by the fact that net profit/surplus is commonly the way in which the performance of senior management of an organization is finally judged.

This final result, the net profit/surplus, often sets the boardroom scene, the mood, and often the time spent on examining the accounts. Unfortunately this can mean that if it's a good result the accounts can be subject to less scrutiny and if it's a bad result then they often dominate the meeting. On occasions an acceptable net profit can obscure poor performance in one or more areas of the business, although this practice should be avoided. Who is to say that the result shouldn't be better still? It is within the role of the accountant to highlight the areas that need attention whether the net profit is good or bad, and graphical tools will greatly assist in this function.

When a board is establishing a required net margin for a budget or to meet its own or shareholder expectations it will have a number of measures in mind: earnings growth, return on capital employed, increasing earnings per share, interest cover, cash generation, and/or a profit/surplus safety margin, etc. Net profit is critical to all these.

When setting these targets, it is this value, the bottom line, the net profit/surplus that the board will be keen to achieve after all the detailed planning of income and costs have been budgeted. It is not uncommon for budgets that have been prepared by management to be rejected by a board because they fail to reach the net profit/surplus the board has previously decided will meet the expectations identified above, and this rejection can happen more than once. It is a clear indication that net profit/surplus is indeed the most important line of the budget.

The effect of this is that the planned net profit becomes the anchor point to which all costs are related, every line on the P&L account becomes subsidiary to net profit. N.B.: even in nonprofit organizations this bottom-line approach is just as vital, and in fact could be considered even more important, because there is less margin of error. A planned break-even can be difficult to achieve and such an organization will not want to slip into deficit. Net profit/surplus is also very influential to cash flow and this is important whatever the organization.

Fig. 2.2 illustrates how net profit should sit in the order of priorities:

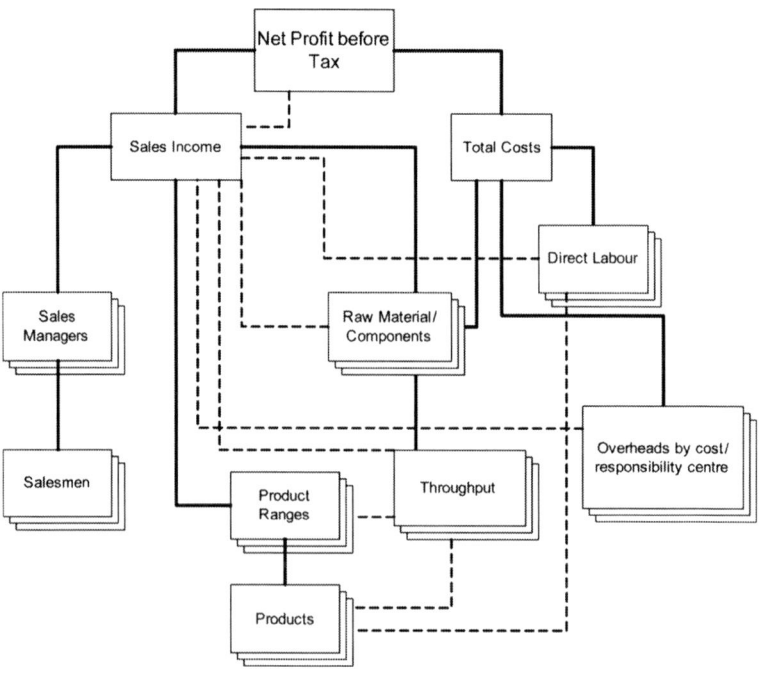

*Fig. 2.2*

*N.b.: the dotted lines indicate cost-income relationships.*

*The importance of cost structures*

The question that arises from the proposition that net profit is the anchor point is how this priority can be used to monitor and control costs and income in the management accounts and enable the *cost structure* of the organization to be monitored and controlled.

Just to clarify the term "cost structure," it could be helpful to look at a simple example that applies percentages to all cost groups. The following percentages are simply a datum from which to plot the way in which cost proportions may change:

- Net profit is 10 percent of turnover (turnover represents 100 percent)

- Material cost of goods sold 13 percent
- Direct labor cost of goods sold 13 percent
- *Gross margin, therefore, 74 percent (100-13-13)*
- Factory overhead 9 percent
- Internal sales and customer services 11 percent
- External sales 16 percent
- Advertising 5 percent
- Accounting and other admin 7 percent
- Board salaries, etc. 5 percent
- Accommodation costs 11 percent

These percentages are the cost structure. Any variation in the actual performance of each line will have a direct effect that will be reflected by a movement of the net profit percentage. Net profit is the balancing percentage.

*N.B.: there may be occasions where a change in percentage of one cost line is offset, partially, or fully by another; e.g., where one type of cost is incurred to save another.*

Monitoring the actual percent of each cost group on a twelve-month rolling total basis will indicate not only what changes have occurred in the percentage of each cost group, but also where each percent cost trend is headed; i.e., whether it will remain in the same proportion to turnover or not. This helps management to decide whether such a change is acceptable; e.g., "Are we content to allow our external sales cost to assume a continually higher percentage of sales income at the cost of net profit?" "Will we allow savings in one cost group that benefits net profit to be consumed by an increase in another cost group?" "How can we tackle the increasing percentage of turnover being consumed by our advertising bills?" Etc.

These questions become obvious when trends of the cost percentages are constructed and the changes to the cost structure regularly monitored.

When turnover and costs are varying from month to month and cumulatively, it is very difficult from conventional monthly management accounts to spot how these costs are varying in proportion to one another; i.e., how the cost structure is changing. In numeric accounts it is rare to find overheads/fixed costs expressed as a percentage of turnover and even if this was shown in these traditional accounts, it would still be impossible to see any trends that may be occurring on the cost structure because the only figures visible are the latest month and the cumulative for the current financial year.

It is common for companies to take variable costs as percentages of turnover in conventional numeric, tabular management accounts, but it is uncommon for organizations to use percentages of their fixed costs/overheads to income either in their management accounts or any other practical way. In view of current practice with regard to the way costs of different qualities (see Fig 2.1 above) are mixed together, even if these percentages were taken they would probably produce very inconsistent results depending on the incidence of the optional costs identified.

As far as these so called fixed costs (overheads) are concerned, managers would usually utilize a simple comparison with the budget as the main means of monitoring/control even though the dangers of relying too much on budgeted cost levels are well known; organizations persevere with fixed budgets despite their shortcomings. If you are in any doubt about these deficiencies, they are highlighted in the next chapter. Using graphical presentation combined with trends offers an additional cost-control mechanism, because these cost proportions can be monitored not only by examining the trend, but also by examining the budget—both are portrayed on the chart.

In summary, it is evident that organizations are failing to adapt their management-account-reporting systems to the rapid changes that are going on around them. These changes often mean that budgets are out of date very soon after their creation, and management accounts haven't changed to respond to this. The processes that have existed in reporting financial results for decades aren't doing the job anymore, and there is little indication that a change is imminent.

Examining the changes to cost structure and in particular the trends in these mutations provides an early warning to management. This is not possible with current methods of reporting. Trends allow managers to forecast how cost groups are changing. This prompts review and corrective action much sooner than would otherwise be the case. These trends in cost structure provide a complete change of perspective from those currently available to management, and such information can only improve reaction time.

A simple example of twelve-month rolling total graphs based on the cost structure we examined above can be seen in figures 2.3 to 2.12.

N.B.: the timeframe covers three financial years (last year, this year, and next year as previously outlined. The dashed lines are simply a reminder of the datum level and the black line the twelve-month rolling total of the actual percentage achieved.

The datum line in these graphs is not actually shown on a graphical representation of the management accounts; the datum is shown here *only* to provide a visual point around which to see the variation in the twelve-month rolling totals (trends) for each element of cost and profit. In practice, a budget and forecast would be shown on the chart and the method of application of these will be covered in the next two chapters.

Note the abbreviated scale in the vertical axis.

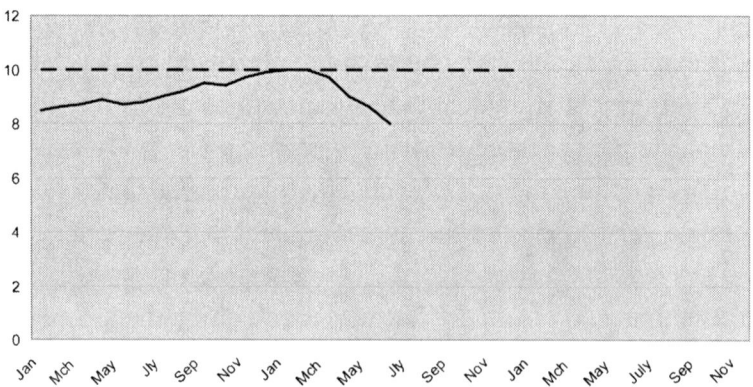

*Fig. 2.3*
*Twelve-month rolling total of percentage net*
*profit/surplus bears to income*

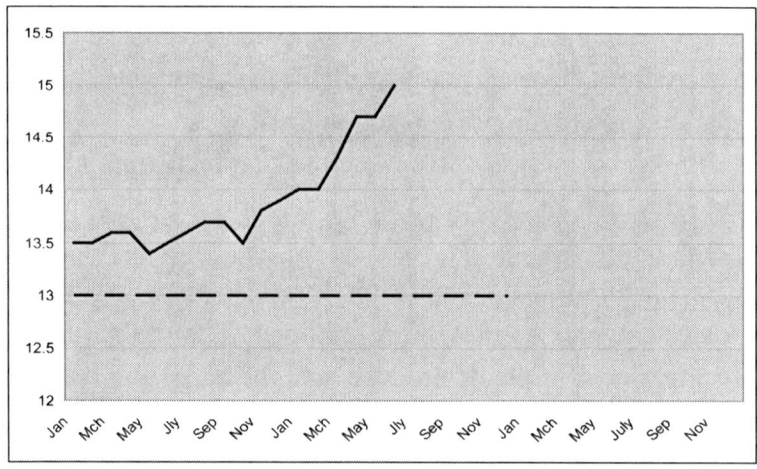

*Fig 2.4*
*Twelve-month rolling total of percentage that*
*material cost of goods sold bears to income*

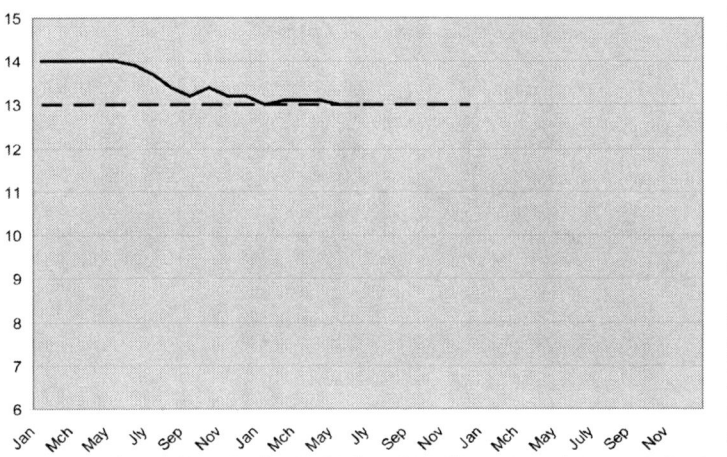

*Fig. 2.5*
*Twelve-month rolling total of percentage that*
*direct labor of sales bears to income*

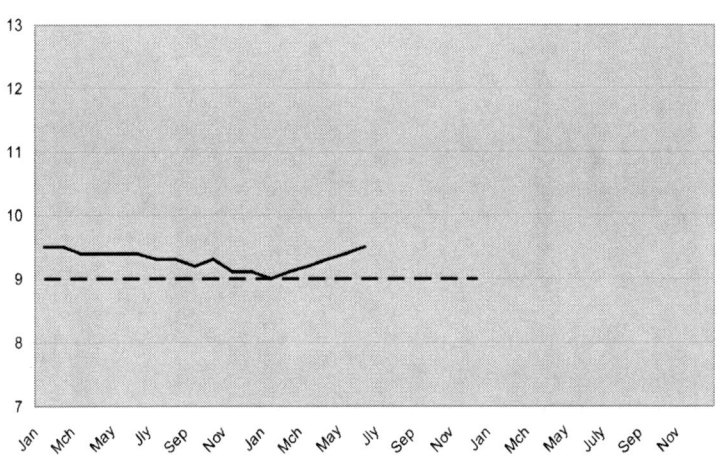

*Fig. 2.6*
*Twelve-month rolling total of percentage that*
*factory overhead bears to income*

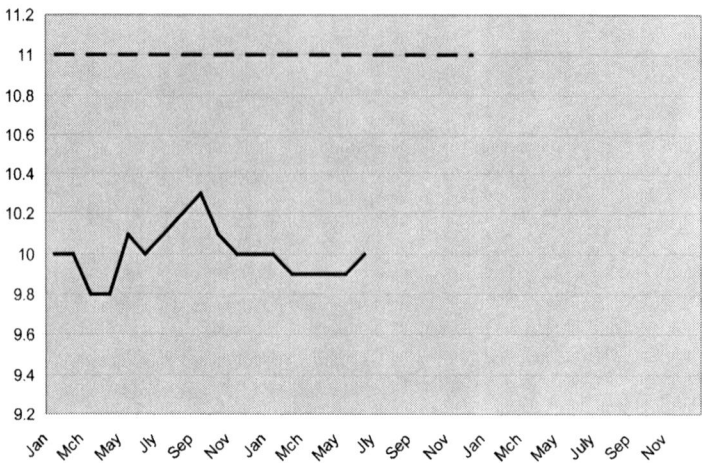

*Fig. 2.7*
*Twelve-month rolling total of percentage that internal*
*sales and customer service bears to income*

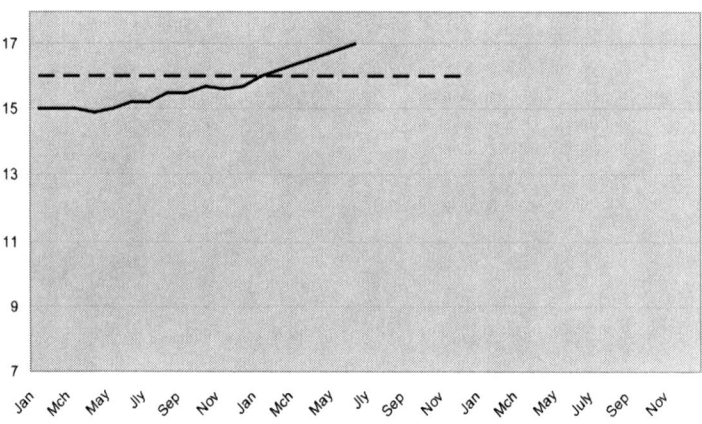

*Fig. 2.8*
*Twelve-month rolling total of percentage that*
*external sales bears to income*

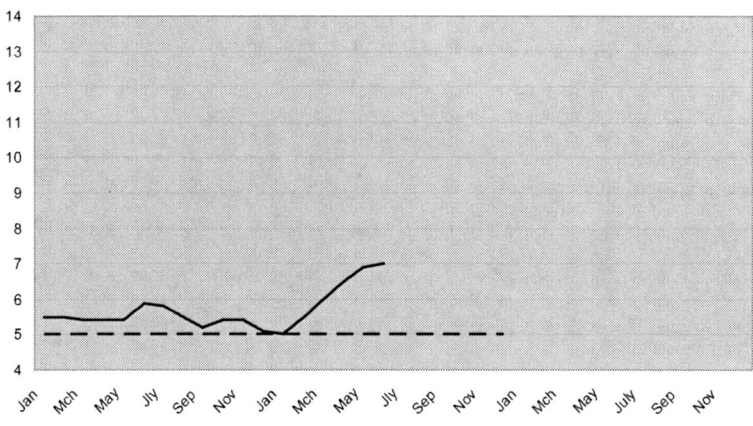

*Fig. 2.9*

*Twelve-month rolling total of percentage that*
*advertising bears to income*

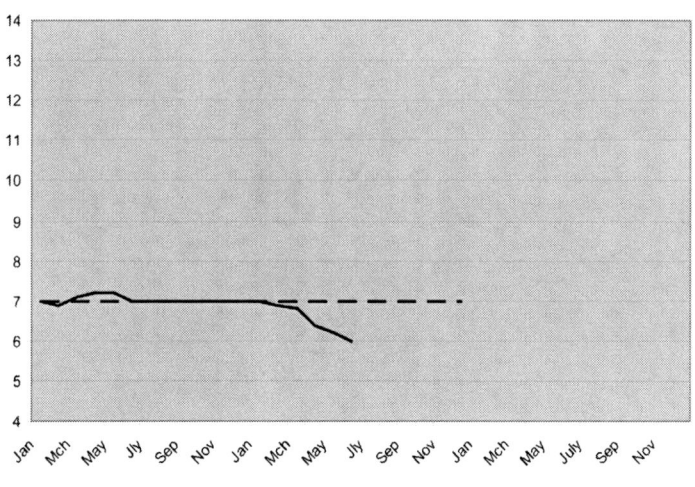

*Fig. 2.10*

*Twelve-month rolling total of percentage that*
*accounts and admin bears to income*

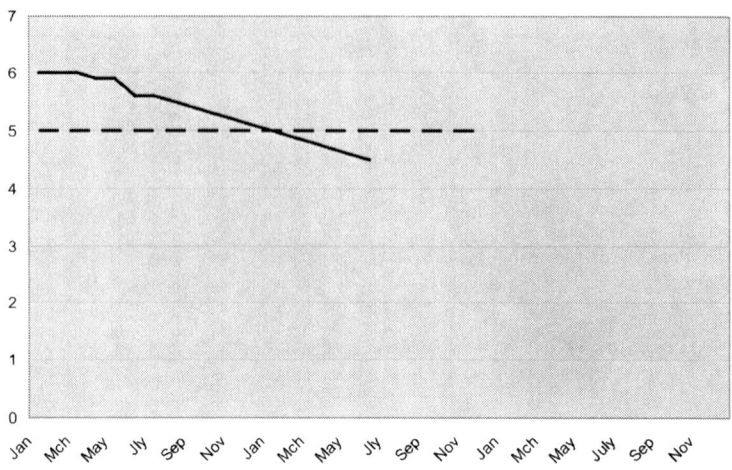

*Fig. 2.11*
*Twelve-month rolling total of percentage that*
*board salaries bears to income*

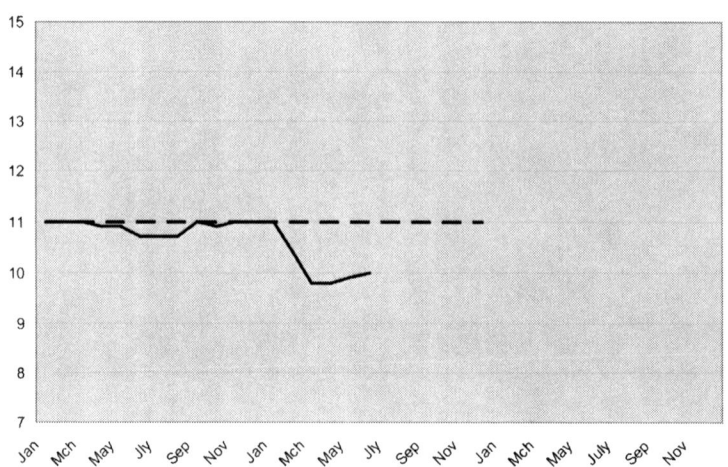

*Fig. 2.12*
*Twelve-month rolling total of percentage that*
*accommodation costs bears to income*

These graphs tell their own story and the movement in cost proportions can be clearly seen; at any point it is immediately apparent what percentage point a cost variation has contributed or detracted from net profit.

It is evident that annual net profit margin, Fig. 2.3, is down from 10 percent in January of the current year to 8 percent in the twelve months ending June, having risen from 8.5 percent to 10 percent in the last financial year. This significant reduction is due to a number of factors:

- Annual material cost of goods sold, Fig. 2.4, is up by 1 percent of income since January and rose .5 percent last year, showing an overall upward trend over eighteen months. Where will it go from here? These trends can take some time to reverse, so worse may be to come.
- Annual external sales, Fig. 2.8, shows a similar pattern; upward trend in cost percentage over eighteen months with about 1 percent in the current year. What will happen over the next twelve months, the trend is ominous.
- Annual advertising cost, Fig. 2.9, was contained last year, hovering between 5-6 percent, but clearly the campaigns for the current year have had a significant impact on profit; advertising is up by 2 percent this year. Perhaps it's time to evaluate the effectiveness of our campaigns
- Thankfully all other costs are running at about the same annual percentage or less, and this has offset the increases to some extent, netting out to the 2 percent reduction in net profit.
- The downward trend in annual cost percentage for accommodation, Fig. 2.12, and direct labor, Fig. 2.5, appears to have ended so these cannot be relied upon to continue to finance those costs that are increasing relative to income.

Many questions arise as a result of these graphs and it is not necessary for us to hypothesize here. One thing that will strike all readers is the glaring necessity for forecasts in these graphs, and this is a major subject covered in chapter 4.

Finally, although not shown here, it is necessary that the twelve-month rolling totals of the actual *value* of the costs, as well as their percentage to income, are also plotted on sister graphs. The full magnitude of actual values is then revealed. This is clearly demonstrated in the chapter that portrays the system in practice.

This is a very simple example designed only to demonstrate the need to graphically depict cost percent to sales so that cost proportion variations can be plotted against those budgeted. Without percentages it is simply not possible to see whether financial cost variations are relative to changes in turnover or not.

In reality greater analysis of these values and percentages may be needed; there are numerous other factors that may need to be taken into consideration:

- Sales price and mix, and material price and volume variances:

*These variances, commonly used in standard costing, are particularly important in organizations where margins from service to service or product to product vary significantly and/or where there are appreciable variable or semi-variable resource differences between products or services offered.*

- Different products/ranges
- Different branches or profit centers
- Different sales staff and so on

All these analyses would be produced as multilevel charts subsidiary to the headline charts as pictured in Fig. 2.2. It will be found that once completed this allows easy comparisons between branches, sales staff, products, etc.

It is worth repeating that in a set of conventional, numeric management accounts the only figures available are the values last month and the year to date. There is a dramatic difference between the information provided by these two types of presentation that will now be clear to the reader.

It should be noted that the impact on Net Result of just small changes to the percentage of any individual cost group can be significant. For example, if turnover is 100 percent and net profit margin target is 10 percent then costs account for 90 percent. If say a department's cost is 0.5 percent of income more than the budget, then it's clear that if net profit is budgeted at 10 percent this department is responsible for a 5 percent reduction in net profit against the budget (10 percent down to 9.5 percent is a 5 percent reduction). This change of perspective relating to the impact of adverse cost changes can have an immediate and obvious impact on management. It allows each manager of a line/s in the management accounts to understand the impact they are having on the bottom line. A 5 percent reduction of net profit is clearly a more powerful fact than a department's cost being .5 percent over on cost.

It may be found when the concept of monitoring cost proportions and the percentage that overheads bear to turnover is introduced that the first reaction from many managers may be negative. Likely comments might include: "But if income is down and my costs are fixed then of course my costs will be a higher percentage! I don't have any control over income, that's the sales manager's job, so how can I be expected to keep my costs in line with them?"

This predictable reaction highlights on the net result, the need for thorough preparation and induction of management before such a system is introduced.

It is essential that managers accept a new order of things, there is no such thing as a fixed cost anymore. Managers with cost responsibility need to understand that turnover/income is monitored and controlled in other ways and turnover/income is the core value to which all costs and net profit must finally relate. Income can't be expressed as a percentage of anything, so it is controlled by alternative measures; e.g., by examining detailed product/service sales against target, examining trends, by scrutinizing sales by individual salesman/branch/subsidiary or changing quotation conversion rates or sales campaign/promotion results, introducing new products or services, etc. In public bodies it is likely to be determined directly or indirectly by government. In charities it depends on the success of fundraising campaigns. Managers have to accept that sales/income, while not under their direct control, is probably under even greater pressure than their own overhead costs. They do need to understand that if net margin percentage is to be maintained and their costs actually increase in percentage of income, then another department must operate at a lower percentage of income if net profit percentage is to be maintained. There will be a need for a new understanding among managers as discussed above. It is a matter of cutting the coat according to the cloth.

This problem is further exacerbated when the finite *value* of net profit must be retained as the budget/target rather than just the net profit percentage margin. In practice this is usually the case, and its impact is that when income is below budget all costs must actually operate at even lower percentages because net profit will assume a larger percentage of income. Conversely, when income is above budget costs can expand to higher percentages (although in the latter case top management would likely be looking for net profit percentage increases too so cost percentages may be required to reflect this).

## Cost percentages become a key control factor

Whilst graphical presentations still portray value variances from budget it is the examination of comparisons of the percentages that costs bear to income that become a key principle in any new graphical presentation of the management accounts. This reveals changes to the *structure* of costs, and more importantly the *trends* in the changes to structure. In addition it offers greater control to management and this leads to earlier decision-making. It affords them the opportunity of reassessing the investments made in each area of its business, and if costs need to be tightened, will guide them to those areas that may need to be addressed. Management accounts that include this information provide a new vision, additional intelligence, and a better understanding of their organization's financial structure.

The division of costs into those that move in sympathy with income and those that don't (as described in Fig. 2.1 that describes cost categories) will make the variations in the percentages more consistent and relevant. Removing the costs that do not move in sympathy with income will provide more accurate trends in those that do. Showing those costs that are more optional or unexpected in nature separately (those that appear in the oval and round boxes in Fig. 2.1) will highlight the impact they are individually having on net profit percentage, and since many of these are subject to individual management decisions, may be separately considered.

*Would an overhead cost taken as a percent of gross margin be a better way of monitoring cost structure?*
It was suggested when we introduced this system that taking overhead costs as a percentage of gross margin may be more appropriate than as a percentage of turnover. This has been explored but offered no benefits. The advantage of all costs using turnover as their base is that when added together with net profit they equal 100 percent, so identifying the full structure and division of costs.

*There is a very important watch point when calculating a twelve-month moving average of a cost percentage.*

The arithmetic must be completed using the twelve-month moving totals of cost and income, not the twelve-month moving average of the monthly percentages itself. The latter fails to take account of the weighting caused by the varying values from each month. This proves the rule that "you can't average percentages." This is particularly relevant to seasonally affected organizations.

In summary, it has been described how tackling all costs on a percentage of turnover basis enables management to monitor how cost relationships are changing in relation to income level, how they are individually adding to or deducting from net profit percentage, and how it will facilitate the direction of effort to those areas that either need more resources or less. It may also limit, postpone, or accelerate those optional areas of expense.

It has also been explained why the alternative way of looking at cost behavior and classification as set out above can be relevant. We have seen that some rearrangement of costs in the nominal ledgers and management accounts, as set out above, is therefore desirable, especially where those contained in the oval and round boxes (see Fig. 2.1) are currently summarized or grouped together for presentation purposes.

For clarity it is repeated that any cost that is unpredictable or unexpected should be shown separately in the management accounts.

It must be made clear to managers that the main point of taking percentages of cost is not to create a stick to beat them with, it is to monitor what is happening to the structure of costs and income within the organization, to look at the trends in these relationships, to establish cost priorities or direct effort to areas of necessary cost reduction, or to answer questions such as why particular costs are rising or falling over time in relation to income. There will be occasions when a board decides to accept an increase in a cost percentage or prompt a reduction. This might be those costs related to a new product line or new salesmen that will later raise turnover and so be forecast to reduce the percentage at a later date, or it may be decided to cut certain programs that are considered to be no longer affordable. These decisions would be reflected in the graphical forecast. The illustration that is provided by utilising three-year graphs, therefore, so depicts cause, decision, and effect.

All this gives management greater knowledge and control, and enables an historic trend to be seen, as well as provide a vision of what may happen in the future and this will lead to faster and better decisions.

Managers can also see the direct impact that their cost responsibility is having on net profit. This too can have a controlling impact that also lowers the management structure level of the decision.

In the last chapter we dealt with how sales income is represented in graphical format and how the use of rolling twelve-month totals helps us to determine trends. In this chapter we have dealt with presenting costs in graphical format and the importance of taking cost percentages to enable more intelligent comparison with budget and monitor cost proportions. None of this entails changes to the principles of twelve-month rolling totals or the time spans represented in the horizontal axis and considered in the last chapter. This must stay the same throughout the management accounts whatever cost or income is dealt with.

## Do we need cost percentages if our income doesn't vary?

When first considering the display of costs in chart format, it appears to be fairly straightforward; just take the actual cost and plot the value on the graph in the same way as you would have done for sales income. But as seen in this chapter, this alone can be misleading and has limited value and this why also graphically illustrating the percentage is vital. But if you are an organization that has a fixed income—that is, no sales volume or mix variation from month to month or any seasonal factors—then it may be possible to take the simple approach; that is, avoid the need to produce cost percentages.

This may apply to some public organizations that are allocated fixed funds for a specific purpose at the beginning of a financial year that are phased equally over the accounting periods. Plotting twelve-month rolling totals of cost values will indicate fairly accurately, when using the twelve-month rolling total process, whether the trend in each individual cost type/cost center shows a rising or falling position and can be directly compared to budget without distortion.

However, it is emphasized that this won't apply to organizations and businesses susceptible to variable sales/income/volume/value or which suffer seasonality. In this case market and other forces will force changes to many costs, so simply plotting these cost values and examining any trend displayed will not provide an accurate picture of whether costs are rising or falling in or out of proportion to sales income, volume, or mix.

This chapter has highlighted why it is necessary to consider a new way of dividing cost by type, monitoring cost-to-income relationships and variations in cost structures. All this is essential to gain full value from the utilization of trends within management accounts. The benefits of this will be further enhanced when budgets and forecasts are given the same treatment. This will be examined in the next two chapters.

Readers will be pleased to know that so long as the few rules introduced in this chapter are followed it doesn't matter what cost/margin terminology you use in your organizations or what layout you use in your management accounts. This will not affect the basic use of the presentation system outlined.

A very important factor, however, as in any regular management report, is consistency. Failure to present results in a consistent manner or changing the format too often or in an untimely way will cause misunderstandings and could lead to wrong decisions.

# CHAPTER 3
## Trends, Graphs, and Budgeting

"Budgeting, as most corporations practice it, should be abolished. That may sound like a radical proposition but it would be merely the culmination of long-running efforts to transform organizations from centralized hierarchies into devolved networks that allow for nimble adjustments to market conditions."
(Hope and Fraser, *Harvard Business Review*, February 2003)

"It sucks the energy, time, fun, and big dreams out of an organization. It hides opportunity and stunts growth. It brings out the most unproductive behaviors in an organization, from sandbagging to settling for mediocrity."
(Jack Welsh, "Winning: The Ultimate Business How-to Book," 2006)

Jeremy Hope and Robin Fraser, authors of the renowned book "Beyond Budgeting," have led the argument for change from traditional budgeting processes that have existed since the 1920s. They claim that intense market pressures, globalization, the instability of once-stable Western economies, and even terrorism add up to create a need for change. These conditions have significantly worsened since Hope and Fraser first made this statement.

The cause was reinforced by Jack Welsh, the icon of American business, former CEO of General Electric and one of the world's most revered and respected leaders. Who better to promote the cause of renouncing company budgets?

The arguments have been continued by the "Beyond Budgeting" round table that claims to have more than fifty corporate members around the world, with some large international players. Their work was described and the cause reinforced with more examples of organizations that had switched away from budgeting in an article by Russ Banham in *CFO Magazine*, September 2012. Interestingly the article does not mention the founders of these ideas, Hope and Fraser, but it is claimed in the article by a leading professor in the US that one hundred companies from around the world have adopted this practice. This has to raise the question of why, despite these distinguished recommendations consistently expounded over ten years, the vast majority of organizations still practice conventional budgetary-control processes today. Managers are not ignorant of the problems attached to budgets, but they appear not to have been convinced there is a satisfactory alternative or a better way. We shall examine some possible reasons why in this chapter.

There is no question that budgeting is burdened with numerous shortcomings, but rather than encourage "throwing the baby out with the bathwater," this chapter will take a more pragmatic approach. How can the practice be improved, led by the fact that so few organizations have as yet succumbed to the reasoned arguments outlined by the "Beyond Budgeting" group. We shall examine in more detail the criticism and challenges that exist in producing effective budgets and the case for retaining them. Crucially, this chapter will show how graphical presentation of management accounts can improve the budgetary-control process and enhance its accuracy and efficacy. It will also reveal a new perspective that will lessen the impact of budgeting defects. But while it won't solve all the problems attached to budgeting, it can improve this established and durable process, which at the current rate of change is likely to subsist for many decades more.

Note that the practical process of conversion of budgets into twelve-month rolling totals and their introduction into the charts is not as straightforward as it may seem. There are some important principles for application, and these will be covered later in the chapter.

## The pros and cons of current-day budgeting

It is clear that there is still widespread controversy over this subject and strong, valid opinions against budgetary control that perversely contrasts with its widespread use. So what drives this common management-accounting practice when there is so much evidence against it and its alleged negative impact on an organization?

Most will have read or experienced in some way the plethora of adverse comments and hostile criticism published over the last two decades; budgeting and its pros and cons, mostly the latter, is probably the management accounting and financial planning subject most written about over that time. No doubt it will be the subject of even more books, studies, research, and articles in the future, but despite all the flak it not only survives, it still dominates as the key financial-control measure adopted by most public and commercial organizations throughout the world.

The old phrase "to fail to plan is to plan to fail" could be a succinct, underlining reason why traditional, once-a-year budgeting is still practiced by most organizations. A budget offers a simple and familiar way of financial planning, and this provides a certain security, however erroneous this feeling may be. This is supported by research from the consulting firm the Hackett Group in 2007, which affirmed that in world-class organizations, where most areas of finance costs have been reduced, there are two areas where more is being spent; one is compliance and the other is financial planning (budgeting and forecasting). Their quoted reasoning is:

"It's no secret that budgeting is the bane of the CFO's existence. It's an annual battle to wring information and concessions out of operating units while generating 45,000 spreadsheets that in the end provide a best-guess at the upcoming year's results. But time-consuming as it is, the budgeting and planning (B&P) process is also one of the finance department's best opportunities to truly play the role of strategic partner to the business units. The top finance teams know this and are spending more on B&P even while their overall finance spend declines . . ."

The organizations that contributed to this research are those that perform in the top 25 percent on a variety of efficiency and effectiveness metrics. They claim that in these firms they spend 5 percent more of their total finance costs and planning than the average; 23 percent rather than 18 percent. So rather than cutting the costs of their budgeting, the organizations contributing to this research are spending more. We can only speculate as to why; they want to improve their current practice and/or today's economic and business environment forces them to. Whatever the reason, they clearly believe that budgeting is still fundamental to their financial planning.

The case for budgeting has also been reaffirmed from other research funded by the Chartered Institute of Management Accountants in the UK and carried out by David Dugdale and Stephen Lyne, who first reported their findings in the UK magazine, *Financial Management*, November 2006, and later in their book "Budgeting Practice and Organizational Structure."

This research found that "there is little evidence to suggest widespread dissatisfaction with traditional budgeting." The research entailed examining the practice of forty organizations, and all but one of the companies in the survey used budgets as part of a whole package of control systems. Most confirmed that they also regularly reported variances from budget. Generally they all felt that budgets were important for planning, control, performance measurement, coordination, and communication, although the use of budgets as a motivational tool was less well supported.

Dugdale and Lyne concluded that the apparent conflict between their findings and the views of Hope and Fraser could be explained by the difference in focus of the two studies—the former concentrating on managing operating units, and those of Hope and Fraser on managing the relationship between operating units and the corporate center. Hope and Fraser's main argument is that if the corporate center sets output controls for autonomous, decentralized business units then the use of tight budget controls can be counterproductive.

What can be concluded from the diverging views of these two research projects? Probably that there is no "cure-all" solution, that some businesses are structured in a way that would allow them to minimize budgetary control systems in favor of setting output controls combined with the implementation of a scorecard approach, while others, the vast majority, find that more conventional budgeting is the best way of satisfying their financial measurement and cost-control needs.

There is much evidence, however, among those using budgetary control of a general acceptance that the budgeting process should be improved and its many flaws addressed.

In their publication, Dugdale and Lyne found that new technology and increased management education have encouraged more sophisticated techniques in budget preparation. In addition, budgeting has been integrated with non-financial measures in general and the balanced scorecard in particular. This indicates that instead of abandoning budgets, as advocated by the "Beyond Budgeting" movement, there are clear indications of a move toward more enlightened budgeting that considers the outputs and business drivers too—an apparent combination of the two approaches.

One of the clear benefits of budgetary control is that the annual process of creating a budget can help to focus the minds of managers on the future. It *should* be an in-depth scrutiny of all aspects of the business and its markets and it *should* be integrated with the process of a strategic/operational review. Unfortunately the practice is not always the in-depth exercise it should be, and it's possible that abuses of the process have contributed to budgetary control's poor reputation.

In the worst cases from my own research, budgeting has been degraded to simply adding a percentage to the previous year's anticipated result, "anticipated" because the budget is usually produced before a financial year-end result is finalized, so the end-of-year result has to be estimated. This lax practice only serves to exacerbate accuracy and the derision from the critics.

While budgeting is condemned by the "Beyond Budgeting" movement, most critics do agree that the practice of budgeting can't be abandoned without the introduction of alternative controls and motivators. Unfortunately, standard approaches that might provide a template for an easy alternative to budgets are hard to find, and it is easy to see why. Most of the examples quoted or reported upon are bespoke systems that have been developed for a specific organization and based upon the principles of one of the "Adaptive Processes" or "new general management models" identified in Hope and Fraser's book "Beyond Budgeting," published in 2003. The alternative systems developed would likely not apply to most organizations, so they do not stand as models in themselves, although they do set examples of how the basics can be adapted. The research indicates, therefore, that there is no "one fit" alternative system to budgeting that can be readily adopted by all types and sizes of enterprise; alternatives have to be fashioned to suit their individual requirements.

Consequently, replacing budgets with a range of measures stretching from NFPIs to balanced scorecards can feel like a "shot in the dark" to many, lacking the clear link to financial performance provided by their trusted budget, even if this trust is sometimes misplaced. It is not easy for an organization to get such a change right the first time, so much caution is necessary.

Most ventures into "Beyond Budgeting" are driven by enthusiastic individuals or groups of individuals, because a move away from budgeting is a courageous one and any alternative needs a big commitment to ensure that the alternative works. Generally these transformations can only happen if they are supported by passion and dedication, and this usually comes from an individual fairly high in the management structure.

The approaches adopted are various and it is worth examining some of these in a little more detail.

First is the often-quoted abandonment of the budgeting process by Svenska Handlesbanken in the 1970s. They are reported to be one of the first to do so. This Swedish banking organization had 550 branches around Scandinavia and the UK, and it's interesting to note that following this groundbreaking decision it began to outperform its rivals and became one of the world's most cost-efficient banks. Prior to this major change in its financial planning in the late sixties, it was losing customers to its local rivals.

It has to be said that the abandonment of budgeting was not the only change; they recruited a new CEO and streamlined their management structure to only three levels. They made each branch a profit center and gave power to the branches to agree to their own customer loans, prices, discounts, and choose what products they wanted to sell (this all actually reduced their bad debt rate too). It's of interest that branches knew that they had to achieve cost-income relationships of around 40 percent. (Is this a form of budgeting, one wonders, or is it ensuring that costs remain in proportion to income?) What it did provide was freedom for the branches to be flexible in their management of costs. In fact, it was their allocated responsibility to reduce costs while satisfying customer needs and boosting income. Another change was the introduction of a branch league table that was published to all. Clearly this too must have been a factor in their success; no manager would want to be dwelling at the bottom of the league, available for all to see, for long.

What this story appears to say is that the abandonment of the budgeting process doesn't come alone, it must be accompanied by a range of other changes. But it does prove that a business can do without a budget; of course, to what extent the change in the company's fortunes changed because it abandoned its budgeting and what profit improvements were due to all the other changes that were made is a split difficult to evaluate.

Other organizations have taken different approaches. For example, BP, GE, and a number of other multinationals implemented a system that didn't waste time discussing the difference between top-level targets and achievement levels targeted by management at lower levels. In other words, they have abandoned the process of agreeing and negotiating targets or budgets between board and management and there was no direct pressure on managers such as occurs in the common annual process of "agreeing" the budget. The targets are set by the board according to the experienced vision of the top management. Having set the target, they simply allocate the difference between this and the manager's forecast, across the departments, and "challenge" the managers to close the gap.

There are many examples of companies adopting "Beyond Budgeting" techniques from across the business world, although not all the results are well documented, so it's not easy to determine to what extent success has been achieved or whether the system adopted is still *budgeting* but under another name. It is clear, however, from the examples that are known that systems replacing budgets have to be adapted to suit the circumstance of the organization.

In addition, one should not underestimate the importance of there being a champion—fundamentally changing an embedded financial-control system like budgeting requires considerable boldness, drive, hard work, and persuasion—even if the instigating manager is the CEO.

Adopting a balanced scorecard or dashboard approach is also a culture change for an organization, and staff must often alter their behavior and be prepared to use their own judgment and initiative without the familiar boundaries imposed by a budget. The organization may also need to embrace empowerment principles that entail managers making more decisions, gaining a better grasp of the part they and their departments individually play in the achievement of strategic objectives and company values. This often means much better in-house communication systems, a matter often ignored or underestimated during the process. They must also learn a new way of evaluating and measuring the financial implications of their decisions, as well as the limits they have.

Many companies are already training their staff in these practices but it can take many years, especially when managers have been reared on a diet of just "meeting their budgets," only reacting to their bosses' direct instructions, and abiding by the controls their budgets decree; use of initiative has often been suppressed, knowingly or not, and it can take much time to reinvigorate.

The *status quo* situation, therefore, to continue the existing budgetary control system, is an easier option for most; it is indeed a simple concept and easy to understand, accede to, and operate within. It also avoids the risk or necessity of culture change, a process that is easily underestimated and often fails.

When more liberal approaches are embraced or when implementing new ideas, the support of managers and other staff must therefore be elicited. If the people think it's a good idea, they will approach it willingly; but if they are only going along with it because they are told to and/or it is against their interests, there is much less enthusiasm and it becomes an uphill struggle. Expect to find laggards in such a process.

Designing a replacement system for budgeting that will comprise a network of alternative measures and carrying the staff with you is therefore not just daunting and risky, it's also a skilled task, and many organizations will not have the skills or experience to achieve it.

Despite these challenges, balanced scorecards and dashboards are valuable tools and often expedient in today's business environment. Many companies have completed the transformation, replaced their traditional budgetary-control systems with these new ideas and have achieved reported successes. Many other organizations will have adopted such techniques to varying degrees alongside the budgetary-control systems and no doubt their use will likely continue to expand, but to expect organizations to abandon their familiar budgetary-control systems overnight after several decades of use is probably asking too much. Budgets are regarded as a financial control "safety net." Whether this trust in current methods is justified has been a matter of wide discussion, and the apparent security budgeting provides can be a delusion. If the process is abused through mismanagement or attention to its shortcomings ignored, it can be damaging as well as failing in its purpose. Some shortcomings are however very difficult to overcome.

As we have seen, in the final analysis most organizations continue to operate within the comfort of the financial plan provided by a budget. Evidence suggests that it offers a form of assurance in the minds of managers, and abandoning these ingrained systems in favor of a set of indicators that can appear to have imprecise or tenuous links with financial performance is an action that appears too big a step for many.

Some critics of budgeting maintain that better financial performance arises from competitive strategies, not from better financial measurement. Of course, success stems from competitive strategies, but to compare it to better financial management is a false argument. From the time budgetary control was first used several decades ago, it is clear from the literature of that time that the introduction of budgeting was not a replacement for competitive strategies. It is a tool for cost control and monitoring financial performance against a plan. And while it can help to support competitive strategies, it never purported to drive or replace them. That is not to say that in practice some misguided organizations may rely on it overmuch at the cost of strategic planning, but this is bad management practice. Budgeting was never meant to replace strategic development.

Despite its popularity, traditional budgeting is flawed. The critics do have valid criticisms; even when done well it has numerous problems. But it is not the intention in this chapter to re-examine in detail the arguments against traditional budgeting put forward over the last twenty years. This has been done many times before, and if more information is required a trip to Amazon reveals thousands of books on the subject. In the final analysis, the problems and downsides of budgeting are mainly common sense and already known to most managers. But to enhance the clarity of this chapter, it is worth reviewing a summary of the main criticisms. These are not in order of priority:

Budgets

- take a long time to prepare, often many months, absorbing much management time and so can be costly to construct, and they can distract managers from their prime responsibilities.
- can be inward-looking and encourage short-term management; they are usually prepared for one year only.
- fail to consider non-financial business drivers
- are very soon out of date and become progressively less relevant as the financial year advances.
- can lack strategic focus because too much emphasis is placed on costs rather than value creation.
- can be too detailed and therefore restrictive

- are prepared in discreet twelve-month, financial-year periods, meaning that forward visibility is progressively reduced as the financial year moves on.
- can encourage managers to spend up to the budget, perhaps unnecessarily, and can lead to a "spend it or lose it" philosophy in managers. Many do not understand that a budget is not a license or reason to spend, it is a *limit* of spend.
- can be subject to cost padding and soft targets.
- can constrain responsiveness and flexibility, and so becoming a barrier to change.
- can encourage vertical control.
- can be based on unsupported assumptions and guesswork.
- can cause resentment vertically in an organization when an employee's budget is exceeded by the decision of a more senior manager.
- are usually departmentally based, so tending to reinforce rather than dismantle barriers. Costs incurred in one department as a result of errors in another can cause considerable friction.
- can lead to "getting what you measure." This can be to the detriment of the business if measures are not thoroughly thought through before implementation.
- can result in sales staff "taking their foot off the pedal" when they have reached the budget, sometimes even saving orders to help them achieve next month's budget.
- can lead to a lack of clarity in the performance levels set in the budget. It is not a target, but nor should it be soft. It should be realistic while moderately stretching management performance—not always easy to achieve.
- are often linked to remuneration, which can affect employees' behavior, sometimes to the detriment of the organization. Incentives based on budgets have to be very carefully constructed.
- can create too much focus on variances, leading to a lack of time to investigate future business opportunities.

In an effort to improve the practice and discover managers' views on their budgeting process, there has been research directed to an organization's dissatisfaction with its budgetary-control system. This research appears to be in accord with many other views:

Clarke and West, in their article "Rolling Forecasts" (*Financial Management*, the UK publication from CIMA for its members, April 2007) carried out an investigation in the Avon Rubber Group.

In view of dissatisfaction with their budgeting processes, managers were asked to rate separately the "importance" and "effectiveness" of a range of budget purposes.

There were eighteen purposes to rate on the basis of *importance* and *effectiveness*. *Importance* rating spread from "immaterial" to "vital," and *effectiveness* from "very good" to "very poor." The questions are shown below.

As far as *importance* was concerned, "Communicate with investors" scored 80 percent, "vital." As can be seen from the list below, this was the most important attribute of budgeting.

"Setting long-term goals" was the bottom scorer, which only rated 20 percent, not far off from "immaterial."

The questions enumerated below are in numerical order of being vital in the view of the managers, and therefore, in percentage terms are spread between 80 percent and 20 percent in descending order

1. Communicate with investor (80 percent vital)
2. Help to manage risk
3. Set short-term goals
4. Control costs
5. Basis for rewards
6. Involve people in planning
7. Coordination
8. Resource allocation
9. Manage capacity
10. Inform strategic planning
11. Empower managers

12. Basis for early warning
13. Internal communication
14. Basis for appraisals
15. Set medium-term goals
16. Improve efficiency
17. Control behavior
18. Set long-term goals (20 percent vital)

It is interesting that in this research study budgeting is still fairly vital when it comes to setting short-term goals, number 3 in the list, but "setting medium-term goals" appears at fifteenth place, not far above the least "vital," which is the "setting of long-term goals." This confirms that Avon's managers have reducing confidence in the *importance* of the budget as it ages.

Only three of the eighteen questions above, when rated on *effectiveness* of budgeting, were considered "very good," but even these only just crept into this category. These were "basis for reward," "involve people in planning," and "coordination." All others were rated in varying degrees as poor to "very poor."

The research concluded that, "Budgets were used to do much in their business, but to little effect."

In overall terms the result of this survey illustrates the poor opinion that Avon managers had of the importance and effectiveness of their budgeting system as an internal management tool, and this is supported by my own research and experience.

It is likely that a majority of organizations feel there is "room for improvement" in their budgetary-control system and processes, but regardless of this the practice still thrives with little evidence of significant changes being made. This paradox indicates that many organizations captured in this budgeting dilemma must be hungry for a better way, perhaps because of the paucity of radical ideas on how to do it. It is fair to say that when more attention is paid to the well-known downsides listed above then budgets can be improved, but even this will not solve some of the key criticisms that are unavoidable because of the nature of the process.

So when all know the shortcomings, why do organizations persist in the annual labor of budgeting at all? What do managers say?

The most vacuous comments in my research included: "we've always done it" or "it's the big stick we need to beat the managers with" and "how else can we calculate manager's bonuses?" More admissible reasons were "to satisfy the demands and requirements of the owners or shareholders, stakeholders, or boards of public bodies or auditors or lenders." Others include "cost targeting for managers," "targets for salesmen," "information to other stakeholders," "managing investor expectations," "planning," and "exercising control." Some simply say "they can't find a better way." Many of these reasons have considerable validity.

As mentioned in this list, a budget is often obligatory; boards, owners, lenders, etc. can insist upon them. Indeed this may be a major obstacle to change because owners do need some prior to financial-year affirmation of their investment and to be assured that internal financial controls and results are adequate. Most public-financed organizations are in this category. Many organizations, therefore, have no alternative, and I suspect it would be difficult to persuade these stakeholders otherwise.

A word about zero-based budgeting. The process of combining the budget process with a full strategic review does not imply the adoption of zero-based budgeting, where every function is required to review costs starting with a "zero base"; that is, without reference to previous expenditure levels or simply seeking incremental increases on last year. Strategic reviews rarely start from a zero base, so neither should the budget even if there are "one-offs" in previous actual costs that may be carried forward into the new budget. Rather than ignore all the history, it is better to identify these "rogue" costs and assumptions and ensure that they aren't brought forward.

With zero-based budgeting, each budget-line must be justified in detail from a zero starting point. Zero-based budgeting has merit if it truly is "starting from scratch"; for example, the launch of a new division or branch, etc. It may also be used with certain lines on a budget where last year's actual results would not be of assistance; e.g., advertising campaigns, other optional expenditures, etc. In established organizations, zero-based budgeting for the whole budget would be an even longer process than traditional budgeting: it is also usually unwise for managers to ignore the history, which can have real value in guiding managers to more accuracy in their budgeting and forecasting.

## The game of budgeting

The fact that most boards have usually made up their minds what the bottom line should be before the budgeting process starts can have the effect of relegating the detail of the main body of the budget to a process of negotiation, shows of strength, and *gaming* among managers as they argue their subjective demands from the organization's predefined funds. Everyone knows the tactics: ask for more costs than needed and underestimate the sales income lines because all want to beat their budget when the final line is drawn. Some of these propositions will not be agreed by top management and the figures tightened, but many will slip through the net and contribute to what is often termed a "soft budget." This guileful exercise leads to trade-offs and juggling of income and cost lines until the final result considered by the board as satisfactory has been reached. This *gaming* has its winners, and it is often not the best managers that win the game.

## The time it takes to produce a budget

The length of time it takes to achieve completion of the budget each year was researched by Cranfield University in the UK, and this indicated that the majority of organizations take three months or more to finalize their budgets. This time span appears to be generally accepted. It is not uncommon for a board to return the budget to managers a number of times because they haven't attained the bottom or top line result the board has already targeted. This takes time.

Clearly there is much substance in the criticism that the process is long and absorbs management time, and since management time is widely described as the most valuable resource within an organization this can indeed be costly. Little wonder that the full budgeting process is reduced to just once a year and revisions resisted.

The other factor is that the earlier the budget is started the longer the predicted period it covers becomes and therefore the less accurate it will be; some budgets may even be out of date before the next financial year has started!

## Common inadvisable shortcuts

As mentioned above, an important reason for budgetary control is that it can, if intelligently integrated, assist senior management with the formation of strategy and long-term business plans as well as monitoring financial performance. The annual budgeting exercise can then concentrate the minds of management, at least once a year, on a full business plan, a detailed examination of strategy, growth, competition, resources, costs, new products, past performance, and marketing, etc. Notice the word *can* in the previous sentence; management must try to avoid the annual budgeting process becoming a mechanical exercise that is limited to simple percentage increases in the previous year's income and costs, just a reflection of inflation, ambition, and aspiration. Many organizations still slip into this trap. Such budgets fail to consider all the strategic factors and ignore trends; it is not uncommon to find budgets that actually show positive trends when the trends of current actual performance are heading in the opposite direction! Graphical displays of twelve-month rolling totals clearly indicate this irregularity and play a significant role in defeating it.

The previous financial year's results are usually a starting point for next year's budget but these are likely to include recognized inadequacies in last year's performance and management must aim for the new budget to eliminate these. Last year's result must therefore be examined in detail to ensure the same deficiencies are not carried into the new financial year by simply adding an inflationary increase.

Sometimes budgets become a form of *target* justified by the words: "well, we should be able to manage a 10 percent increase in business next year" or "I see no reason why this cost shouldn't be cut by 5 percent next year, we just need to try harder." This is pure aspiration unless a defined and feasible plan accompanies it. It does not make for good budgeting.

Note also the rounded sums. These casual percentage increases often appear to be 2.5 percent multiples, much the same as many price increases. It gives the impression that little thought or investigation has been invested in coming up with a calculated percentage; one that can be evaluated later if variances occur—a process that only has value if the criteria for the increase has been recorded.

Clearly this form of budgeting is unproductive, sometimes reckless, and just strengthens the critics' view that the practice of budgeting would be best "abolished."

## Out-of-date budgets

This is perhaps the most common and difficult problem with conventional budgeting; in the fast-moving business, commercial, and public world we live in the annual budget is very soon out of date. Worldwide, advanced communication systems and IT were never dreamed of when budgeting was first introduced. In those days the pace of business was much slower and the problem with aging dramatically less. Despite these technical revolutions budgeting is still much the same now as it was then, consequently the problem of aging and accuracy are much more acute.

In the worst cases budgets can become meaningless altogether, but in most cases many lines in a budget will become of declining value as a performance and cost-control measure during the course of the year. It's almost impossible to keep up to date month by month in the management accounts with which lines of a budget are now invalid, and managers will sometimes struggle to counter variances that have arisen because circumstances have changed since the budget was agreed. One wonders just how much time is wasted investigating and reporting on variances when they have arisen because of:

- strategic and other decisions taken that affect future costs,
- unforeseen events,
- declining/rising sales levels,
- unexpected competitor activity or innovation,
- macroeconomic factors,
- an unannounced calamity,
- and many other unpredictable events that could not have been considered in the original budget.

To compound the issue, the same questionable variances are frustratingly presented in the cumulative totals during every future month's management accounts for that financial year, and this can trigger even further investigation and interrogation because the reasons expounded in the preceding months have been overseen or forgotten. It isn't difficult to understand why the practice has been so heavily criticized.

A budget is a plan, but like most plans it can only consider facts that are known at the time it is prepared, the rest will be an estimate, some might say "guesstimate," of expected events and perhaps include allowances for other unknown contingencies—values that are often just grabbed out of the air without any real logic attached to them.

## Amending budgets midterm

Consider the similarities of a budget to a pilot's flight plan before the aircraft ventures on a trip across the Atlantic. The pilot knows the time of departure and the due time of arrival, which may be considered the profit target set by the board. These two critical times for passengers are important criteria on which the performance of the airline is judged.

To meet the due arrival time, a plan must be devised before takeoff that considers wind speed and direction at various points on the route, prevailing weather conditions at different altitudes/locations/timings that will affect the comfort and safety of the passengers and the airspeed and groundspeed of the aircraft, the routes and altitude of other aircraft/levels of traffic, and finally the economy of fuel on the journey. It's a complex situation, but so are most businesses or public enterprises where like the flight plan most of these factors are subject to "forecast," none are for certain.

As the aircraft moves toward its target location and arrival time, the speed, altitude, and direction of the plane will be changed to accommodate the actual circumstances encountered along the route. At each stage the conditions ahead are reviewed and amendments made to the flight plan as necessary.

All these changes are made to accommodate the target arrival time at the destination. This would only be changed if in trying to meet it the safety of the passengers and aircraft would be jeopardized.

So here is a plan, call it a budget, that is constantly adapted to accommodate the unforeseen circumstances encountered so that it reaches its destination on time.

Thankfully few businesses have to change plans by the minute as the pilot and his crew have to, but the principle is clear. If a plan is to be of lasting value then it has to be changed at intervals to accommodate and consider events that were not anticipated in the original. The challenge, therefore, is to find a way to reduce the changes and speed up and simplify the process so as to avoid the costs of lengthy management time. Clearly such budget resets can't be a full business review every time, but then neither is a pilot's flight plan necessarily rewritten completely at every stage of the journey; however, one thing remains constant in the pilot's plans, the end objective: to arrive on time. This would only be sacrificed if all else failed. To use this aircraft analogy, it could be compared to the net result in an organization we could say that the *net result is the keystone* around which other changes are made or measured.

The remarkable fact is that the need for revising a budget during the course of a financial year is nothing new. In *Information Note* 55, "Managerial Aspects of Budgetary Control," published by the British Institute of Management in October 1966, the introduction says:

> *"Flexibility should be designed into the budget. The system should be able to adjust to major problems, such as a sharp drop in sales, without the collapse of the whole program. Also, to prevent criticism and ridicule which may destroy the budgetary system, standard procedures must be installed to take care of minor adjustments during day-to-day operations."*

So as long ago as the 1960s, the recommendation was that the budget should be revised for unforeseen factors.

The same thoughts are echoed by the then Institute of Cost and Works Accountants in the UK; in its Terminology of Cost Accounting in the 1960s it says:

> *". . . the establishment of budgets relating to responsibilities of executives to the requirements of a policy and the continuous comparison of actual and budgeted results either to secure by individual action the objective of that policy or to provide a basis for its revision . . ."*

It is clear that from the beginning of budgetary control it was recognized and recommended that budgets must be updated and reviewed as they were overtaken by events. But research indicates that only a minority of organizations actually do so; the common reason put forward for this failure is that it takes up too much management time. To use a common expression to react to these statements, "if you think revising your budgets costs money, try not doing so." Cost control can be lost, the confidence of managers damaged, and their attitude can change to one of contempt for the budget.

It is staggering that after massive advances in business technology and IT no practical universal approach has yet been found to carry out these revisions and that is now in common use.

Many would say this is an indictment of the accounting profession, but then so is the fifty-year-old numeric method of presentation of management accounts that this book promotes to change.

### How do trends help?

The ideas and target audience of this book are senior and middle management, not shareholders, business owners, or stakeholders (unless they are also managers). It is directed to those who manage the business day to day and it doesn't matter for the purposes of this book what approach to budgeting is adopted, although it is hoped that having read this chapter many might be incentivized to re-examine their processes. The main objective in this chapter is to describe how a budget is presented in graphical format, how it compares and links with the actual financial results of an organization, and how graphical display can be used to improve budgeting techniques leading to better financial control and greater accuracy.

It can be seen that budgeting is full of pitfalls, but so long as managers legislate against these dangers many of these problems can be mitigated. There are, however, defects integral to the process that are difficult to overcome however diligent the manager. These more difficult areas can't be avoided and so must be identified and budgets improved during its *term*, rather than during its preparation. This is where graphical analysis is of major assistance. The portrayal of trends in actual performance and forecasts overlaying those of the budget clearly highlight those areas where the budget may have either been prepared negligently or when it was unable to consider factors that have only come to light since the budget was prepared. Trends in financial performance help to pinpoint areas that need rectification in future budgets as well as identify likely future performance and improving or worsening variances. They are also of major assistance when preparing the budget for the following year since the trends of actual performance and forecast performance are clearly visible. This subject will be considered in more detail in chapter 5.

## *Net profit/loss/result is the keystone*

As mentioned earlier it is common practice for a board to have in mind minimum levels of net profit and perhaps sales growth at the start of the budgeting process. A board must have vision for the future of the business, and these targets will usually form part of that ambition. It would, of course, be expected that the board would have views on the top and bottom lines of the budget. The board is privy to all aspects of the business, the requirements of its stakeholders and its market, and it is responsible for the long-term growth and strategy, it has a breadth of vision. It also has to satisfy the needs of the shareholders or owners of the organization. Individual managers would not always be aware of the scope of these factors.

It is not unreasonable, therefore, for the board to set bottom-line targets and the parameters within which the managers must operate when they are formulating the budget.

As a financial year of a budget progresses, the budgeted growth targets for income, and particularly profit/surplus levels, will generally remain sacrosanct despite what may have happened to all other budget lines during the course of the year, whether these have been caused by unforeseen events that overtake a budget or not. Budget resets of a net result are normally the last thing that an organization will want to change; this is the *key result* that has received the approval of the stakeholders, who while tolerating variances in income and expenses don't like net profit warnings.

All know that the regular process of line by line comparisons of variances between budget and actual income and costs will often prove ineffectual; it is a fallible exercise because circumstances and management decisions are reflected in the *actual* values but not the *budget,* which remains as originally drafted. Such variances then persist month by month as the financial year progresses because they become part of the cumulative variance and therefore often the subject of repeated discussion at the presentation of each set of management accounts. Even then the budget isn't often changed however justifiable the variance. Clearly this is unsatisfactory and it is one of the most important criticisms of budgets; they are out of date almost as soon as they are prepared and as the year moves on they get progressively worse. The fact is that change is endemic to every organization: people change, competitors change, products change, economics changes, plans change when results fail to meet expectations, and management's ideas change too.

This can often make any persistence from the board that original profit targets be met appear unrealistic, yet these original budget objectives remain till the end of the financial year. It is as if up to the last month there is unreal hope that something will happen out of the blue to correct a situation. As a financial year progresses, the incidence of these variances increases to the extent that sometimes many lines on a budget lose their purpose altogether. This can be very damaging; when budgets fail to be revised then those budget cost lines that should be reduced are not attended to and this can lead to unnecessary overspending. In the meantime those lines that should be legitimately increased are not, but this does not necessarily mean that these increased costs can be stemmed. So here we have a net detriment to bottom line that has been caused simply by failure to amend the budget.

So is the answer to change the budget during the year?

In view of the time it takes to prepare an annual budget and the fact that it may have been approved by the stakeholders, it is unlikely that starting again with a budget during a financial year is either practical or possible. If this is so, what else can be done to legislate against this inevitable defect?

It has been proposed that the only figure that management is reluctant to change in a budget is the last one, the bottom line. It doesn't matter if this is a budgeted profit, breakeven, or even a loss as it might be in nonprofit organizations, this is the figure that most stakeholders prioritize; earnings growth is a key measure for investors in commercial organizations, who are much less concerned by variances in the lines above the final line in the profit-and-loss account. This insouciance can be used positively to introduce more flexibility in the cost and income lines within a budget to reflect changes in circumstances. This prolongs the effective use of the budget throughout its life. The only criterion is that such changes balance out and leave the bottom line intact or improved. On the face of it this may sound naive, so let's examine it in more detail. To begin with, just because a particular cost has been overspent against a budget does not mean that the same cost should be cut to meet a budget. The overspend on a budget line may be vital while a cut to another budget line may be perfectly acceptable, so why not change the budget lines to suit? This practice of *virement* in a budget is not widely utilized but it should be. Virement is the utilization of a budget for one purpose to finance another purpose; i.e., transferring the budget from one cost type to another. Generally speaking, this arises within a single responsibility/profit center but there is no reason why it can't be adopted in a wider sense. Such minor changes to the budget would usually require only lower-level approval.

Of course virement of this nature can be avoided or reduced by significantly reducing the number of budget lines. Is it really necessary to bog down a budget by detailing a value against all minor cost items? This is usually a level of micromanagement that simply isn't necessary. Grouping all costs together for a particular cost or responsibility center and leaving it to the manager to manage within this sum will not only reduce the number of variances, it will also provide greater freedom, empowerment, and job satisfaction for the manager. If he or she wants to create limits of individual spend within the department they manage, it can be done *off budget*. In this process care is needed to separate out in the management accounts those start-up, speculative, consequential, temporary, once-off, and optional costs as depicted in the round and oval boxes in Figure 2.1 from the base structural and base correlative costs as described in the previous chapter. This is to facilitate meaningful cost-to-income percentages that were also described in the last chapter.

Major changes to circumstances since the budget was created beyond those that can be managed by virement would need board/top management approval, especially if they concern income levels or significant cross-responsibility boundaries. These are best dealt with utilizing cost-to-income relationships that monitor cost structure within the organization as described in the last chapter. The charts for cost percentages and their trends provide an easy method of indicating areas that have slipped out of, or will slip out of budgeted proportion to the net result, and this provides the agenda for discussion about re-budgeting those cost percentages.

Using a graphical approach that shows trends in management accounts, especially when forecasts are also depicted in the charts, can also facilitate budget revisions during the course of a financial year to reflect happenings and decisions not foreseen in the original. The graphs will pinpoint those areas that are slipping out of kilter to turnover. Used wisely, the charts can shorten the time taken with this process. This will not only save management time, but more importantly it will help to retain and increase the value and credibility of the budget. The next chapter deals with the inclusion of forecasts in the management accounts and an appreciation of this will reinforce how graphical presentation of management accounts will improve the budgetary control process and address many of its shortcomings.

By the judicious display of actual, budget, and forecast, combined with the monitoring of cost proportions (as described in the last chapter), the interplay between these trends is revealed; this mitigates a major weakness in conventional budgeting.

*How can graphs assist accuracy in end-of-financial-year budget
to actual projections?*

In the previous chapters we have seen how twelve-month rolling
totals can enlighten management by revealing a trend in the results
long before the year-end. Using considered forecasting techniques,
that include any new information and initiatives, it is not difficult to
extrapolate this trend. This will provide a view of the likely financial
year-end result. By plotting the budget on the same charts as actual
income and costs, the performance gap is now clearly revealed. It
is the widening or narrowing gap between the trend lines that is
particularly important; it highlights the differences between the two
trends (actual-forecast result vs. budgeted result) and the rate at
which any divergence is taking place.

With traditional numeric management accounts it is very difficult
to visualize how the year will end. The change month to month,
revealed as the current month variance, reveals no discernible
pattern, and the cumulative value doesn't add much information
either; it can be seen whether the variance has grown or reduced
in the month but any consistency or trend is invisible. Seasonality
also adds to the difficulty. This prevents even growth in the results
month to month, so attempting to predict a result using proportionate
increases is also inaccurate. Nor are any changes to cost proportions
(percent of turnover) available because most numeric management
accounts do not include percentages, so there are no indications of
cost relationships to income or the direction the trends are headed.

This information is instantly visible when viewing graphs of
twelve-month rolling totals. Not only does this bring a note of realism
to budget-actual relationships and the feasibility of meeting end-of-
year profit targets, the information revealed in the trend charts for
individual costs and income lines will also make it very clear where
the divergences have occurred. We shall examine this integration of
budget and actual on the same charts later in this chapter and discover
how this integration of budget and actual performance trends will
prompt action earlier than is achievable with conventional numeric

accounts. It is those lost months without action that once gone are often lost forever; those missed opportunities are unlikely to be recouped within the same timeframe.

## *Trends work with or without budgets*

It is not the objective of this book to advocate any particular form of budgetary control or promote dispensing with the budget altogether in favor of other approaches. This must be a matter for each organization to determine for itself. Whatever decision is taken will not affect the graphical approach to the presentation of the management accounts. If there *is* no budget it is simply left off the chart, leaving just the trends of actual and forecast results. This still adds significant value. Not only is it still clear what direction each income and cost line is taking, the impact of the forecast and its feasibility is also revealed. Some may argue this is all that is needed anyway, although I have to say that I believe for purposes of once-a-year focus and planning together with intermittent revisions that maintain cost controls there is still value in the budget so long as it is completed thoroughly and considers the numerous downsides we examined earlier. On the assumption that a budget is shown, then graphical presentation substantially improves the understanding of budget vs. actual relationships. All further examples in this book make the assumption that budgets are still produced.

## *Displaying budgets in graphical format*

The incorporation of a budget into the same chart as the actual performance requires important arithmetical considerations. These are best illustrated by considering the example in Fig. 3.1

This chart displays the twelve-month rolling total of actual turnover and budget for the previous financial year together with the twelve-month rolling total for budget for the full current year and the actual turnover to date. The budget is indicated by the bars and the actual performance by the continuous black line. In this example the financial year is January 1 to December 1.

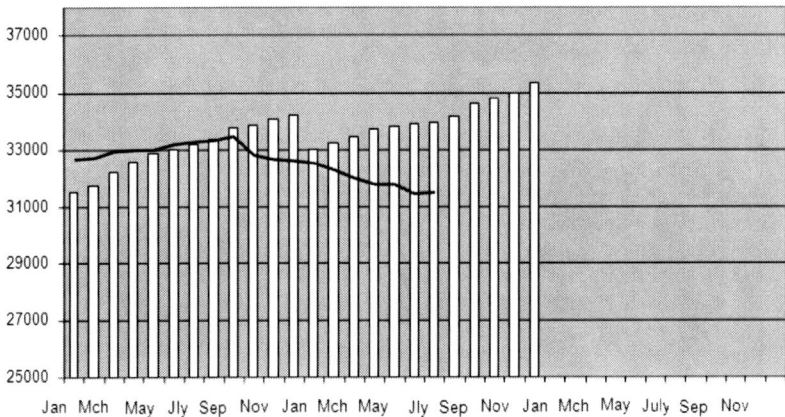

*Figure 3.1*
*Twelve-month rolling totals of sales, budget and actual*
*(Note that this graph only displays the top of the vertical axis*
*[25,000-37,000] this accentuates the slope on the graphs)*

There are a number of points that immediately become visible in Fig. 3.1:

1. Last year's trend in actual turnover was growing almost month on month and this turned down in October. Since then there is no sign of this downward trend changing and sales have clearly underperformed for some time. Even at the beginning of last year, when sales were above budget, the advantage was not maintained. Note the narrowing gap between sales and budget from January to June last year. This advantage ended in June, and although budget was met for a couple of months the actual result then started to slip away. The downward trend continued to the current month of the current year. On the assumption that the budget for the current financial year was prepared during October-December last year, it is likely that serious questions were arising about the sudden decline in sales. It is also likely that action was taken to turn the trend

because the budget for the current year indicates expected sales growth for the current year, although the graph indicates the action taken did not work.

2.  In the current year the divergence from budget continues to widen, raising a serious question mark over achievement of budget for the current year. There will be a significant shortfall from budget if current trends continue.

3.  There is a curious step in the rolling total of the budget at the end of the previous financial year. This is explained below.

4.  Although a three-year timeframe is shown on the horizontal graph (last, current, and next year), there are no entries as yet in the next year. As yet it is too early for next year's budget to be entered as this will probably not be completed until toward the end of the current year. In addition, the graph shows no forecasts; this subject is covered in the following chapter.

## Calculating the budget rolling total

It will be noted that the budget rolling has a step at the crossover from one financial year till the next (as mentioned in point 3 above). To explain this it is necessary to describe the way in which the current financial year's budget twelve-month rolling total (the middle year above) is calculated:

The starting point is a phased *budget* (month by month) for the current financial year together with the phased *actual* result of the previous year. All this information is held by the organization's accountant.

The rolling total of the budget for January (current year) is calculated by taking the budget for January and adding the *actual* turnover for the previous eleven months. Then in February the calculation would be to take the budget for January and February and add the last ten months' *actual* turnover to this, and so on until the end of the year when in month twelve the full budget for the year will be included in the rolling total. *The gap, therefore, between the actual and budget rolling totals represents the true cumulative variance of*

*budget and actual performance that arises from the current year's
budget only.*

The requirement of mixing actual and budget values in the twelve-
month rolling total is not immediately obvious, so further explanation
may be necessary. A business is usually measured against a budget
over a twelve-month financial year and at the beginning of each year
the previous year's budget is *forgotten*. At this stage it has served
its purpose and is now superfluous, as well as being totally out of
date. This fact applies whether management accounts are presented
numerically or graphically. If the budget rolling total were calculated
by using the previous year's budget (rather than the *actual* values),
as might first be thought, then up to eleven months of the budget
rolling total would comprise the immaterial budget from last year
mixed with the current year's budget. In view of its irrelevance, last
year's budget must be disregarded; management is only interested
in their performance against the current year's budget. This is what
they are measured against, and there is little point in calculating
a rolling total that includes such obsolete numbers. The method
of calculation prescribed above means that the budget rolling total
displayed becomes the line that managers aim to meet or exceed both
retrospectively and in the future.

By using the same "actual" values from last year in the budget
twelve-month rolling total as those used for the twelve-month rolling
total for actual performance, the performance gap (variance) revealed
in the graph will be attributable *only* to the current year and the trend
in the budget will be directly comparable to the trend in the actual
result. The gap between the actual rolling total sales trend line and
the budgeted sales line is the variance, and this value will be the
same as would have been shown as the *cumulative* variance in a set
of conventional numeric management accounts. This is the value that
managers are measured by.

If the rolling total of the budget were to have been calculated
using the budget from the previous year instead of last year's actual,
then the resulting trend would have exacerbated the problems arising

from out-of-date budgets, and the resultant comparison would be meaningless to managers.

As shown in Fig. 3.1 above, this method of calculating the budget twelve-month rolling total accounts for why the budget and actual are close to coinciding in the early months, because at the beginning of any financial year the difference between actual and budget is usually quite small; the variance from budget is for one month only at the end of January. If the budget is continually missed as the year progresses, the cumulative difference grows just as any annual cumulative variance would grow in a conventional set of management accounts; in the graphical chart this is depicted as an ever-widening performance gap. In the event that the budget is achieved then the two values would coincide on the graph and no gap would appear. Likewise, if following a period of a growing variance action is taken to rectify it, meaning the budget each month is achieved, then the two lines would continue as parallel lines, illustrating the stability of the situation.

It is appreciated that this is an apparent *mix* of rolling totals but it does portray the information needed within the management accounts and in no way detracts from the trends in actual and forecast performance.

The difference between graphical and numeric presentations is that in the graph the trend in the variance is revealed; it can be seen whether the gap/variance is widening or converging and the rate at which this is happening. In the numerical accounts this is invisible; only the cumulative and current month's variances are visible.

At this stage the chart shows only the budget for the remainder of the current year. When a forecast is added it will appear as a continuation of the actual result and this clearly indicates the end-of-year result predicted, so revealing the performance gap from budget at year-end.

The impact of this calculation method for the twelve-month rolling total of budget on the graph is illustrated by a *step* in the twelve-month rolling total, a phenomenon not usually seen in twelve-month rolling totals but arising because of using the actual result from last year in the twelve-month rolling budget total rather than the out-of-date budget from last year. Such a step up or down is likely at the end of any financial year when the rolling total of the budget for the previous year is replaced by a revised rolling total for the forthcoming year, all as explained above.

In Fig. 3.1 it may be assumed that the step *down* in the budget indicates either a too optimistic budget for the *previous* year or poor income performance or both.

Likewise, if the step in the budget had been up rather than down the opposite would be true, either soft budgeting or better actual income performance than budget.

### *The importance of percentage graphs for costs when comparing to budget*

As mentioned in the previous chapter, every cost or cost group will be represented with two graphs: the twelve-month rolling total of actual value and the twelve-month rolling total of the percentage that same cost bears to turnover. This achieves three main objectives:

1. It keeps managers in touch with the actual values involved compared to budget actual value forecast.
2. The percentage that each cost bears to income reveals any change in the cost proportions and the impact on net result, as well as the budgeted percentage.
3. It will be found that on occasions actual cost value will be rising while the percentage cost to income is falling and the reverse.

Figures 3.2 to 3.3 are samples of such graphs for material cost of sales. This is a base correlative cost; i.e., a variable/semivariable cost that changes with the level of volume in a business. It may be close to or directly proportional to volume of sales and it will be more variable than fixed.

*Note that actual values/percentages are shown by the continuous line and budgets by the vertical bars. So as to simplify the graph, only the current and last year's results are shown.*

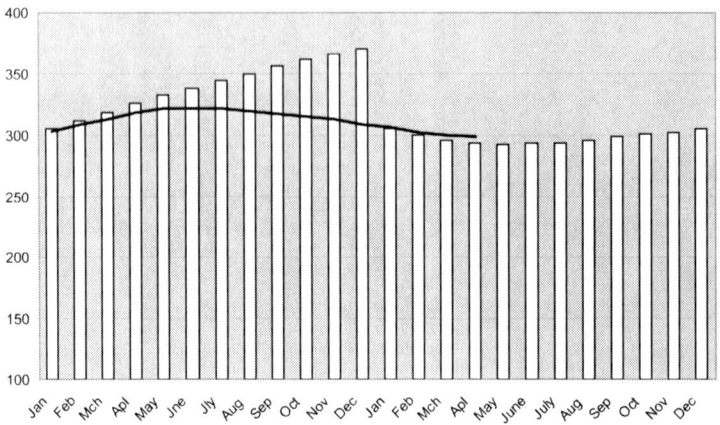

*Fig. 3.2*
*Twelve-month rolling total, value of material*
*cost of sales to April of current year*

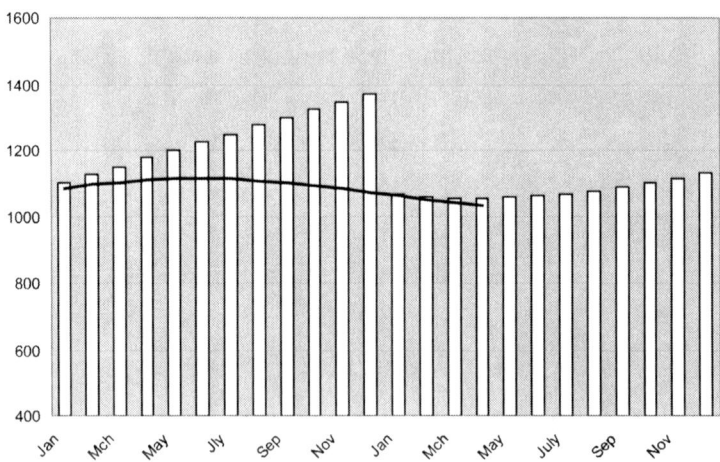

*Fig. 3.3*
*Twelve-month rolling total of sales*
*(actual and budget) at April (current year)*

In figures 3.2 and 3.3 material costs appear to have fallen more or less in sympathy with sales.

The sales graph in Fig. 3.3 shows a budgeted growth in sales last year that did not materialize; in fact, sales started declining in August last year. The budget for the current year reflected this downward trend and expects a recovery in the last six months of this year but *actual* sales show no sign at present of turning the downward trend and have just started to dip below the budget.

Sales and material costs are continuing on a downward trend but are costs moving *exactly* in sympathy with sales income. The graph plotting value looks to be more or less in proportion to the sales reduction; however, consider the graph shown in Fig. 3.4:

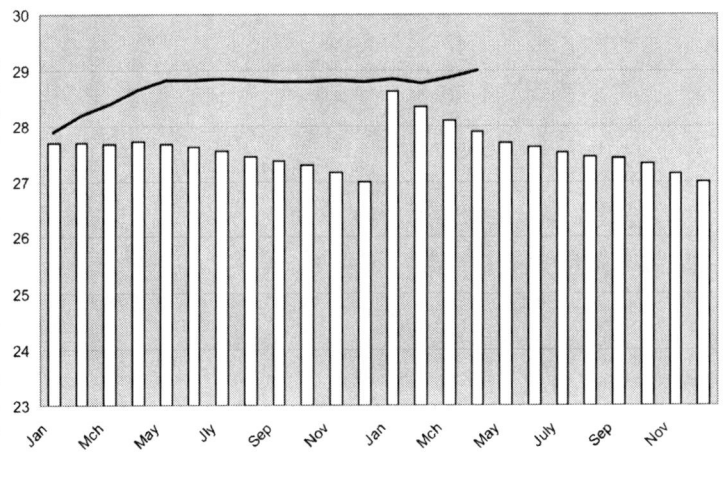

*Fig. 3.4*

*Twelve-month rolling total, material cost percent of sales value*

It is evident from this trend graph that during the early part of the previous financial year material costs themselves either rose by about 1 percent or sales price or mix changed to the detriment of margins.

N.B.: note that sublevel graphs for each of these variances would identify the trend in each of these factors.

Following this rise margins have stabilized; the percentage then remained steady for nine months. The budget indicates a reducing material cost percentage for the current year, so some action may have been proposed to reduce material costs or some change in sales mix or price expected. However, in the last two months material costs as percent of sales has risen, now touching 29 percent, so whatever assumption was made appears to have been incorrect.

This fluctuation in percentage appears quite small, spreading over just a 2 percent range and would not be easily detected from conventional numeric accounts. But such fluctuations have a much larger impact on net profit than may appear at first sight; if net profit percentage was 10 percent of sales then this 2 percent reduction in margin amounts to a 20 percent reduction in net profit. This would be clearly indicated in the graph for net profit to sales percentage chart.

This very simple example demonstrates how plotting the percentage that costs bear to income can reveal even small variations in cost proportions and margins that would not be easy to spot with conventional numeric management accounts or even just from the sales and material graphs themselves. Whilst small however their impact on the bottom line is of a larger magnitude as demonstrated above.

*In summary*

The resilience of the budgeting process despite the known weaknesses and the alternative strategies offered by the "Beyond Budgeting" movement, has been proven through the research of Dugdale and Lyne. From the evidence available it is not easy to see at this time how significant changes away from budgeting will take effect over the next decade or so. Research has indicated that incremental improvements are emerging; Dugdale and Lyne's research found that a combination of ideologies was already happening in some organizations.

As mentioned earlier the alternatives to budgeting appear to be bespoke to the organization adopting them, and perhaps this is one of the factors that dissuades potential adopters; it is a challenging and risky venture if the budget is actually abandoned. What is not clear from the many examples studied is to what extent the enthusiasm, drive, and perhaps pride of the instigator, plus the enthusiasm and imagination of the management support, is the reason an alternative works or not. To what extent are these essential to the change rather than the nature of the system adopted? Furthermore, to what extent a system persists beyond the reign of the instigator is also an unknown factor—new brooms often sweep clean.

This is possibly a major challenge for bespoke or radical approaches. They do require faith, conviction, culture change, and iron determination and unless this is present it is likely that an initiative to move away from budgets will not succeed.

On the other hand, there is security and familiarity in a developed universal system such as budgeting despite all its drawbacks. It does not require a determined advocate to drive it, and it is second nature to accountants.

In this chapter we have summarized the criticisms and advantages of budgetary control and how budgets are incorporated into the graphical presentation of management accounts. The application of trends to actual results and budgets demonstrates how these graphical presentations clearly indicate the trend in any divergence from budget and the rate at which this is happening; it provides management with an instant vision of how current performance is likely to affect the final financial year-end result compared to budget. Trends depicted in this way highlight and pinpoint budgeting weaknesses, and if acted upon, will improve the budgeting process.

It is reiterated that turning a trend in actual performance, particularly one that has been consistent over several months, is unlikely to happen overnight and requires significant corrective action by management. A view over all the charts (income and costs) will highlight the extent and direction of those efforts. It is very easy to underestimate both the difficulty of turning an adverse trend and the time it takes to do so. On many occasions I have seen forecasts and budgets that have trends turning favorably in the future when subsequently they have either not turned at all or the turn has occurred much later than predicted. There appears to be a natural optimism and an underestimation of how difficult a trend reversal can be it can require considerable management time and can have cost implications. This bullishness is a common occurrence and one that should be viewed with some skepticism whenever it is seen in the charts. It is essential to take note and beware of such false optimism. This subject occurs again when considering the preparation of forecasts.

The reader may well ask, following this review of current budgeting convention, how should we change our current practice? As observed above, the advice of the "Beyond Budgeting" fraternity petitions that budgets should be downgraded or even abandoned in favor of other measures centered on a balanced scorecard, and dashboards but such a dramatic move appears to be too big a change for most organizations. It could even prove damaging as well as introducing significant risks to the business.

For many organizations, management has to live with the budgeting process because it is obligatory, actually demanded by most public organizations and in many private companies too, particularly when owned by private equity partnerships or financed largely by banks. Many shareholders also insist on budgets. It is therefore not easy for these organizations to abandon them even if they felt it expedient.

While graphical presentation of management accounts can lessen the impact of some of the downsides of budgeting it is still essential to review and tackle some of the other defects listed earlier. Here are a few recommendations for consideration:

- Ownership of budget lines by an *individual*
- A "bottom up" approach
- Budgets must contain realistic, achievable objectives that err slightly on the side of stretching the manager. A budget is not a target that is designed to be almost beyond reach, often given to sales staff. Nor is it a forecast that is designed to depict what is likely to happen if something doesn't change.
- Budgets should address and coordinate with the strategic plan
- Budgets should allow flexibility within each manager's responsibility, with generous virement (*the agreed transfer of money from one budget line, income or expenditure, to another within a financial year*). This will help to alleviate the wasted questioning of the many variances that occur at lower levels often arising because of unforeseen happenings or opportunities. This gives a manager greater freedom to manage. Even virement can be avoided if budget lines are reduced; it is simply not necessary to budget down to each individual cost. Costs can be grouped to allow managers freedom to operate within their cost-group budget.
- Budgeted costs should adopt a percentage of turnover approach as outlined in the previous chapter to control and monitor changes in cost proportions.
- CEOs should encourage a variable approach to so-called fixed costs.
- Boards should resist the temptation to base incentives on individual manager's control of cost within his/her department. Incentives are best based on organizational or divisional outcomes to encourage team performance; this also promotes peer pressure.

The "Beyond Budgeting" group has been promoting the abandonment of budgets in favor of a balanced scorecard since 2003, but the vast majority of organizations stick to their traditional budgets, so this chapter takes the pragmatic way forward to improve current budgeting practice rather than renounce it—but it can be slowly moved to a better place. Trends and forecasts will offset many of the problems attached to budgeting and perhaps, when you have introduced a system of graphs that depict the trends in the management accounts and seen the benefits that accrue from the inclusion of forecasts, you may even reach the conclusion that you don't need budgets anymore.

# CHAPTER 4
## Including Rolling Forecasts in Management Accounts

In this modern age it is unthinkable that oceangoing ships would proceed around the world without the aid of modern, sophisticated, forward marine visibility and weather-forecasting systems, constantly scanning the horizons and airwaves for unforeseen or changing circumstances and obstacles. The consequences of not doing so can be catastrophic, yet many large multimillion corporations run their businesses with crude and irregular forecasting processes; it is like sailing a ship with your eyes closed.

Investors, shareholders, financial backers, trustees, etc. are more and more cautious because of the turbulent times in which we live, and it is more vital than ever for all organizations to manage their stakeholder's expectations carefully, these interested parties will have greater trust in an organization that consistently meets its own forecasts. Organizations that raise expectations too high and miss their targets will surely lose that confidence with consequent damage to their share value and/or esteem. Those that don't forecast at all risk losing even more. And don't run away with the idea that forecasting is only applicable to oceangoing ships, it applies just as much to smaller vessels too. Very often the smaller the organization the more vulnerable it is to unforeseen events. It has less mass to absorb unexpected difficulties and often much less cash to cope with it.

The problem is that accountants have not "grasped the nettle" of forecasting. Very often the initiative comes from the CEO or another board member when it should be accountants pioneering the way. But forecasting isn't all down to the accountant, it is group effort and all have to be on board with its importance; it is an accountant's skill set to amass data, coordinate information, and introduce cohesiveness. It is the accountant that should be badgering managers and leading the way and establishing it as a routine internal management exercise. Unfortunately it has not had the regular, thorough, systematic examination and implementation that it deserves, and which the accountant has been trained for.

It is a process that is difficult to do well and it takes up management time, which effectively means it is relegated to a lower rank compared to other accounting practices. How many of us have fallen into the trap of doing the easy jobs first? In the fast-moving environment in which firms operate it should be near the top of the priority list, not dwindling near the bottom.

In this day and age forecasting should be as important, if not the most important duty of an accountant; it should be reflected in their training, their objectives, and their job descriptions. It should be a natural continuation of the management accounts. Last month's financial result should be seen in the context of what has happened over the previous months and what is expected over the forthcoming months, not in isolation as is the case in conventional profit-and-loss statements, which fail dismally in this respect. Forecasts should be viewed in the same context, as an extension of the trends in actual historic financial performance.

There is a woeful catalogue of evidence of widespread failures in this vital area. One such study from the Hackett Group, REL, and the NACT revealed that four out of five of the largest companies were unable to forecast cash flow accurately. The study is based on responses from eighty-five US and European companies with average revenues of over $12 billion. If this is the case with the largest organizations, which probably have the most sophisticated IT processes, then it is likely the statistics will be considerably worse in smaller organizations.

Hackett says that this uncertainty creates a potentially dangerous scenario when combined with the lower levels of cash on hand in most industries as well as reducing revenues, shrinking margins, and limited availability of credit and cash from other external sources.

The Hackett study found that only 22 percent of companies say they can forecast operating cash flow two to three months ahead to within 5 percent accuracy, and previous Hackett research showed that only one in three companies can forecast their turnover to within 5 percent accuracy.

The organizations considered to be at the top of the forecasting performers list achieve significantly better financial results than others. They also complete their forecasts in less than half the time it takes typical companies and require fewer staff to complete the process, perhaps indicative of and testament to their commitment to developing a reliable, regular system.

The best companies also have cross-functional teams with extensive operational involvement in the process, which is important given the number of groups outside of finance that have a critical role. A related Hackett survey also found that while forecast accuracy is measured by most companies, 80 percent don't set accuracy targets.

"It's disturbing to think that most companies are virtually flying blind in this critical area," said Hackett's chief research officer, Michel Janssen. ". . . this problem is by no means a new one, but it's been exacerbated by the current economic climate, where it's more critical than ever for companies to be able to understand and predict their cash flow from operations."

According to REL president Mark Tennant, "The bottom line is simple, you can miss the mark on sales or earnings forecasts occasionally and survive, but you can only run out of cash once. Companies would be well advised to consider whether they're leaders or laggards and how they can make changes to improve cash-forecasting accuracy."

This research clearly highlights the potential for improvement across a swathe of organizations throughout the Western world, and it is reiterated that good cash forecasting is extremely dependent upon good revenue and expense forecasting—the subject of this chapter.

It is common to find management accountants burning the midnight oil in their struggle to produce last month's management accounts to today's tight deadlines. Their priority is to produce the financial statement in time for the monthly board meeting or other such diarized event. The relentless push all over the world is to reduce the time of their production, but what does it achieve? All it means is that accountants have little to no time to question the results or investigate anomalies and variances and so come to meetings without answers. So what if we manage to see the accounts a few days earlier? What difference does it make? They are still *history*! Talking about historic variances three to four days later than usual will make no difference; in fact, if the few days involved means the accountant can come up with some valid answers to questions on the accounts then this will probably lead to better decisions. I too am "guilty as charged." I also have been behind this push (and subject to it too in my accounting days long ago). I look back on it now with contrition.

In view of the actual comments of managers that deride the value of their management accounts, as described in chapter 1 this immense effort to meet deadlines by the accountant has to be questioned. It's not a waste of time, but is it time well spent when the final result is not appreciated by managers as a valuable tool?

Supposing they were to take a little longer and include forecasts and trends, their worth would dramatically improve and the delay need not be a disadvantage. The fact is that last month's result would have been announced within the forecast from the last set of management accounts, probably two weeks before the accounting period is due to end. This is much more valuable than examining last month's account one to two weeks after the end of the month. The extrapolation of twelve-month rolling totals in the form of a forecast can be surprisingly accurate over the short term, but even more importantly, the quality of management discussion that follows examination of these trends and forecasts is significantly enhanced. The subject of historic variances is replaced with expected performance shortfalls in the future.

It is not common to find forecasts that run into the following financial year in conventional management accountants. Some do include a forecast to the end of the current financial year but rarely further forward than this.

Even when such end-of-year forecasts are included within the body of the P&L statement, the thoroughness of them can be questionable. In my experience such forecasts are not tackled in-depth and can often be drafted within the finance department with little or no reference to other managers, so no management ownership is achieved. They also often rely too much on the future budget for their information, and we know how outdated this can be. In fact their main purpose is to illustrate whether the budget is going to be achieved, not tackle critical questions that arise from changes to trend lines. To describe these as forecasts is a travesty.

Even when more consideration and collaboration has been invested in such end-of-year forecasts, their usefulness reduces as the financial year progresses because the timeframe it covers lessens with each successive month as the year progresses, limiting their value to the current year only.

Current practice often means that even when longer term forecasts are produced they can be *ad hoc*, often prompted by adverse results or triggered by an emergency—a cash deficiency is a common reason. This spasmodic approach is far from satisfactory, lacking the planning, thought, and honing that comes with a considered regular exercise that also measures forecasting accuracy.

At the present time, even when an organization approaches its forecasting processes more thoroughly and intelligently and projects further into the future, they are generally presented as a report separate from the management accounts. This is better than not producing them at all, but the benefits of overlaying them in the management accounts so that the respective trends can be compared are missed. While the management accounts would be consulted and used as a starting point, a base, the numerical management accounts do not show detailed month-by-month history or indicate trends, so their usefulness in building a forecast is limited.

It is also common for forecasts to be just a guess, driven by natural optimism or aspiration with no deep investigation or research. I suspect that most experienced managers would have heard the words "I think that we should increase income by about 10 percent for next year." These magical round-sum increases span all types of organizations. They are a sign that little consideration has been invested and this pretence at forecasting just serves to bring the science of forecasting into disrepute. Most good forecasts start from the bottom up of the management structure, and the sum of all these parts doesn't usually add up to a "nice round sum." This does not mean that a rounding up or down is not sensible in the final totals: $1,001,567.32c is just absurd in a forecast.

It is also vital that the criteria used for a forecast are recorded. How can any analysis of why the forecast was wrong be achieved unless the reasoning behind the forecast is known? There is always an element of judgment contained in a forecast, but judgment means considering all the facts, and this is what differentiates it from guesswork.

The subject of forecasting is included in this book, because when producing *graphical* management accounts that include trends in actual performance the addition of a forecast becomes a natural extension of the trend but I emphasize this does not imply a simple extrapolation; the future is rarely predicted simply by consulting history, although as mentioned above it is fair to say that existing trends may persist over the short-term even when circumstances are changed because these changes usually take months to take effect. When entering a system of rolling forecasting that looks forward until the end of the following financial year, forecasts will include much more than extrapolation; they will be influenced by anticipated future events, some within the control of management and many that aren't.

Unforeseen happenings clearly can't be forecast, although some element of contingency may be included, given that *major* unexpected events may exceed such contingent reserves. This does not make forecasting a less valuable tool, and the impact of these unpredictable developments will be better controlled by more frequent forecasts.

A vital aspect of regular forecasting concerns management having an appreciation of how quickly it can take action and how prompt the reaction time to such unpredicted occurrences. All too often the results following management decisions are not as quick to take effect as they would like, so regular forecasting predicts the impact of these promptly. More on this and the subject of forecast frequency later.

A worthwhile, reliable forecast can take time, and this fact alone is probably the main reason why forecasts are not as regular as they should be. There are, however, techniques contained within graphical presentation that will shorten the exercise and these will become clearer as this chapter progresses. But the fact is that some investment of time is necessary whatever system is used; most worthwhile practices do take time. There is no magic solution to this, and unless managers are persuaded that forecasting is worthwhile then the exercise will be futile because less attention will be paid to its execution. This means that it is essential to perfect the system and not take risky shortcuts because this will contribute to its failure. You will see that the inclusion of forecasts in graphical management accounts not only helps with their accuracy but also pinpoints where they can be improved.

The regular construction of forecasts should be a core management exercise, but it must not be underestimated; a forecast is not a tool used intermittently, simply to illustrate the effects of a new income stream, reorganization, or crisis. When completed routinely, they assist organizations recognize deteriorating situations faster and so trigger quick responses to unpredicted or underestimated events. Following the dramatic economic events of the last few years it is now more evident than ever how quickly the fortunes of an organization can change. Once the routine of regular forecasting is established managers are better equipped to anticipate and respond to these unexpected factors.

When forecasts are incorporated into the trends within graphical management accounts, they become an extension of them into the future. It becomes immediately obvious when examining the slopes of the trend lines whether forecasts appear optimistic or pessimistic and how management decisions and plans can affect an organization's future results. Reliable forecasts are also essential for resource planning, ensuring that internal departments and suppliers are given sufficient notice to gear up or down to accommodate these changing future demands more promptly.

However, the consequences of poor forecasts can be very damaging to an organization, sometimes even worse than no forecasts at all. For example, an over-optimistic sales forecast may lead to an investment in new plant, stocks of materials, and recruitment of more personnel to meet the expected extra needs, all at significant cost, and this may prove detrimental to the final results. Forecast reliability is therefore a big factor, and we shall examine how graphs can be used to achieve continuous improvement in their reliability.

The process of representing forecasts graphically is fairly straightforward and will be covered later in the chapter, but it is important to describe the scope of the subject, its applicability to management accounts, and some of the most important principles first.

The preparation of forecasts is a matter that has been the subject of much debate and volumes of publications over many years. A brief search on Amazon revealed over 8,000 books on the subject at the last search.

Despite this daunting choice, it is recommended that relevant and selected material is referenced before embarking on the journey of introducing a formalized forecasting program within your organization. I have only touched a fraction of this literature and the readers should explore for themselves but be selective. I did find that a good practical guide at an affordable price is "Future Ready: How to Master Business Forecasting," Morlidge and Player, 2009. This book helps to lead you through the process in a practical and straightforward way without getting bogged down with an abundance of mathematical formulas. Many other books cover these complex statistical processes should you need them later, but frankly only a minority will require the use of these more complex approaches.

There are many pitfalls and much valuable practical advice contained in examining other writers' experiences that will speed your progress and enhance the reliability of your forecasts, so some research on the subject will be time well spent. Experienced managers will know that it is difficult to create forecasts that other managers will have confidence in and considerable planning and time is required to begin the process and obtain credible and reliable results. A period of trial for any new forecasting system can be worthwhile. This means that patience at the beginning is required but the return from the invested time can be rich. In business today, any organization that is unable to forecast and respond quickly to what they reveal risks missed opportunities and even financial loss; in the worst cases it can lead to failure of the enterprise.

There is also a body of opinion that forecasts can help drive a business to better results. In view of the fact they are formulated and agreed at all levels of management and force regular critiques of performance and strategy, it is quite likely that they do provide a payoff beyond that which arises from faster reaction time to unforeseen events or unexpected results. Forecasting can become a brainstorming of new ideas if the process is well managed, and if this becomes a more regular occurrence it is to be promoted.

In my view, the forecasting of financial results is the most important function of an organization's accounting operation. Most other management accounting activities are subsidiary to this, although many of these are essential and integral to the construction of credible forecasts. No other accounting output is more valuable to management than a financial report that looks into the future and reveals the likely result of past, present, and future events, as well as other planned or spontaneous business decisions. In the final analysis it is *only trends that matter,* whether the organization is improving or deteriorating; will we hit our targets?

But while forecasting should be accounting led, the production of business forecasts is not wholly an accounting responsibility; they rely heavily on input from all managers and other staff, they are a pooling of all an organization's experience and brainpower. However, the financial function's coordinating, marshalling, and supporting role, combined with the guidance that a finance controller and his/her team provides, can be invaluable to the process. It will become clear that the trends revealed by the production of graphical management accounts will be of considerable help in the construction and feasibility testing of these forecasts. Dependable forecasts of turnover and costs are also critical to accurate cash forecasting, another vital responsibility of a management accountant.

*Is it necessary to use specialist IT software to assist with the forecasting process?*

The decision to go this route will depend upon your organization's size, complexity, and the depth of your pocket. There is a legion of packages available offering a wide range of software, and it is impossible in a publication of this type to give guidance in their choice; not only are many directed to particular types of organizations, they are also being constantly reviewed and improved and any advice would soon be out of date. They can also be highly sophisticated although in the end they are all dependent on the accuracy of the raw information so you will need to be sure that this can be relied upon. As they say, "garbage in, garbage out." In some cases, however, they are the only way of analyzing and comparing mass data that would not be practicable without such software to do the number crunching. But don't run away with the idea that if an organization doesn't have the resources for such advanced and sophisticated systems that its forecasting will be inferior or beyond reach. They are not needed by most organizations, and there is a lot to be said for a manager's considered judgment rather than complex algorithms.

*What can you, or not, actually forecast?*

There have been some classic examples of how long-term forecasts have been dramatically wrong. These were described in "Financial Management" (CIMA, March 2007).

- 1943: "I think that there is maybe a world market for five computers."
- 1949: "Computers of the future will weigh no more than five and half tons."

- 1977: "There is no reason why anyone would want a computer in their homes."
- 1981: "A memory of 640kb ought to be enough for anyone."

And the last comment was from Bill Gates, so even the best can get it dramatically wrong. Who would have known the market better than him at that time?

When these comments were made, they were realistic projections of the then state of the industry. Of course, few, if any, could have forecast the advances in technology that subsequently took place. And even had they possessed the foresight, would they have been brave enough to voice their thoughts? Many listeners would have thought they were deranged.

But most business forecasting is much more concerned with the imminent and visible future. It can't consider the unforeseeable gigantic leaps in technological advances; it can only react to them as quickly as possible if they happen. It must, however, consider all the factors it does know, and even this is hard enough.

## What is a forecast?

To begin with it is important to fully understand how a forecast differs from a budget and a target.

The *Oxford Dictionary* describes a forecast as "a calculation or estimate of something future." In view of the fact that the end result we seek is usually expressed in numerical terms, then a business forecast may therefore be described as a calculated and/or estimate of the future financial outcome given known historic results/trends, market intelligence, details of firm/existing plans of action, and the economic circumstances in which the organization operates.

A good forecast will not include ideas or thoughts about actions that *might* be taken in the future, or managers' aspirations, or include plans and strategies that have as yet to be approved for action. A forecast may well *prompt* action, or at least a plan of action and these may be considered in the next forecast. But such plans, unless they become definite unusually quickly, are often too late to be incorporated into a current forecast, which is usually being produced to a deadline and may not allow sufficient time for any corrective plans to be properly evaluated, approved, and become definite.

A forecast is therefore an objective, *realistic* assessment of where an organization might be at given times in the future, which considers all the above factors and especially those that were not known or inaccurately assessed when a budget or previous forecast were set. This is where it differs substantially from a budget and a target.

Forecasts still have to make assumptions about what might happen, and even a forecast carried out three months ago will often turn out to be wrong because times change and events are unpredictable. We must accept, to begin with, that it is highly likely that most forecasts will be incorrect. These inaccuracies must be expected, and because of this there must be a mechanism for monitoring error so that improvements to accuracy can be identified, implemented, and monitored. There are simple ways of doing this graphically within the management accounts that will be demonstrated later.

Forecasts reveal weaknesses, areas for action, and opportunities that assist an organization get back on track. This is the main reason for a forecast: to support decisions and prompt action, helping to *create* the future rather than just *reacting* to it. There is nothing fatalistic about future business results; with good forecasting the future can be largely foreseen and action taken to change it.

A budget is described in the *Oxford Dictionary* as "the amount of money needed or available (for a specific item, etc.)." It has a very different meaning from a forecast but this is not to say that a forecast may not be the same value as that previously budgeted. Perhaps there have been no other unexpected factors since the budget was produced. In a business context, however, we can take budget to mean the amount of money needed or available to reasonably and commensurately satisfy a particular level of sales or allocated income. When applied to costs it can be described as *a limit of spend, not a license to spend*. In other words it is not an instruction to spend the budgeted value when a lesser sum would suffice, although unfortunately some managers either don't understand this or abuse the situation by spending up to their budgets even when needs do not justify it. How often have you heard the phrase "well, if we don't spend the budget in this financial year we shall lose it; it won't be carried forward and next year's budget will be cut." I came across this more times than I can remember when approaching the end of the financial year with public authorities/departments when there can be a frenzy of spending to reach the annual budget.

In commercial or public organizations, unlike the dictionary definition, the term *budget* is not limited to costs, it is applied to the income lines too. Budgeted income is not difficult to establish when an organization is told what it will receive, as in most public sector organizations. Others in the commercial world often find sales forecasting much more difficult. It is generally much harder than cost forecasting (unexpected costs set aside) but it is an important subject because it is usually the precursor for the cost lines; many costs cannot be determined until the income lines have been budgeted.

The terms *budget* and *target* are sometimes confused, so let's dwell for a moment on the term *target*. Using the analogy of a shooting target, as in archery, it may help to better understand the difference. In this context the bull's-eye may be described as the *target,* it is what the archer or marksman aims for. But in practice we all know that it would be unrealistic to expect even a skilled sportsman to hit the bull's-eye every time. This would be optimistic and there is no room in a budget for optimism. Budgets must be set at an achievable, realistic level, and this, in the case of the marksman, may be the inner ring of the target rather than the actual bull's-eye itself. A target is therefore best distinguished from a budget by saying a target is what management aspires to while a budget is what management reasonably expects to achieve. The budget may *stretch* employees a little, the target stretches them further.

In practice targets are often used for salesmen while a sales budget may be set, say, a few percent below that level. The term *target* can have a range of meanings and this differentiation may not necessarily apply to your organization, but it is important not to confuse the two terms. Occasionally cost budgets can inadvertently become targets even when they are still described as budget; e.g., if such a budgeted cost is cut as a result of downward management pressure without certainty that it can be achieved at a lower cost, then the budget is in danger of becoming a target. Such processes need to be very carefully managed if management is not to be fooling itself and/or demotivating a manager at a lower level. Such instructions have, therefore, to be objective, realistic, achievable, and constructive. The word target is also misused in practice when a manager says of a budgeted cost: "this is our target." It is not a target, and managers need to take care of misleading staff. A *target cost* will therefore be less than a *budgeted cost* and be accompanied by a plan of action to reduce it below that level budgeted.

Cost targets are often set during the design of a new product; when a market price is often set before a product design is completed, a cost target will be set for designers to work to so that a target margin can be achieved. There is nothing wrong with using the word *target* in this context, although a cautious accountant may well not use such a target cost in the future budget or a forecast.

Another way of differentiating between a target and a forecast is that targets are usually top down while forecasts should be bottom up.

*Recognizing the problems of producing reliable forecasts and learning to deal with them*

There are a range of considerations:

- As described above it is not difficult to find sophisticated computer programs to assist the forecasting process and these may help certain types of organizations construct more reliable forecasts. However, the final decisions, the formula, algorithm, data type, formulation of action plans, and more often than not the whole process, are designed and carried out by human beings. This is the biggest problem to be aware of. Humans can be optimists, pessimists, cautious, influenced, frightened, worried, irrational, want to please, uninformed, follow the crowd, unmotivated, motivated, hubristic, unsure, egotistical, and just plain wrong in their judgment. In practice they are more than one of these. All these states of mind can influence the quality of a forecast and they are not easy to mitigate. They introduce bias into a forecast that can be persistent, and it is essential to have an awareness of them. Do not underestimate the potential error that can be introduced by these human factors. For example, those who are responsible for producing forecasts are likely to be vulnerable to influences from others that provide information prior to the forecast. This phenomenon is known as "anchoring" and was first identified by psychologists Amos Tversky and Daniel Kahneman back in 1974. Their research identified that such focus on the particular number given in advance created a fixation that can substantially alter the judgment of the recipient. Various studies have been completed to verify this and in one such study a group of currency traders, all working for the same firm and therefore expected to come up with similar forecasts, were divided into two groups for the study. In each case the groups were asked the same question but with different numbers. The first group was asked if they expected the Euro–US Dollar exchange rate to be above or below 0.6. Their average guess within the group was 0.79. In the second group, they were asked whether the exchange rate would be above or below 1.6, and their average guess was 1.28. The huge gap arose because each group "anchored" on the number first presented to them.

Even worse than this, it has been proved that even entirely unrelated information can have this effect. Dan Ariely of MIT carried out a mock auction with his MBA students. Before the auction he asked them to write down the last two digits of their Social Security numbers. This clearly had no relevance to the auction process yet the half of the students that wrote down higher numbers bid 60-120 percent higher than their peers. These huge differences demonstrate just how powerful anchoring can be and how those who forecast can be subconsciously influenced. It confirms just how important it is for the forecasting team to be totally uninfluenced before the forecast process and why it should be a team effort, not an individual one. One last point on the matter of human factors. There must be no incentive payments for forecast accuracy. Any such temptations and motivations may lead to effects on business performance and these are likely to be negative. Under this financial influence a forecast becomes a soft target they are sure they can hit.

- Forecasts will also be subject to distortion if those who receive them do not recognize that their behavior will affect the conclusions of the forecast team. Above all else they must recognize that a forecast is not a target or a budget, it is essential not to put subjective pressure on the forecast team to come up with something better. A forecast is worth nothing if it produces a result that meets a previously set budget or target only because the forecast team has been derided or placed under pressure to do so. Neither should a forecast be used as a mechanism just for setting higher targets. As soon as a team gets wind of that, then you can expect lower forecasts. Senior management must recognize that reliable forecasts are a best calculated and considered view of what will happen given all available data available at a current date. They may lead to action that will change the future, but unless a forecast is uninfluenced it will cease to be a forecast and instead become some form of target. This sounds easy to achieve, but in practice, when pressures of business abound, it is very easy for senior management to fall into the trap, so they must maintain a constant awareness of the potential problem. There is a fine line between objective advice aimed at improving a forecast accuracy and subjective pressure to come up with something better. Some organizations actively discourage pessimism, which is often interpreted as disloyalty. The bearers of bad news can become pariahs, shunned and ignored by other employees. If pessimistic opinions are suppressed while optimistic ones rewarded, an organization's ability to think objectively is undermined. A good mix of managers, ranging from pessimists to optimists, is no bad thing.

- Good forecasting involves many in the management team. Usually the most detailed knowledge of any department's whole operation is that of the manager that runs it, so his knowledge should be harnessed. Using each manager's expertise in this way also encourages *buy-in* and this bottom-up approach is considered by many as the best approach to reliable forecasting. It is, however, important to recognize the potential bias from the manager of the subject department and also to understand that groups can become homogenous; after working together they can begin to think alike, which also introduces bias to the forecast.

- If statistical methods are used to help the forecasting processes that contain algorithms and other mathematical formulas, then this too can introduce incorrect assumptions into a forecast: who decides on the formulas or which factors to include in the calculations, have they made the right choices, introduced the right constants and weightings, etc. Have these formulas been updated and reassessed in the light of the latest circumstances? When these formulas go wrong once, then it can happen automatically and often unnoticed in further forecasts.

- When forecasts are being made relating to something new, say the introduction of a new product or service, then different problems arise. This was thoroughly investigated by Dan Lovallo and Daniel Kahneman in the report of their research "Delusions of Success: How Optimism Undermines Executive Decisions," published in *Harvard Business Review*, July 2003. They state that "Most people are highly optimistic most of the time. Research into human cognition has traced this optimism to many sources. One of the most powerful is the tendency to exaggerate their own talents, to believe they are above average in their endowment of positive traits and abilities." Another is the tendency to misperceive the causes of certain events such as taking credit for positive outcomes and attributing negative outcomes to external factors such as weather, other people, or inflation. Yet another is to exaggerate the degree of control we have over events. Their analysis of start-up ventures in a wide range of industries found that more than 80 percent failed to achieve the market share that was forecast. Neglecting competitor reaction is also common. It is not unusual for a number of competitors to be preparing and attacking the same market at the same time, each oblivious of the other when it is forecasting its likely impact. The likelihood of this must be considered in the forecasting process.

*So how are these potential distorting factors addressed?*

- *Firstly, be aware of them.* Whenever they are spotted, investigate and rectify them. Better still, avoid them, using the right systems and training.
- *Look for independent supporting evidence when forecasting new income streams.* When the forecast is for a new product/ service, as described above, then one view as expressed by Lovallo and Kahneman is to take the "outside view." This

entails selecting a reference class, a similar situation that has happened before, then documenting and examining the outcomes of a number of these and using this guidance to forecast your new project's prospects. You will often find this forecast to be less ambitious than you first thought.

- *Utilize the entire organization's knowledge.* Use the senior management team, if this isn't the team that actually carries out the forecast process, to advise or brief the forecast team, not to influence them with actual values and figures but by defining strategy, market knowledge, facts of which the team may not be aware, and matters concerning the board's future plans, etc. The senior team will often have knowledge that will enhance the accuracy of a forecast and a forecast should pool all such knowledge. This is where it is easy to fall foul of the situation described above; such advice must be objective, avoid direction or instruction, and not place a forecast team under pressure to come up with a better result. Often, in fact, such advice may even lower a forecast. This approach captures all the available intelligence vital to better forecasts.

- *Test the forecast's reasonability.* This is where the trend analysis introduced in earlier chapters will help you. Consider the chart in Fig. 4.1. Note that these are twelve-month rolling totals. The vertical bars represent the budget and the solid black line the actual result to August of the current year. The dashed line is the forecast rolling forward. Also be aware that only the top of the vertical scale is represented; i.e., from 25-37,000:

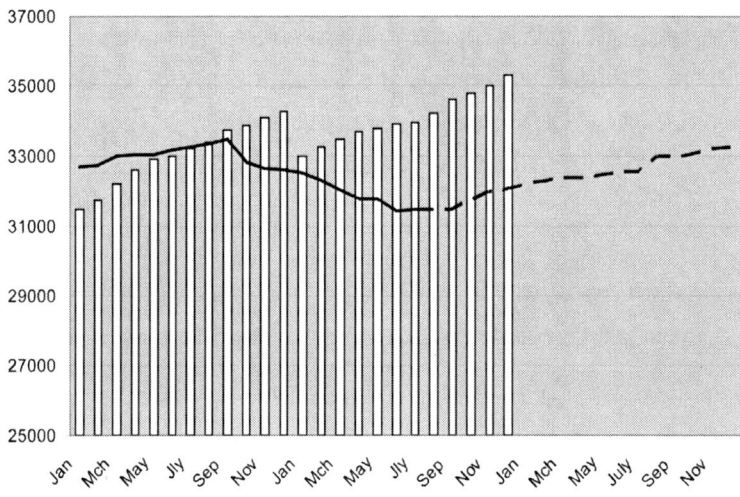

*Fig. 4.1.*
*Twelve-month rolling total of income showing*
*budget, actual, and forecast.*

It is evident that there has been a downward trend in the actual result from October last year to August this year and a gradual divergence from budget that had anticipated growth. The forecast shows a recovery; initially, a flattening of the downward direction, followed by an upward trend. "Is this reasonable?"

On the face of it, it is questionable. At the very least it would introduce a serious challenge, so more information is needed. What has or is going to change to alter this downward trend? It may be new products, new salesmen, a new pricing strategy, a competitor dropping out of the market, an expected growth in the market size, a forthcoming advertising campaign, etc.

Such justifications may be applicable and objective (although they would need to be reasoned and quantified) but many answers won't be. "We think that sales should rise by about 7.5 percent next year" or "sales always go in cycles" and so on. Trend changes like this may just be aspiration. Perhaps the budget also was in this example.

It is also important to allow sufficient time for the change in a trend to take effect. It is a common error to be too optimistic in the time for new initiatives, customer reaction time, etc. to take effect.

Such questions are essential to prove validity of the forecast but they will also help to improve the accuracy of the forecast and test its reasonability.

- *Learn from previous mistakes.* It is important to reexamine previous forecasts and investigate errors to establish where it may have gone wrong. This entails keeping good records of the assumptions made and criteria used in reaching forecast conclusions to pinpoint such errors. In other words, learn from previous mistakes. Narrow down and reduce the areas of error. Previous forecasts can easily be displayed on the twelve-month rolling total charts. See Fig. 4.2.

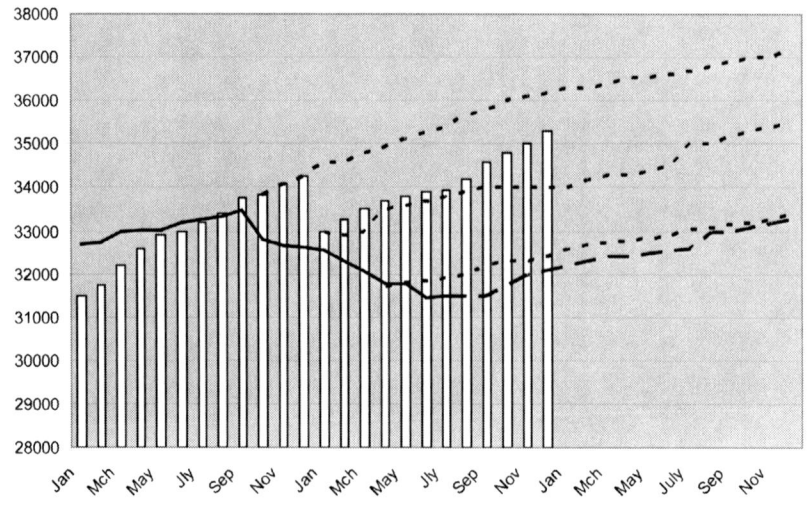

*Fig. 4.2*

*Twelve-month rolling total of sales showing actual, budget, latest, and three previous quarterly forecasts*

Fig. 4.2 is the same chart as Fig. 4.1 but the previous three quarterly forecasts have also been shown on the chart as dotted lines. The current forecast is shown as a dashed line.

In this example forecasts are carried out every quarter, and it is clear that all three previous forecasts (those made in September, December, and March) have been too optimistic, although the last two forecasts (March and June) are fairly close together, indicating that there may be some improvement in the organization's forecasting process. The same questions as those asked in the previous example are naturally relevant and in fact would have been consistent with two out of three of these forecasts because they indicate a rapid reversal of a downward trend. It has been said before in earlier chapters but reiterated because of its importance, rapid reversals of any slope on a twelve-month rolling total is not easy to achieve, it usually requires quite a dramatic change in the month-to-month result year on year caused by a very significant event. In the first forecast illustrated the mistake appears to be that the forecast was merely extrapolated and also followed the budget without due consideration of the fcat that the trend in the actual result was just beginning to show signs of reducing.

The example shown in Fig. 4.2 is exaggerated to demonstrate how graphical displays can assist in improving forecasting reliability. It would also be hoped that those responsible for producing such forecasts would have seen this history of error and taken steps to correct it themselves; managers would naturally not want to be seen to repeat their forecasting mistakes.

Due care must be taken to avoid driving managers in the opposite direction; that is, under forecasting income or over forecasting costs in the belief that this is to be commended. Unlike a target or budget, there is no prize or praise in beating a forecast. All it means is that the forecast was unreliable and potentially damaging to an organization. Under-forecasting can be just as damaging as over-forecasting. It is *reliable* forecasting that matters and only this should lead to a pat on the back.

## *Calculating the twelve-month rolling total for a forecast to appear graphically.*

A forecast's starting point is where the business is *now*; any previous forecast is not considered in any future forecast or the 12 month rolling total save for portraying it as such on the chart as illustrated in Fig. 4.2 by the dotted lines, where it is included just to highlight *former* forecasting error.

The calculation of the current twelve-month rolling total of a forecast comprises a combination of actual results and future forecasts. Any forecasts for previous accounting periods are now irrelevant, only the actuals from the past until and including the current month are included in the rolling total. Note that to calculate a twelve-month rolling total for the forecast it is necessary to forecast the future result on a month-by-month basis, giving due consideration to any seasonal or other factors.

As an example it is suggested that the month end is June for management account purposes and that the financial year runs from January to December. Under the system described in previous chapters we need visibility within the graphical representation of the previous financial year, the current financial year, and the next financial year, so a forecast produced at the end of June in the current year will look forward a period of eighteen months until the end of the next financial year.

Since the current month is June, the first individual month forecast will be July and the last month forecast will be December of the following year.

The calculation of the twelve-month rolling total to the end of July in the current year will be the value of the forecast for July plus the previous eleven months' *actual* result. The twelve-month rolling total for August will be the forecast for July and August plus the previous ten months' *actual,* and so on.

It is not, therefore, until June of the following year that the twelve-month rolling total for the forecast comprises wholly of forecasted monthly results.

The forecast twelve-month rolling total for the end of July would therefore comprise eleven months' actual results and one month's forecast result. If the forecast for July happens to be 100 percent correct, the twelve-month rolling total of actual result at the end of July will be exactly as forecast at the end of June.

## How often should forecasts be completed?

Another Hackett Group survey (2008) found that of the 20 percent of organizations that reported their firms could change dramatically within the space of a month (80percent of them) produced quarterly forecasts. This statistic appears to indicate that despite the possibility of dramatic change occurring with a month's notice most firms still only produced quarterly forecasts, which will often delay their reaction time. The only explanation appears to be that practical factors such as the time their business forecasts take maybe too long. This factor has been supported by further research carried out in the UK by Richard Barrett, ALG Software, and Jeremy Hope, author and research director of the Beyond Budgeting Round Table (BBRT). Here is an extract from their research:

*"Purpose*: more frequent re-forecasting is becoming an important topic on corporate agendas and is seen by many to be the only way to keep financial performance on track at a time when revenues are becoming less predictable. The paper aimed to investigate this topic:

*Design/methodology/approach*—For the past four years ALG Software has commissioned a study of the re-forecasting practices in a sample of the top organizations in the UK by revenue. The objective of the study is to benchmark how frequently the UK's leading organizations currently reforecast and what their goals are for the future.

*Findings*—The results show that the majority of organizations remain dissatisfied with the frequency with which they reforecast and wish to reforecast more frequently. However, the findings also show that many organizations feel that they cannot reforecast as often or as quickly as they would like. In fact, evidence suggests that little, if any, progress has been made during the last four years since this survey was first commissioned. This is due to either the amount of time it takes operational line managers to re-forecast their resource requirements, or the amount of time it takes the finance function to complete a round of re-forecasting. The type of application used for budgeting and re-forecasting appears to make little difference to the time it takes organizations to produce an annual budget or complete a reforecast. Central to this issue is the use of non-financial or operational data that predicts future resource requirements and the limitations of the budgeting systems that organizations currently employ. Regardless of the type of application used for budgeting or re-forecasting, much of this modeling is still done offline on spreadsheets."

The lengthy time it takes to reforecast is clearly a widely experienced and significant problem, and reducing it seems to be a major challenge that as yet remains unsolved by many. However, there is a danger to more frequent forecasting even if this is achieved: the risk of repetition. Due to lack of time there would be a tendency for managers forecasting every few weeks to simply carry the last forecast forward without the level of consideration that is required. Clearly the shorter the period the less new information there will be to consider, and care must be taken against incorrect assumptions. It is easy for managers to slip into this trap.

There is no standard approach to the question of forecast frequency. It is for each organization to consider the implications of more or less frequency for itself. What may be necessary in a bakery, trying to forecast how many loaves to make tomorrow, will be very different from a local authority's garbage collection service that knows well in advance how many homes it has to visit every week.

Below are some of the main factors that need to be considered when making this decision. However, I believe that it is unlikely a frequency of less than each quarter will provide the benefits that are available.

- *Your management accounts cycle*—monthly, quarterly, four weekly, or weekly—may influence *when* you reforecast, but the regularity is still more likely to be determined by the factors below. The regularity of forecasting is not linked directly to the regularity of management accounts but would coincide with an edition of the management accounts if you are to display the forecast in graphical form within the management accounts.

- *The time it takes to produce a reliable forecast.* Do not be tempted to shortcut this important process. Remember that an unreliable forecast is worse than no forecast and can lead to incorrect and damaging decisions. Note, however, that forecasts over the short-term tend to change every time you forecast while longer-term forecasts have a tendency to remain more stable. It is also obvious that longer-term forecasts will be less accurate than short-term forecasts; forecasts degenerate as they age. This is not to say that less care should be taken with their construction, just that the assumptions on which they are based may not change so often. This factor may help to reduce the time spent on the forecast because longer-term assumptions may not be changed as often as those for the shorter term. It is true to say that once a system for regular re-forecasting has been established and it has bedded-in the process time will be lessened as staff becomes accustomed to the systems and more confident in the process adopted.

- *The speed of events and changes within your organization's scope of activity.* Any business activity linked to "fashion" is likely to suffer fast changes in the market, and this will prompt rapid changes within the organizations that operate within that industry. At the other end of the scale, publicly-owned bodies may find that changes are slow and infrequent because changes to income are usually signaled well in advance. Each organization needs to determine where it fits in the range and design the forecasting frequency accordingly. Some business changes will, however, still take time. It is clear that the need for greater regularity of forecasting will be higher the faster the speed of change in the sector and therefore the necessity to make rapid changes in the business. Many proposed changes may require market research, product research and development, new tooling or plant on extended delivery, and specialist staff recruitment. This too will figure in the decision concerning frequency.

• *The time it takes to review the forecast, decide on any actions, seek approval for those decisions, implement them, and the reaction time for their effect.* If you are an SME still run by its owner, a sole trader, or a small partnership then you can probably complete all but the effect of the decision in days, if not hours. But if you are large centralized multinational or a public-owned authority, the process can dramatically increase; it can sometimes take months to go through the approval process for a proposed significant change. If your decision implementation time is at the longer end of the scale, your forecasting frequency should be greater so that the instigation of the decision is prompted at the earliest time. If your reaction time is fast, less frequent forecasts may suffice.

• *It is not necessary to start from scratch every time you forecast.* A forecast is not like a budget that once a year demands a re-evaluation of every income and expense line. With a forecast it is only necessary to examine anything that has changed since you last forecasted, particularly the *assumptions* that were made. This may require examination of the non-financial drivers of the organization and consider any new initiatives or decisions prompted by the last forecast. It is much easier to carry out the re-forecasting process by focusing on changes rather than doing it from scratch.

## Including unconfirmed/unapproved decisions in a forecast

On occasions when an unsatisfactory forecast is produced, there is a temptation to introduce anticipated decisions to correct this deficiency before these proposals have been detailed, approved, or implemented. This enticement is ever present and should not be underestimated, it has many guises, from minor assumptions about what might happen to major potential events. This subject prompted significant controversy when we faced this dilemma the first time the system was introduced. This desire stems from wanting to produce a better result, which while being a natural human reaction is not desirable in a forecast. It was finally concluded that we should only include agreed, definite, and authorized changes in our forecasts; that is, use the forecast only to depict what will happen if we don't change. This decision didn't delay any such potential change; in fact, it probably hastened their implementation. This does not apply to those planned future changes that all are secure in the knowledge will happen and which have financial forecasts/plans attached to them.

## The tools needed for better forecasting

Good forecasts are not grasped from midair, they depend upon access to many sources of information and a structured approach. The elements to consider are:

- *A forecast team*—comprising a knowledgeable manager from each division/department who has a detailed knowledge of the latest decisions, actions, strategy, and plans for their departments. Each manager may individually have their own team of members drawn from their own departments, and this bottom-up approach helps to achieve buy-in and ownership of the forecast. It cannot be emphasized enough how important the bottom-up approach is. At no time should middle managers be in the position to say, "Well, it wasn't my forecast. How can I be responsible for the fact that we got it wrong?" Forecast responsibility has to be close to those that are "accountable." Senior management must recognize that they must not hand down forecasting edicts.

- *A strategic overview*—it is essential to see the bigger picture. Accurate forecasts can't be produced with a silo mentality; a manager can't lock himself away in a backroom and produce a forecast in isolation. It is a group activity, each party must have an understanding of the inter-relationships within the organization, the business plan, and future strategy. Any overall final forecast must be cohesive and consistent across the organization.

- *History*—previous financial results are essential, and for this purpose there is no better way of expressing them than in the form of a trend, depicted through the medium of the twelve-month rolling total. It does not start with a top-level trend; i.e., the grand totals. It will usually start with income because this is often the base for determining many costs. Sales or other income would require the individual trends of each product range, service type, or other type of income, because each of these detailed trends can independently be going up, down, or be flat and the rate or incline or decline can be different. Some products will be in their ascendancy, some will be approaching or have reached maturity, and some will be in decline. The balance of such variations in lifecycle and the rate of change is a vital component for consideration. A further complication is that different income streams can have different margins, and it is important to evaluate the impact of these margin variations on total contribution/gross margins. These variations mean that just examining top-level, grand-total trends will be inaccurate and unreliable; it is the amalgam of all these detailed forecast income types that will form the final total sales income forecast. This approach is vital for tracking where a forecast has gone wrong. It is not possible to identify the reasons for an incorrect forecast without being able to "mine" for this information, and this will only be available if forecasting starts at the bottom. The same will apply to cost information, which once again starts at the bottom level and works up, guided, where appropriate, by individual income stream trends. It will also be helpful to have cost-to-income percentage trends as outlined in chapter 2. Trends are a vital component of forecasting. They act as a check on the feasibility of any forecast. This applies particularly to the shorter term. Remember that trends usually take months to turn following any corrective action and this has to be considered in the forecast.

- *Market Intelligence*—every business needs information lines from the market. Competitors and markets do not stand still and events must be monitored. The earlier you learn of competitor's advertising/marketing campaigns, new/additional salesmen and their whereabouts, new products, changes to their pricing strategies, and improvements in their customer service offer, then the earlier you can react. How will these affect your business? What actions need to be taken to counter any threatening competitor behavior? What impact will these threats and your reaction have on the forecast?

- *A senior member of the financial team*—not just a number cruncher or someone to seek out financial details but a senior imaginative individual who can act as a sounding board, play devil's advocate, add balance to the group, and question any ideas and contribute new thoughts from outside the box.

- *Knowledge of previous forecasting accuracy and where it went wrong*—the rolling total graph in Fig. 4.2 demonstrates the value of this and these trends, for each income and cost line, will clearly pinpoint where, what, and who is responsible for any unreliable forecasting. This is essential information without which it will be difficult to improve the reliability of your forecasting.

- *Knowledge of the economic environment in which the organization operates*—inflation levels/economic trends, impact of macroeconomic factors on your industry, economic growth or recession, etc. It is essential to keep up to date with the bigger economic and political picture.

- *Quotation trends and conversion rates, specification trends, enquiry levels*—these all offer a future indication of what could happen to your sales levels. They are the first indication of sales activity levels and are therefore essential for your forecasts.

- *Limiting factors*—what the limiting factors in your organization are and what impact they will have on your forecast. For example, do you have sufficient plant capacity to cope with the forecast sales growth? Have you the warehousing to cope with the extra stocks required to support this new sales campaign? Do you have the highly skilled staff you will need to support the new customers that this new idea will generate? What about these special extra components required that are on six-month delivery from the Far East? "We just don't have enough people to answer the phone for this new advertising program and we simply can't squeeze any more people into this office." "This will require considerable cash for investment in additional stock and we are on our overdraft limit." And so it goes on. Any of these and many more may restrict your forecast, especially when this is looking twelve months plus ahead; a grasp of these factors is crucial and the time delays incorporated to correct them.

- *Key uncertainties*—factors about which we can't make reliable forecasts. These may be technological advances or macroeconomic collapses. These can't be forecast but the sooner you know about them the better. It is essential that at least one member of the team reads the trade press and follows other media stories.

- *Market research and business plans*—this may apply to new product introductions and sometimes existing products, particularly those that have undertaken some change, a new market approach, or an advertising campaign. Clearly these reports are soon out of date, so they will have limited use until some market experience and forecasts take over.
- *There is an increasing reliance on business drivers to assist in the forecasting processes*—these are often non-financial metrics and NFPIs that managers use day to day. This data can be a valuable source of information for forecasts.

## *Where does the forecast process start?*

Every organization has limiting factors and the recognition of these and at what volumes they apply is a prerequisite of any forecast. If the forecast breaches the limiting factor then this is probably where the forecast starts. For example, a manufacturing business may have a plant that is only able to produce a certain number of products within the prescribed working week. Any type of organization may only have access to limited cash resources. A public body may not be in a position to increase its income level but is obligated to achieve breakeven even when the demands of the service it provides are increasing. Components may be in limited supply or be on very long lead times, specialist staff may be difficult to recruit or take many months to train, there may be a limited amount of production or office space, etc. There is clearly no point in creating a sales or income forecast that exceeds the capacity of any of these limitations. While this may prompt action, introducing new initiatives to overcome them can add considerably to the timescales of the forecast and cost.

Having established the limiting factor, this is usually where the forecast is initiated. However many businesses find that they can supply all the goods or services they are able to sell or that any limiting factors are easy to overcome, so the sales forecast is more often than not the starting point for a forecast.

## Sales Forecasting

It is not intended here to tackle the huge subject of sales forecasting. This subject alone is a book in itself and there were nearly 3,000 such books found on a recent Amazon search, so there is no shortage of material. In addition, there is now a legion of software to help with the process if your business requires this level of sophistication.

However, there are aspects of sales forecasting that may be facilitated by the graphical presentation models set out in this book that are likely to apply to any type of organization whose income is not defined in advance.

The guidelines that follow may therefore be particularly helpful to smaller organizations and/or those that may prefer to avoid the costs of expensive software. The following paragraphs will focus on how graphical presentation will assist in the sales forecasting processes. As mentioned above, it will not attempt to cover the wide topic of enumerating the forecast for complex organizations.

As emphasized above, sales forecasts start at a basic level. They cannot be constructed by adding percentages to grand totals, which may include scores or even hundreds and thousands of product/ service types, branches/divisions, etc., each may be at different stages within its lifecycle or other specific influencing factors or different managers so each will require separate consideration in a forecast.

It all starts, therefore, at this bottom basic level, and it is the summation of these forecasts that build the top line.

If your organization does market hundreds/thousands of products, then the task of constructing a chart for each of these is daunting and would most likely require bespoke software to deal with it. If, on the other hand, your business consists of more manageable numbers, then utilizing spreadsheets may suffice.

Most sales forecasts will commence with the examination of current and past sales, and there is no better way of visualizing these than using the trends as outlined in this book.

In the event that you are forecasting sales for a new product or service, when historical information is unavailable then the numbers from your market research or using the techniques described earlier in this chapter will be your only guide, although an awareness of the pitfalls of over optimism, as outlined previously, is essential. The following paragraphs will relate mainly to established products/ services where previous trends are available. The underlying trends are invaluable as a starting point. They will immediately and at a glance tell you the direction the value is heading and the pattern it has followed over the last twelve to twenty-three months. You will see whether a product has reached a peak or a trough, the rate of change, and any variations in that rate. You will be aware of the reasons for these peaks and troughs from the investigations that will have taken place when they were first experienced. These patterns will be of considerable assistance in determining the forward direction and certainly help check the feasibility of the forecasted figures. You will also be aware of the stage a product has reached in its lifecycle, and this helps to predict when a product will peak and then subside. In addition, you will know what marketing plans are being made and the nature of any research and development taking place to the products concerned. It is also helpful to know your competitors and your market share, remembering that the bigger your market share the more difficult and costly it is to significantly advance it. All these issues will be considered and many more.

Further trends taken from other data outside the profit-and-loss account may be of assistance where such material is available or applicable. This concerns trends in enquiry levels, quotations, and specifications. Consider the charts shown in figures 4.3, 4.4, and 4.5, which monitor enquiries, quotations, and orders of the same product. All are twelve-month rolling totals. Such information can be of much value when constructing sales forecasts if you are an organization that can take advantage of this information; i.e., you produce quotations and record enquiries.

It is important to note that all graphs, whether part of the management accounts or not, should be of similar format as those in your management accounts, although the timeframe may be different if you make the decision not to forecast enquiry and quote levels. In the examples illustrated the timeframe has been limited to the last financial year and to date in the current year.

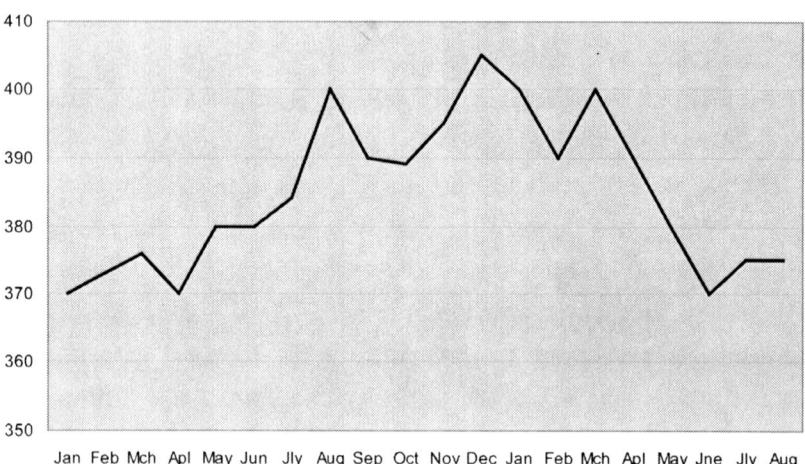

*Fig. 4.3*

*Product A, number of enquiries*

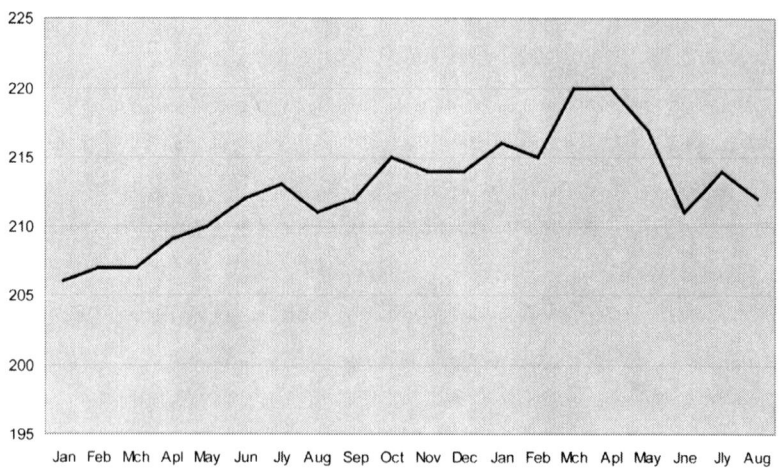

*Figure 4.4*

*Product A—Value of quotations*

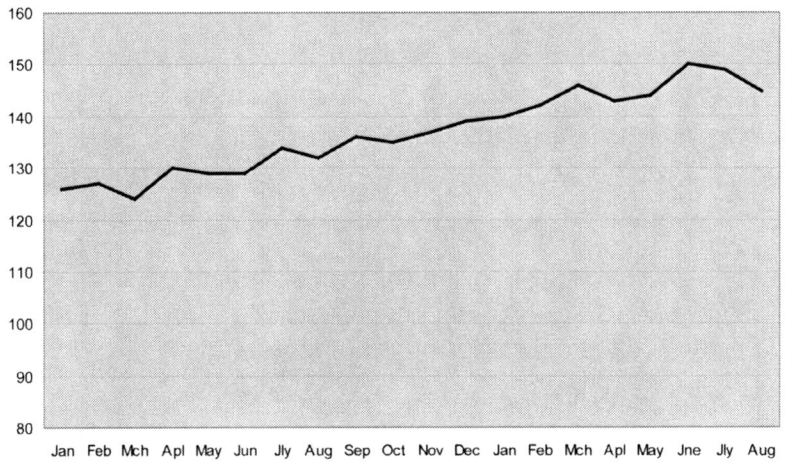

*Fig. 4.5*

*Product A, value of orders*

It can be seen that a peak of enquiries was achieved for the year ending December, since when there has been a decline. Following this, a peak of quotations was achieved in April/May and the same pattern of growth and decline can be seen in both charts with quotations following about three to four months after the enquiry. Orders also follow a similar growth pattern but as yet no significant decline is visible, although there is a slight dip in the latest month, which may be a sign that this will follow the same pattern as quotations over the next few months. Clearly there is a delay in the conversion of an order from a quotation but it is not clear from these charts yet how long that period is; it is clear, however, that unless conversion rates are set to improve then a drop in order values will probably follow, leading inevitably to a drop in invoiced sales. It will also be noticed that enquiry levels have fallen significantly, and although the last month or two appear to have stabilized, it will still need to be watched carefully. This information is of considerable value in predicting sales levels several months ahead. It acts as an early warning system that will prompt faster action.

But this type of analysis will also raise a number of other valuable points and questions:

What's happening to our quotation conversion rates? Are they improving or not? Are we more or less competitive than previously? Are our products falling behind the competition? Are the competitors more active? Why *are* enquiry levels falling or rising? What has been the impact of our latest publicity campaign? Etc.

*Forecasts can originate from customers, sales staff, or branches*

There are other approaches to sales forecasting if sales are made directly by sales staff, whether field or telephone based or from branches.

The process starts in the same way, at the level of the salesman or branch, and each would have their own chart displaying their individual trend of invoiced sales. It may also include charts for their level of quotations and orders to assist the process. The member of sales staff or branch manager would take personal responsibility for forecasting future sales with the support of their immediate manager. In this scenario the history of previous forecasts as illustrated in Fig. 4.2 is essential to help the employee to achieve improving accuracy as the process matures, because in my experience there can be considerable optimism or pessimism introduced by sales staff at this level; showing previous forecasts introduces more realism into forecasts from sales staff. These low-level forecasts tend to go further because other more personal factors are included; e.g., a member of staff on maternity leave, sickness, other personal issues, or a new salesman from a competitor appointed in the same territory. In the case of a retail branch, then other happenings can influence sales: road works outside the shop, a new competitor outlet just round the corner, or new parking restrictions in the area. All these situations can affect the performance level of an employee or branch and will be relevant to the forecast, especially in the imminent future. These factors and many more like them are often unknown to senior management and illustrate why top-down forecasts often fail to be accurate.

*There is also a double check on sales forecasts that should help to improve forecast accuracy. When considered necessary, the totals of forecast sales, through the route of sales staff or branch, can be compared to the totals achieved from the product-by-product forecast route. This can sometimes bring some interesting results and is a useful checking tool.*

It is possible to go further than this if time or suitable IT is available; this will mean analyzing achieved sales by product per sales person or branch. All of these will be depicted by trends. Comparisons of these trends by sales person to sales person or branch to branch can improve the forecasting process and as a by-product, reveal other interesting information that will help guide and coach the salesperson or direct the branch; for example, you will find that the mix of products sold can vary enormously from salesperson to salesperson or branch to branch. You may even find that your best salesperson/branch is not actually selling the same profile of products or services as the norm, perhaps choosing a particular product to focus on, and it will reveal varying trends between branches or salesmen. Maybe a particular salesman enjoys selling a certain line or they know more about it and have the most success with that product. It may even be for selfish reasons; e.g., products have better commission levels or the average selling price is greater; therefore, requiring less effort. It may even be the opposite; the product is very competitively priced, so easier to sell against the local competition because of better features.

There are myriad reasons why these trend comparisons can vary but they will improve the sales management by raising many questions as to why some are achieving greater success than others. This will facilitate decisions to improve.

If relevant, this kind of analysis can also help to determine true profitability per salesperson: by using the sales per product to calculate contribution levels. It will also assist in performance appraisals and training needs analysis for the salesperson and lead to discount analysis over sales outlet. It could also point to the regional strengths of competitors as well as sales territory determination and balancing. It can be a very informative analysis and management tool.

Depending on your business, it is also possible to assist building your sales forecasts around your customers' purchasing trends. This may not be feasible in some businesses but those whose business is of the repeat type revolving around relatively few customers may find this approach beneficial. Forecasts would need to include the addition of new customers and account for some churn, but this is quite manageable. This approach also has advantageous byproducts: customer profitability, trends in customer purchases that raise important questions relating to customer retention and loyalty, product mix analysis that points to extra sales efforts to expand turnover with existing customers, and of course the early identification of dissatisfied customers.

*Sales forecasts have limiting factors too*
One can't ignore, of course, that there are limiting factors within a sales forecast.

This could be that the organization may have reached an "optimum" share of the market; i.e., a share that to enlarge would require extra sales and marketing costs that are out of proportion to the gain they can make with their existing product base that may prompt the development of additional products or services. It is generally the case that the larger your market share the more the unit cost of enlarging it, and this should become clear from the trends that will show a gradual lessening of the upward slope that gives early warning or a potential peaking.

Publicly funded organizations are likely to find that their income is fairly defined by central government, or limits imposed on what increases they are allowed. This makes their income budgets easier, although it may place restrictions and challenges on the services they are able to offer. Others, such as charities, will need to consider their cost of raising donations when assessing their likely future receipts to maintain the percentage of funds they can use for the beneficiaries. These costs may assume an increasing percentage of the funds they generate as the total grows, a factor that can have significant impact on donations if those who give find out how much of what they give is absorbed by administration.

This guidance on sales forecasting is largely drawn from my own experience, so it is reiterated that if you are new to this subject then there is a plethora of material out there to help and guide you to best practice.

Finally, I do emphasize again that in most cases the best forecasts are those completed from the bottom up. Boards sometimes think they know better but they must be conscious of the ownership needs of forecasts. Staff motivation can be damaged if they think that a forecast is edging toward a target set by top management, although senior management is naturally not divorced from the process. It is their responsibility to guide the operation to greater forecasting accuracy, the goal of responsible forecasts.

# CHAPTER 5

# Using Graphical Management Accounts in Practice

Visualize the boardroom of Finishing Touches, a retailer of socks and ties with a major outlet in a big city shopping mall that is now facing a new competitor in the mall, Socks and Hankies.

The board meeting is underway, the minutes have been approved, and matters arising have been discussed. The next item on the agenda is the management accounts, which for the current financial year have been transformed into a graphical presentation depicting trends (twelve-month rolling totals). Finishing Touches also produces traditional numeric accounts but these are now largely for the detail of the cost analysis. They have already come to rely upon their new graphical accounts for strategic and board-meeting decisions.

The organization's financial year starts in January, and after the first half year the retailer also implemented a new business-forecasting process. The latest forecast from October, produced with the September management accounts, is depicted by a dashed line; and their first forecast, which was produced with the June management accounts, is shown as a dotted line.

Please note that the value scales in the charts, like most charts shown in this book, do not start with zero; this can give a visual distortion of proportions, so it is essential to note the vertical scales before considering the slope of the graphs. The actual values shown may be read by adding as many zeros to the values as suits your situation; this does not alter any aspect of the graph. Remember that the bars are the budget, the solid black line the actual performance.

The CEO, David Lancaster, addresses the three-man board. It comprises the Finance Controller Bob Findlay and the Sales Director/Vice President John Grant. David also takes responsibility for procurement, although designs are also bounced off John. The meeting continues . . .

*DL* OK, guys, let's move on to the management accounts. Do you all have the graphs in front of you? Just to put the whole accounts into perspective, let's take a look at net profit, figures 5.1 and 5.2. It's not really a pretty picture.

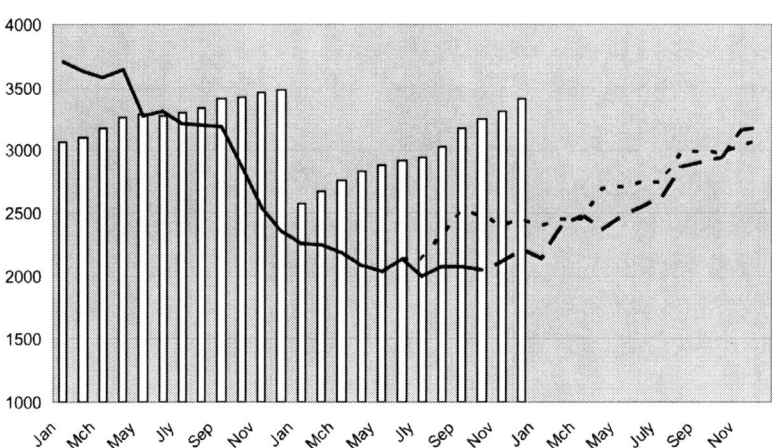

*Fig. 5.1*

**Net Profit %age to Sales**

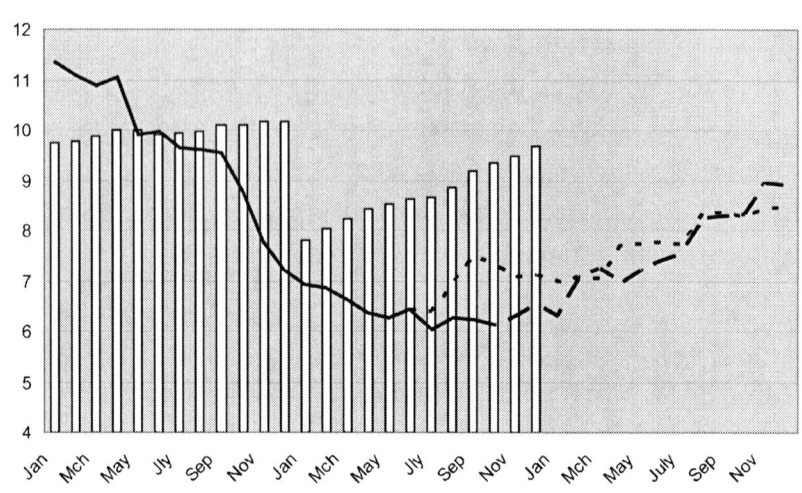

*Fig. 5.2*

It's been a tough eighteen months, although we do seem to be slowly bottoming out of this trend. As you can see, we were riding high at over 11 percent net margin at the beginning of last year (Fig. 5.2) and that's just about halved. We are going to have to provide some good answers to our paymasters at the end of this year. We can't put the entire budget deficit down to the new Socks and Hankies store; we can now see that the downward trend started before they opened last October. We also missed our budget last year by about a third (Fig.5.1), and according to the last forecast we shall miss it by about the same amount this year even though we set it lower. In view of the downward trend last year we should have been more realistic in this year's budget. In retrospect I don't know why we thought we could turn a trend like that so quickly. What a pity we weren't producing these trends last year. I don't think we would have made this mistake had we been doing so. It's very clear now how long it takes to turn a trend.

It's good to see that the trend appears to have flattened now. It's been bumping along on a level for a few months (Fig.5.1), so hopefully we may have seen the worst but we need to do more to turn this trend upward. We know we have a loss of turnover on Socks because of the new Socks and Hankies store, and this is part of the problem. But more on this in a minute. Our total sales turnover is only going to miss the budget by about 4.5 percent (Fig.5.3), so Socks turnover is only part of the story. The important thing now is to look at where we're going and how we can improve the situation further.

Let's look at the total sales graph (Fig 5.3). Do you all have that in front of you? Well, after that rather flat period in our sales in the first half of the year it's good to see that sales are now continuing the upward trend, and we haven't been able to achieve a price increase, so this must be volume growth. It's not all good news, though; our profits have tumbled despite the fact that out sales trend has been more or less flat since the beginning of last year. We are going to have to investigate where the profit leaks have been. Hopefully we should have some answers to this by the time we reach the end of these charts.

The actual sales line on the graph together with the forecast is indicating that we shall miss our sales budget for this year; the adverse variance has been consistent throughout the current year. Look at the growing gap as the year has progressed. Back in June your forecast looked as though you were expecting to hold the position steady and not adding to the cumulative variance. The gap has remained the same for the last six months, but then in August we took another dip in sales against your budget and the gap continued to widen. So what went wrong with your earlier forecast, John?

**Total Sales**

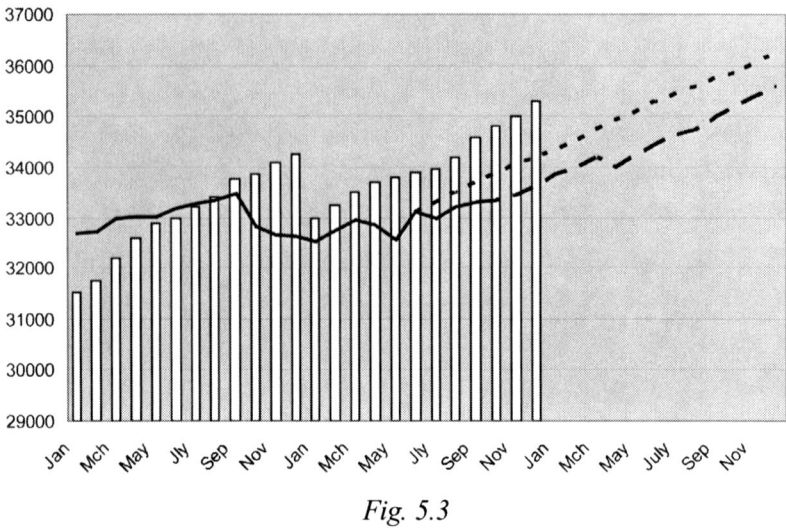

*Fig. 5.3*

JG    Well, you can see that we've been on an upward trend in total sales since June, and all the signs are that this will continue. In my earlier forecast I had more or less continued the trend that was started in June. This is because the economy is growing again after the recession. The independent retail statistics are now showing growth, and all the pundits are saying that things will continue to improve. I can't see why we won't benefit from this. We are also getting more customers come through the door every month, so this backs this up. But to answer your question about the June forecast, you need to take a look at the sales of each of our two product ranges (Figs. 5.4 and 5.5).

**Sales of Socks**

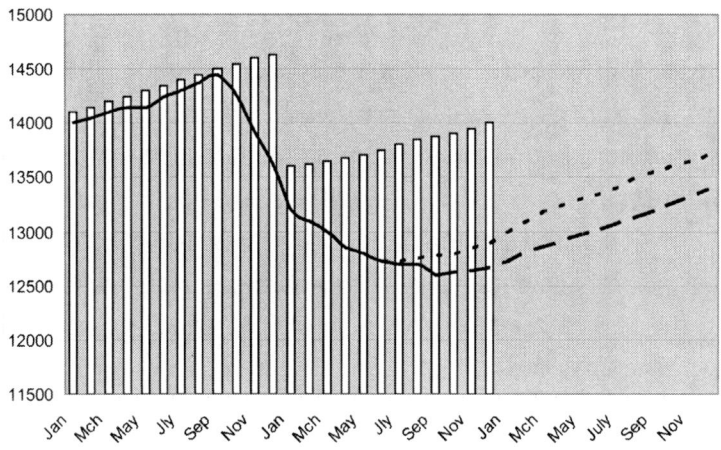

*Fig. 5.4*

**Sales of Ties**

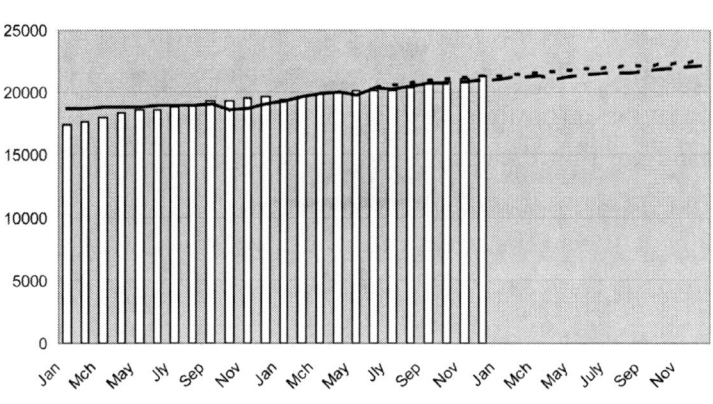

*Fig. 5.5*

JG   The problem has to do with sock sales. As you can see, all the extra sales I forecast were to come from these product lines. This stemmed from the decision to increase advertising to boost the new lines. When we take a look at the advertising trends later you'll see that we forecast a big jump in our advertising costs, and to reflect this I forecast a big jump in our sock sales. We had done all the planning for this marketing campaign, even designed all the adverts, but I pulled the whole campaign before I brought it to the board for approval and before we signed up with the agency. I was worried about the way the profits were going and felt we couldn't afford it. In retrospect it would have been better if I hadn't included the expected sales or costs in the forecast. I did still have to get it approved and I know it was against the forecasting rules, but it just looked so certain. That's a mistake I won't make again. Socks have also suffered as a result of that new outlet of Socks and Hankies starting up down the mall. As you can see from the chart (Fig. 5.4), we took a real hit as soon as they opened last October. And on top of the recession it's been a struggle to hold on to the market. As you can see, the trend has been continuously down since then. Overall we are down about 13 percent. However, things are now improving. As you can see from the shape of the graph, the decline is slowing, so it looks as though we are about to bottom out. We have had some adverse comments from our customers about Socks and Hankies. Their range is looking a bit dated and lacking new designs and I'm basing this turnaround on that.

BF    I have to say, John, that you were optimistic that you could turn the corner on socks. Just look at your budget in the chart, a steep upward trend (Fig.5.4), but this just hasn't happened. Thankfully the increase in tie sales has offset the socks reduction, but the gap on the socks side is worrying. What's to say that this downward trend isn't going to continue? They may get their act together with some new ranges.

JG    Well, when we agreed the budget we had just added the new woolen range and had completed a big advertising campaign, so I was optimistic we could turn the trend quickly. This just seems to be taking much longer than we expected, but sales of these products are now increasing, and this, together with the adverse comments from our customers about Socks and Hankies, gives us a better chance.

BF   The graph shows (Fig. 5.4) that the downward trend has yet to turn despite what you've said. So is it realistic to forecast a turnaround in sales immediately? Granted the current trend is flattening, but do you really think you can reverse the trend as quickly as this? What's changed to make this happen?

JG   Well, I think the new woolen range is really beginning to bite now. It's taken longer than hoped to get the message over to our customers, but with hindsight it was probably too much to expect for it to turn the trend as quickly as we had budgeted. However, we've seen the sales of these continue to grow as the year has progressed. In addition, we have redesigned the window displays to give more prominence to the sock ranges, and the new supplier that David found in the spring has not only made us more competitive, the product is of better quality too. This has already been noticed by our customers, so I don't think we have been too optimistic in the forecast.

We are also continuing the advertising campaign, although the plans are that this will drop off once the current plan ends at the end of the year. All these decisions came out of our July board meeting after I presented our last forecast, if you remember they were prompted by the continuing downward trend. On the bright side, as you can see, ties continue the upward trend (Fig. 5.5) that's been running since the beginning of last year. This had a bit of a boost last November when we introduced that new silk range from Italy, and I don't think we have seen the best of that yet. This supplier keeps coming out with some winning designs, so I think there is a good case for a continued upward trend. We've also been very consistent on our budgeting and forecasting for the tie ranges; as you can see the performance gaps are virtually nonexistent.

DL    OK, well, let's stick with these forecasts for the present, but we will need to keep a close eye on them over the next few months. Let's have a look at our gross margins. Let's turn to the total contribution trend (Fig.5.6). Bob, can you talk us through this?

BF    Well, as you can see, contribution has been pretty flat this year despite the improving sales value, so margins have dropped and this is reflected in the contribution percentage of turnover chart (Fig. 5.7). We were doing fine until February, more or less on budgeted percent margin, but as you can see we lost 0.5 percent in March and haven't recovered from this. All this was down to what happened on ties, but we'll come on to that in a minute.

I can't say as yet whether the forecast improvement is feasible. It looks fairly dramatic to me. This shows a 2.5 percent sales increase over the next fifteen months, so we had better have some pretty good justifications for this forecast. It will depend on whether the other income improvements and cost reductions are also feasible, so we need to see the other charts for those too. Let's look at contribution levels first; this will help us see whether it's in the margins. As you can see from the total contribution chart (Fig. 5.6), the latest trend shows a steepening of the trend line as we move into the New Year. This reflects the increase in sales values forecast that we looked at earlier (Fig. 5.3), but not all of it is down to sales. We are also forecasting an increase in margins on ties; have a look at the contribution percentage chart for ties (Fig. 5.11). This shows a 3 percent improvement next year; we need to have a good reason for this optimism. Apart from this you can see that the earlier June forecast was completely wrong. We just didn't get near the forecast, and I think that John will have something to say about that in a minute.

**Total Contribution - Sales less Cost of Ties and Socks**

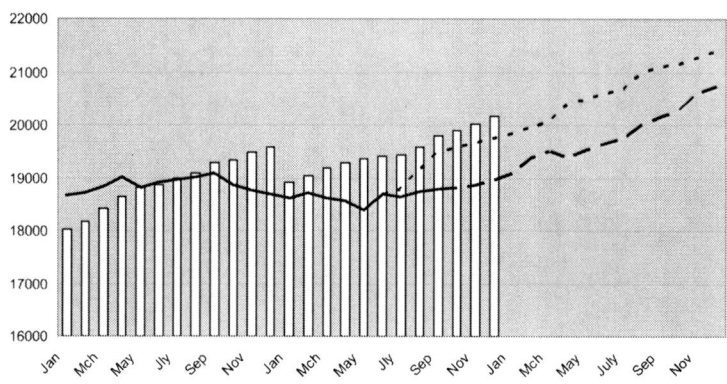

*Fig. 5.6*

**Total Contribution %age to Total Sales**

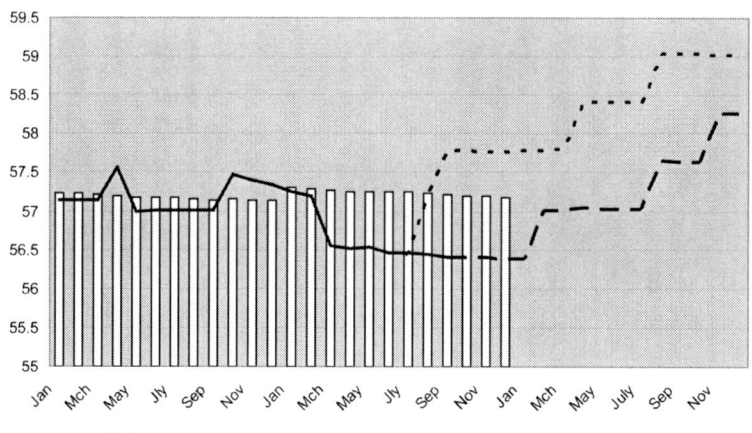

*Fig. 5.7*

It might help to have a look at the charts for contribution for each of our main lines (Figs. 5.8, 5.9, 5.10 and 5.11).

**Socks - Contribution (Sales less Purchase cost)**

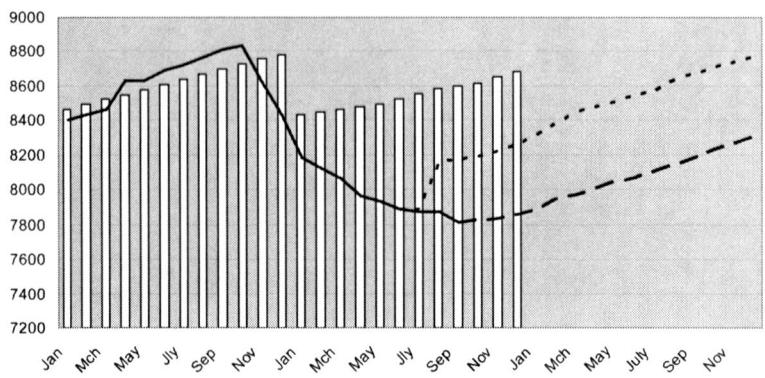

*Fig. 5.8*

**Socks - Contribution %age of Sales**

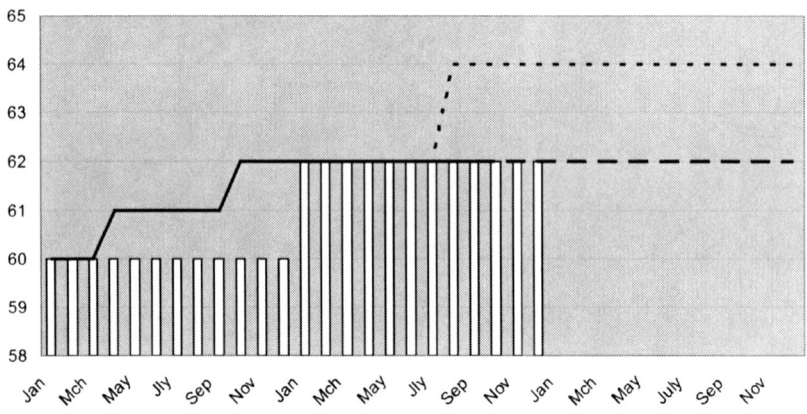

*Fig. 5.9*

Ties - Contribution (Sales less Purchase Cost)

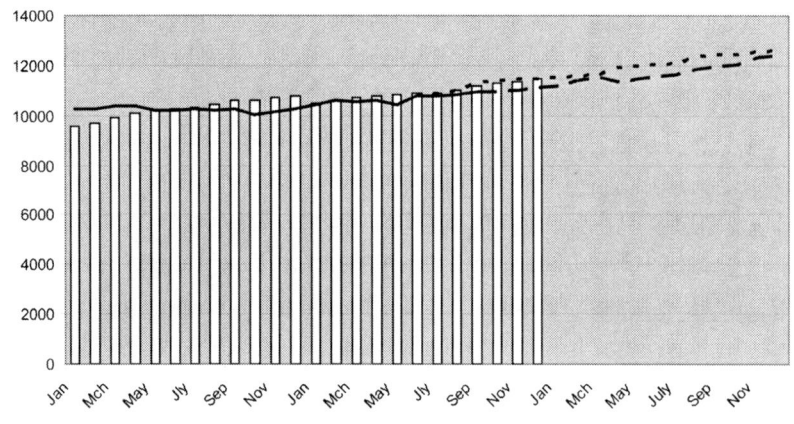

*Fig. 5.10*

Ties - Contribution %age to Sales

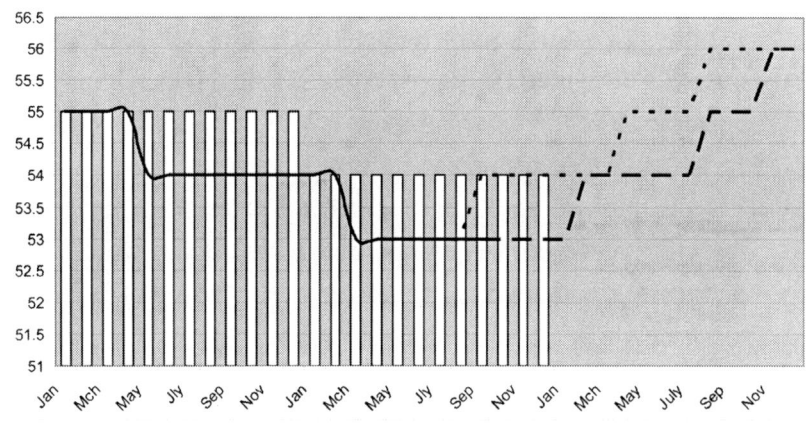

*Fig. 5.11*

BF    In the case of the sock product lines, we have seen an improvement in margins over last year. We are spot on budget and forecasting this to continue.

JG    Back in June we forecast an improvement in margins because we thought we had found a new supplier for the nylon and wool mix range but the deal fell through before it was signed up, but it all looked definite at the time we did the forecast.

DL    This teaches us another lesson, doesn't it? We can't make assumptions about factors in a forecast. Plans must be firm if we are going to base a forecast on them.

JG    Yes, it's a lesson well learned. We shall make sure in future that unless a plan is approved or a deal signed up we won't include it. As you can see we have made no assumptions in the latest forecast, although I can mention that we may have a new deal to report next month if all goes well, so hopefully we can improve the forecast later.

BF    In overall terms, the situation on ties is a bit more hopeful. As you know we experienced a 2 percent reduction in contribution last year and in view of the fact that ties account for about £80,000 more sales than socks; this has made a significant difference to the grand total. The 2 percent increase in cost that came through last year was our supplier's response to the global cost of silk; it rocketed after the political situation overseas disrupted the supply chain. We had hoped it may have corrected itself by now but there is still no sign of a reduction, so we can't forecast any relief in this area yet.

JG    We did look to increase our selling prices but our market research among our key competitors revealed they were holding their prices, and since we are already near the top of the market on price we decided we couldn't move, though I do see from your monthly procurement reports, David, that you expect a significant improvement in the margins of ties (Figs. 5.10 and 5.11). Where is the improvement going to come from?

DL    The situation on the cost of ties is hopeful. The new ranges have really grown in volume, and with increased sales volumes forecast we will move into the new band of quantity discounts as next year progresses. This should make a significant difference by the end of next year, and as you can see by the upward steps on the percentage trend graph I have reflected this in the forecasts. I don't think this is taking too optimistic a view. If you look at our chart for tie sales (Fig. 5.5), there has been a consistent upward trend on these sales since late last year. And now the general economy is turning, so I can see no reason why this shouldn't continue next year.

BF    In overall terms, this year the net effect of these base correlative cost changes caused by the cost of silk is an increase in the percentage of total purchase cost to total sales of about 0.9 percent (Fig. 5.7). This is weighted by the adverse margin on ties; as we know ties sales are larger than socks, so despite the better margins on socks (Fig. 5.9) this reduction on ties has outweighed the margin improvements on socks. This contributes to the overall reduction of about 5-6 percent in our net profit margin, but our overheads account for the lion's share of the deficiency. We need to have a good look at them now. Let's start with advertising and marketing. I've seen some biggish bills come through for this over the last few months (Figs. 5.12 and 5.13).

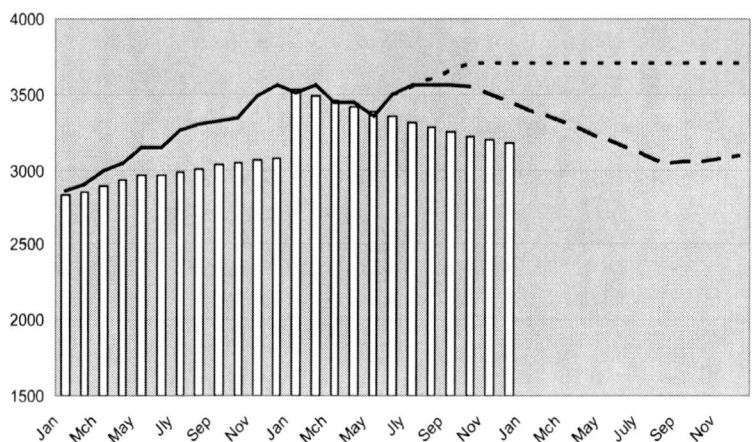

*Fig. 5.12*

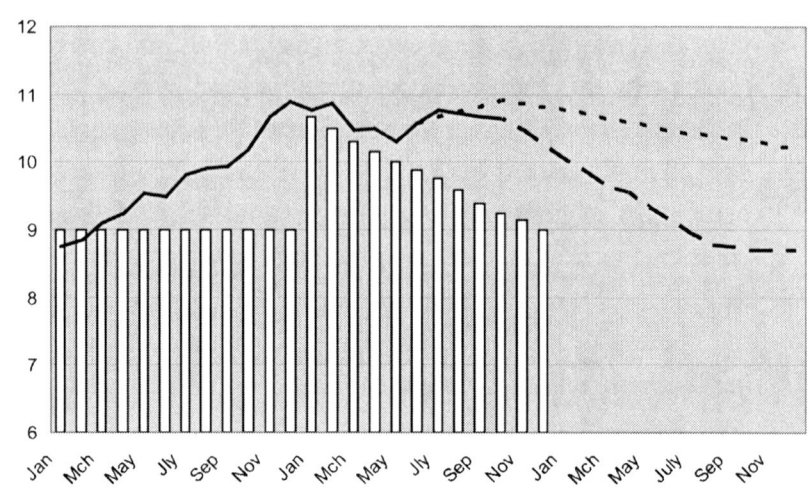

*Fig. 5.13*

BF    Advertising has risen from about 8.8 percent to 10.8 percent since the beginning of last year, so here's about 2 percent of our net margin shortfall. Before we go any further, do you want to say something about this, John?

JG    We did increase advertising early last year over our budget to get some growth in our socks ranges when the new woolen ranges came in, and I had hoped that these extra sales would offset the advertising cost. But as we mentioned earlier, the sales didn't come along as quickly as I hoped. Then the new branch of Socks and Hankies opened in the mall and I had to counter this by boosting the advertising still further. As you can see from the chart I increased the budget significantly for this year with the view to gradually reducing it over the year. We managed to nearly hold budget for the first few months, but as you saw from the socks sales chart (Fig. 5.7), sales just kept falling away. I think the impact of Socks and Hankies, with customers trying them out, went on longer than I had expected, so I've had to hold it at that level really, around an annual rate of 10.5 percent until we could find a better answer to this additional competition, but it's taken some time. Now that we have found these new ranges I'm expecting to be able to reduce the advertising spend; you will see this in the forecast. I'm aiming to try and get it back to around 8.5 percent by the end of next year when the situation between us and Socks and Hankies should have stabilized. But you know how it is, things are changing all the time. We are now at least not adding to the variance from budget this year. As you can see the forecast line and the budget line are parallel, so the actual cumulative variance is not getting worse.

DL    You told us earlier, John, about the plan for a major advertising campaign that didn't come off.

JG    Yes, at the time of producing the forecast we were planning quite a major spend in advertising and this is reflected in my forecast (Figs. 5.12 and 5.13) and also in the sales forecast for socks (Fig. 5.4). As you can see from these forecasts I believed this would have paid dividends later, but before I signed up I got nervous and pulled the plug. The overall results were slipping away and I felt the plans were best postponed. This was just after the June forecast. As I mentioned earlier, we were still waiting for approval on this campaign and I shouldn't have included it in the forecast until this was passed, to do so was a bit misleading.

DL    OK, you have taken the action to reduce it now and as you can see it's important to keep it going down, so keep us informed. Let's move on to our admin costs (Figs. 5.14 and 5.15). Have we all got these charts?

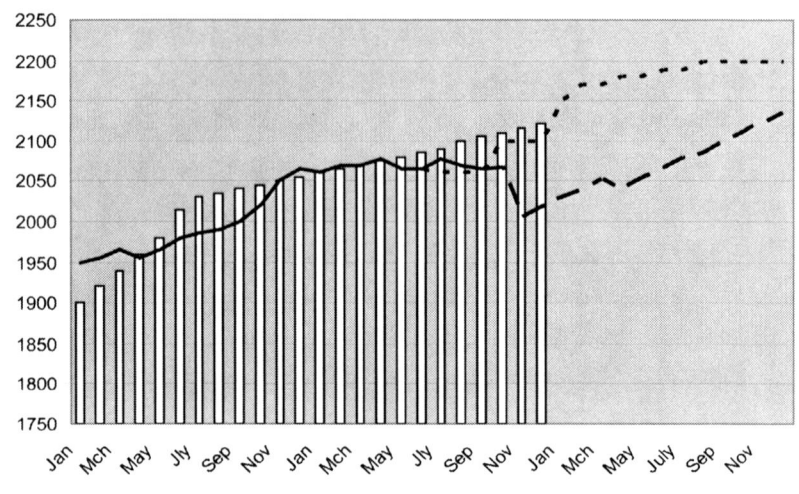

*Fig. 5.14*

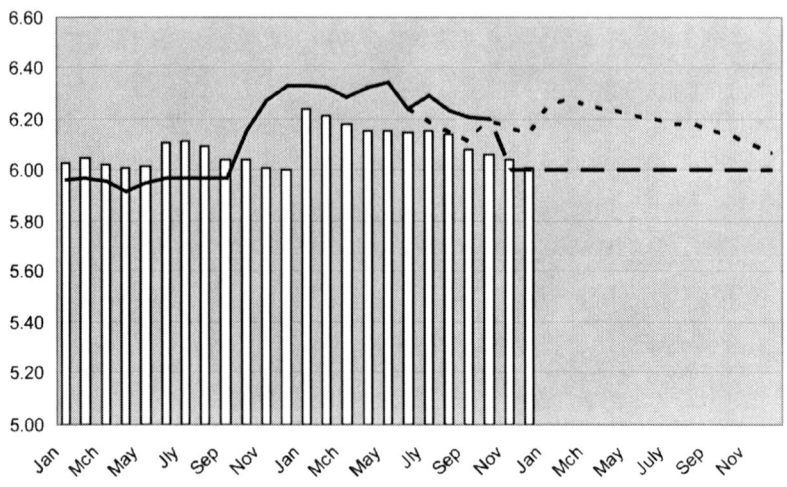

*Fig. 5.15*

BF    As you can see, in percentage of turnover terms these have been pretty flat for some time (Fig. 5.15). There was a 0.4 percent increase last year when we had to take on that new member of staff, but this is now expected to come down within a couple of months when Maggie leaves to have her baby; she's told us she isn't returning. This new staff member is doing well and this means we won't have to replace her, so we will be back to last year's level. This isn't bad in view of inflation and we have been able to offset this with some other savings.

DL    This is good to hear, Bob, but what really concerns me is the growth in the actual cost you are expecting in the forecast next year. Look at the actual cost graph (Fig. 5.14). That's a massive increase. You're following the percentage right enough but we have a good deal of "base structural" costs included in admin and I wouldn't have expected that to rise in proportion to sales value. Are you anticipating something unusual that will cause this?

BF    Well, we were thinking of upgrading our software. There's some systems around now that will help with our statistics, and the nature of this is such that we write it off rather than capitalize it. We had planned to do it earlier this year, as you can see from the June forecast (Fig. 5.14), but we postponed it in view of the results. Perhaps we should delay this again until better times. It is an "optional cost" and we don't have major problems at present, so it may be possible to postpone that action until the year after when things will hopefully have recovered. I'll have a look at it, and if it looks good I'll change the next forecast. This will help to flatten the forecast cost and reduce the forecast cost percentage.

DL    In my view, Bob, you should separate this type of "optional" cost from the "base structural" costs of admin; this will provide better trends of admin cost and allow us to see how the these other costs are influencing our cost proportions.

BF  Yes, I agree, that's a good idea; I'll have it changed in future graphs. Can we move on now to our management costs (Figs. 5.16 and 5.17)?

As you can see these have risen by about 1 percent of turnover since the beginning of last year. They're up from 6.7 percent to 7.7 percent of turnover, and we are now running above budget and forecasting even more rises. Our latest forecast is even worse than that of June in terms of percent of turnover. Even though the value trend (Fig. 5.16) shows our latest forecast being better than our previous forecast, this is deceptive because our total sales level forecast in June (Fig. 5.3) was significantly better than it is now, but when you look at forecast cost proportions you can see that we are now forecasting this cost to increase even further out of proportion to total sales to the tune of nearly 0.5 percent. I know that doesn't sound much but when you think of our net profit level of 7-8 percent (Fig. 5.2). That's still quite a large figure.

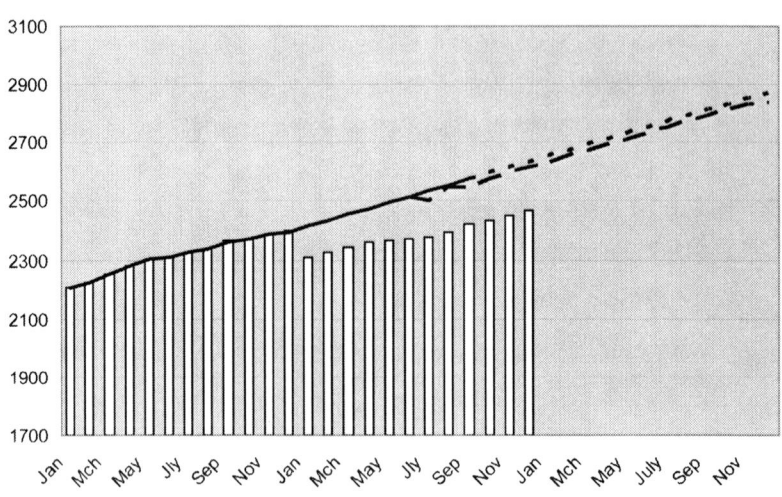

**Management Salaries and Expenses**

*Fig. 5.16*

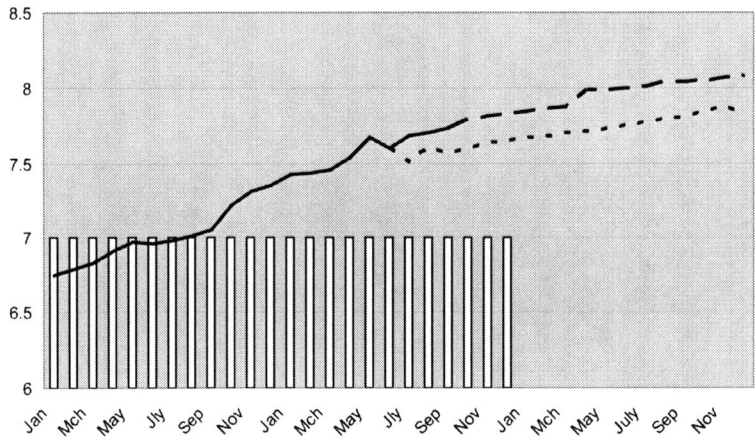

*Fig. 5.17*

DL We were far too optimistic in our budget for this year and I can't really account for that. We weren't producing these trends last year but if we had been we wouldn't have made this mistake; as you can see the trend in our actual performance was on the up and that's really where out budget should have started. As you can see our full 12 month budget for this year is actually above last year's and I suspect all we did was to look at last year's figure in total, add on a small percentage and then take a very inaccurate stab at phasing it. It just goes to prove how bad that practice is, had we seen the trend for last year when doing our budgets we wouldn't have made that mistake. However the cost increase this year has mainly to do with all the extra traveling needed on the continent to source better designs and prices, and as you've seen we have had some success with better margins and some good finds as far as ties is concerned. However, in view of the forecasts I think we have to review this. I'll have another look at it and see whether we can't modify our plans for the 18 months to get us back to where we were. We also budgeted for some bonuses for us this year too, and in view of our reduction in profits these are going to be lower, so we need to get that into the next forecast as well. We can adjust this in the next forecast when I think we can get back close to budget. Let's move on our shop salaries (Figs. 5.18 and 5.19).

**Shop Staff Salaries**

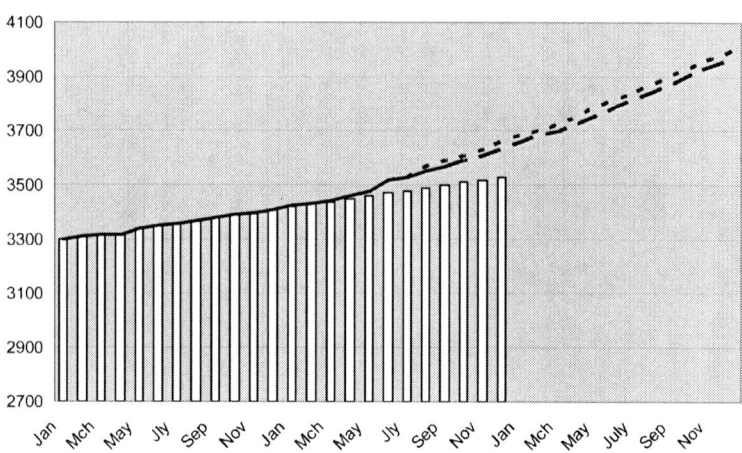

*Fig. 5.18*

**Shop Staff Salaries %age to Sales**

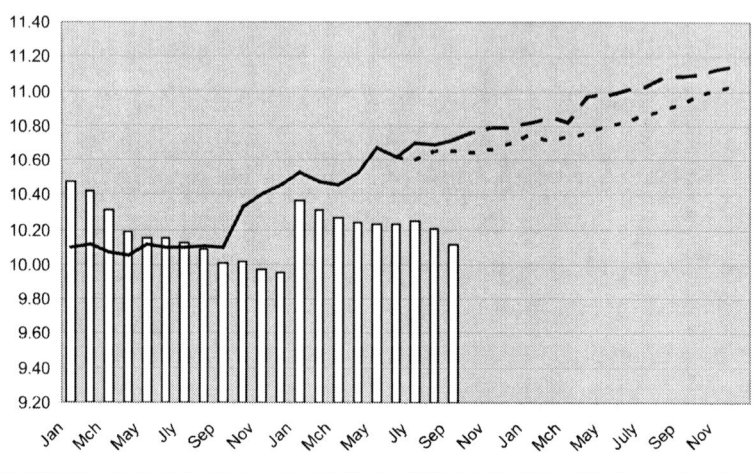

*Fig. 5.19*

BF    We were holding our value budget fairly well until June, but it's drifted away from budget since then and the percentage to sales value has risen by nearly 1 percent over the last twenty months (Fig. 5.19), so this cost is growing out of proportion to income and that doesn't seem right for this cost, which should vary to some extent with turnover. It is really "base correlative." We are only about 0.6 percent off the budget at the year-end but the trend shows it getting worse. I know we took the decision to increase our shop opening times back in October last year, but the increase in cost seems to be out of proportion to the increase in sales value we've achieved. What do you think, John? This is your department.

JG    I did expect this rise in the percentage after the increase in shop hours, but then it should have dropped off. It always takes awhile for customers to catch on to changes however well you advertise them, but this is longer than I had forecast. You can see by the step up in the budgeted percentage (Fig. 5.19) that I increased this for a while at the start of the year and then budgeted to gradually reduce as the sales value grew. Unfortunately sales have not grown as we had hoped. The worry is that the performance gap is widening. The percentage to sales value is growing and our forecast is for it to get worse because we were looking to extend the working hours again. Our June and September forecasts are quite consistent; that adds to the worry.

In view of this we have to review this plan. We'll do some analysis to measure the sales we are making in the extra hours we have already been working and postpone our plans to extend them further until all this is clear. I'll include the results of this in the next forecast.

DL    Let's cover the next cost center, our accounting costs.

**Accounting Costs and Salaries**

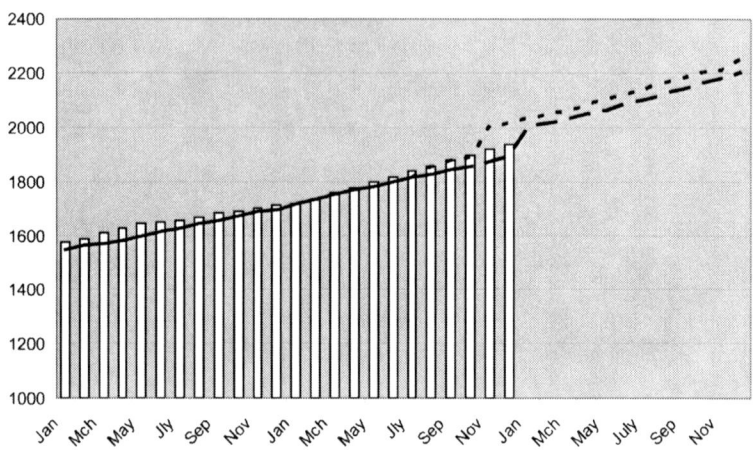

*Fig. 5.20*

**Accounting Costs %age to Sales**

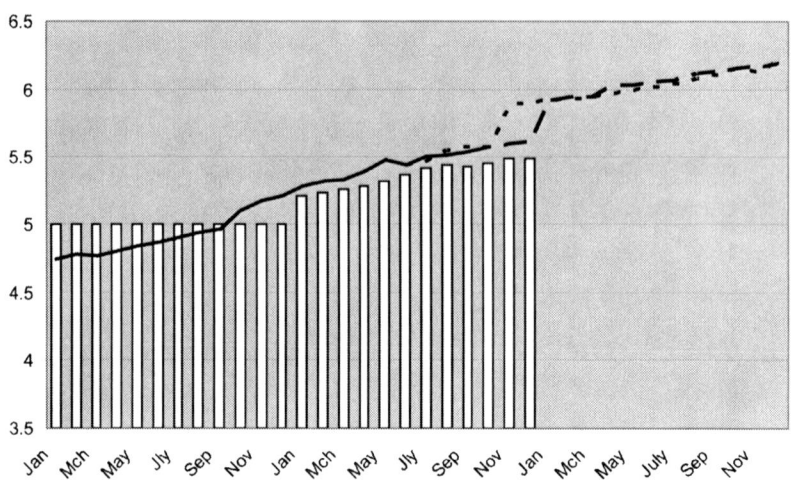

*Fig. 5.21*

BF    As you can see we had budgeted for a small increase in January of this year (Fig. 5.21) and we are pretty much on budget at the end of September. You'll remember that this increase was down to a significant increase in our insurance premiums last year; I've gone out for a number of other quotes but so far no luck. The jump in our forecast is because we need an extra member of staff to cover a long-term sickness. We just can't manage without someone. In June we did forecast this recruitment to take place earlier but we have held off in view of the unsatisfactory figures. As you can see we have now forecast the additional member to join us in the New Year.

DL  In view of the circumstances, Bob, I think you are going to have to find a way of managing. I suggest you get your guys together and see what can be done. We just can't afford to increase our costs by another 0.5 percent of sales value as your forecast is showing. Let me know how you get on.

Finally we have our accommodation costs (Figs. 5.22 and 5.23). Let's see what's happened here.

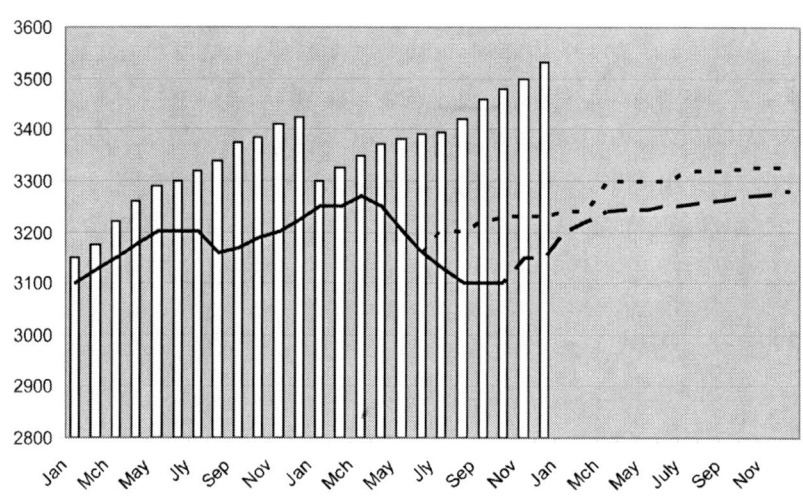

*Fig. 5.22*

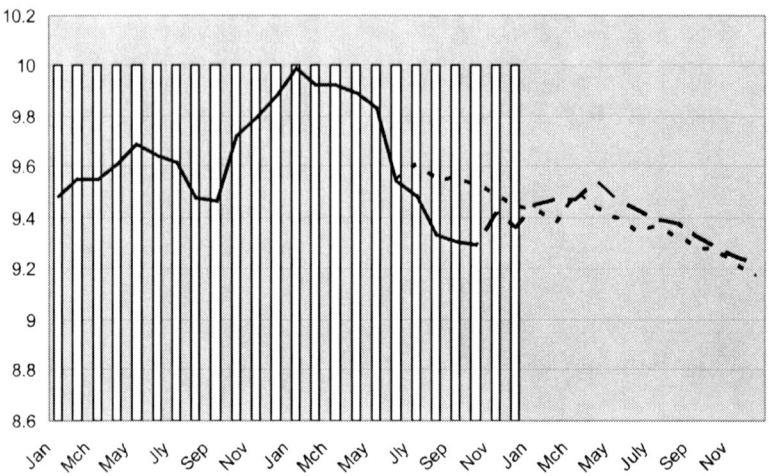

*Fig. 5.23*

DL    Well, thank goodness we're managing to hold something below our budget. This hasn't changed since last year and the forecast looks consistent too. Anything to say about this, Bob?

BF    Well, just to say that we budgeted for 10 percent of our turnover for this year, consistent with last year's budget. As you can see, despite the increase in turnover, we've held the actual accommodations steady. In fact, we've managed to save some money by re-sourcing our utilities. Our latest forecast does show some increases next year to reflect our three yearly redecorations of the shop, but apart from that we have no other foreseeable costs coming up. We may have to review this later if our figures don't respond, but for the moment I prefer to keep it in the forecasts.

It might be helpful, David, to sum up where the net profit has gone. In percentage terms we were doing really well in net profit to sales at the beginning of last year. It was over 11 percent. Now we are down to around 6 percent. That means our costs have risen out of proportion to sales. We can analyze that as follows: cost of purchases is up by about 0.7 percent and we know that a reduction in margins on ties is largely to blame for that; this could have been worse if the margins on socks hadn't improved. As far as the overheads are concerned, all other costs except accommodation have increased relative to sales: administration, 0.2 percent; shop staff, 0.6 percent; advertising, 1.9 percent; management costs, 1.1 percent; and accounting 0.8 percent. On the face of it none of these appear to be significant percentages, with perhaps the exception of advertising, although as we have seen in this instance it is "optional." But when they are added together they combine to halve net profit. I think this demonstrates to you why small percentage variations in cost percentages to income can be very important areas for attention. Armed with the trends and forecasts available to you now, you can see these divergences before they happen. Our decisions today will certainly lead to alleviating the problem areas.

It's good to see that we are forecasting an overall improvement in both net profit value and net profit percent of sales, but we shall need to watch all these forecasts carefully over the next few months.

The critical factors in our forecasts are the turnaround in the sales of socks and the significant improvement in margins on ties, but there are risks with both these, so I think we should also look for some further improvements coming from costs too.

We've already anticipated an improvement in management costs, but I think we have to have a good look at advertising. The forecast on this looks promising but it's showing a significant reduction over the next twelve months and we just have to make sure it happens, so the cost effectiveness of each campaign will need close examination. Shop salaries are also a bit of a worry, so let's get the analysis of sales in the extra hours opening that we've agreed upon completed as soon as possible. The rethinking on the new staff member in accounts will also help the next forecast.

DL    Thanks, Bob. These are useful comments and give us all food for thought. All the actions we've discussed here will be helpful, but should we consider something more fundamental? Apart from some cost-control issues the most significant problem is that we face a new competitor, and there is no doubt we have lost some market share. Socks and Hankies is not going away, so we will have to find ways of coping with it. It seems to me that we can counter this in a couple of ways. We can either widen our product range through our existing outlet or open a new branch.

My concern about the first option is that it will reduce floor space for our core products. We are already pretty cramped and the result of this may lead to a loss of turnover in our core products. We may even have to reduce the size of range we currently offer because we simply won't have the space.

It will also mean taking us on a new market, and we don't have the fashion knowledge and buying skills in this area, so there would be a learning curve. Opening a new branch will need more investment and it will probably reduce our overall profit for a while and we shall need more cash from the bank, but it will allow us to make full use of the expertise we've developed in our existing market. It will also increase our volume of the same products, which will boost our negotiating power with the suppliers and this could lead to better margins all round. What do you think? I think we should put together a business case for this and review our strategy . . .

And so on . . .

Of course this is a highly simplified example but hopefully one that all will understand. It serves to demonstrate the integrated use of a combination of income, cost, and margin trend charts in a boardroom context that will be well known to many readers. However, it also demonstrates how the questions and answers prompted by the charts have moved away from a discussion of historic results and monthly budget variances actuated by conventional management accounts to a much more important discourse that focuses on future plans and actions. This is precisely my experience when the system was introduced. This remarkable transformation and major improvement in the value of board meetings was brought about by simply presenting our management accounts in a different way and adding quarterly forecasts. The same dialogue could not have happened without seeing the trends and regularly considering these forecasts. It is very hard to say to what extent this dramatic change contributed to our success during the following years but our net results increased significantly year on year until my departure from the organization several years later. There is no doubt in my mind that the impact of this new management accounting system was significant.

## Multilevel charts

The application of graphical presentation of management accounts to every type and size of organization is a key feature of the system. It is a universal system, but a degree of fashioning will be necessary.

There is no prescription or *pro forma* for this. The requirements are so varied and the management needs so different that each must decide for themselves, based on the techniques outlined in this book, which charts would best suit their needs. It isn't difficult to determine this. It is very likely that all organizations will have a total income and a total net result (profit/loss/surplus/deficiency). After that it may vary considerably.

Income may be divided up over branch, subsidiary, division, profit center, salesman, product, service, etc.

Direct, variable, or as termed in chapter 2 "base correlative," costs may follow a similar course to income and may lead to striking a gross margin together with its percentage for each branch, subsidiary, division, etc. as above. Each would have its own charts. As we have seen this can prove particularly valuable when comparing branches, salesmen, etc. side by side.

Why should these comparative trends and forecasts for each be different? This will open the gate to many more managerial issues and questions that will lead to better overall control, guidance, and performance.

All other costs will also be divided or departmentalized to suit individual needs, but readers will be reminded to separate those costs contained in oval and round shapes in Fig. 2.1 in chapter 2, which are not connected in any way with the volume of activity within an organization's operation. The percentages that these bear to turnover are likely to be very volatile, and if these costs are included elsewhere they will distort the percentage and trends of the receiving department and it will become very clear how they are changing the cost structure and affecting net profit percentages.

The diagram in Fig. 5.24 that is repeated from chapter 2 for reference purposes here may help to clarify the formation of your chart structure. Note that the dotted lines indicate cost-income relationships (percentages of income) that will need to be charted.

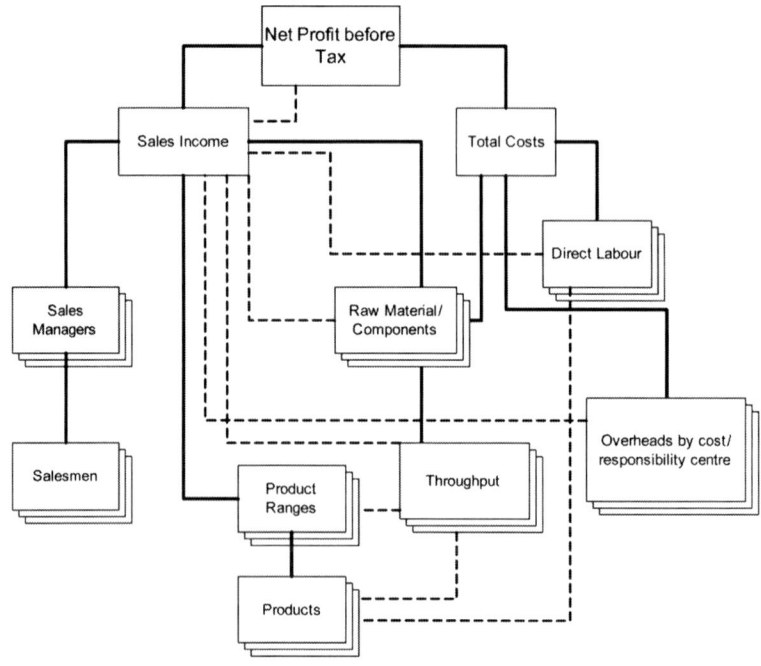

*Fig. 5.24*

Organizations using an activity-based-costing approach within their management accounts may find the graphical approach particularly valuable because of the way in which trends in costs and margins within activities can be monitored.

## Number of charts

There is no specific advice offered for this. It will depend upon practicality, size of organization, numbers of products/services, level of IT involvement, numbers of responsibility centers, personal choice/requirement, etc.

Boards may only be interested in the top-and second-level charts, while managers may only need those areas of business in which they have an interest. Once again these are not difficult decisions. Some will want to start just with top-level charts and add to them as required, others may want to go much further at the outset. Very often the management accounts will be supported with other trends. These might be non-financial, cost or sales orientated, and they might not always be presented at the same time as the management accounts, but they do have something in common: *they should wherever possible follow the same format.* This uniformity or timeframe and trend calculation, wherever this can be achieved, promotes comprehension among managers and provides a base for correlating the trends of financial and non financial indicators. This was adopted for most of the NFPIs and other sales performance data when we introduced the concept of trends within management accounts. One of the most valuable of these extra reports was the trends in our enquiries, quotations, and orders. Not only did this enable us to see the trends each was headed, it also enabled us to monitor the time between each stage of a sale, the relationship between quote and order that enabled us to see the trend in conversion rates, and the lifecycle of the products. This information became invaluable as a management tool; it helped with new product development, competitiveness, and sales effectiveness. When this same information was broken down over one hundred field sales staff it became an irreplaceable sales management tool for field sales managers, enabling comparisons that had not been possible before. In addition it facilitated better forecasting because all the trends were available at the lowest levels, product or individual salesperson, and trends in existing performance led to better forecasting.

There are therefore no limits to how many individual charts this trend approach can be applied to. All will depend on need, practicality, and ambition. The only advice is not to run before walking. In our case the system developed over a couple of years before reaching its full operation. This timeframe gave all parties the time to fully understand, appreciate the power of, and develop the software needed.

## Sales price, volume, and mix

Within organizations that are subject to discounting or multi-product or multi-service organizations, total contribution levels can vary depending on the actual price achieved, the mix of products/services actually sold, and the volume of each. Accountants will be familiar with price, volume, and mix variances that arise when utilizing the technique of standard costing.

For those unfamiliar with this technique imagine a multi-product company that has budgeted to sell a certain volume of each product at a certain price. When comparing this budgeted sales grand total to an actual sales grand total, variances will arise for a number of reasons: the actual result may be different because the mix of products is different from budget, or the price of one or more of the products is different, or the volume of one or more is different from budget. In standard costing the total variance from budget is divided into three variances that arise from these three factors so that the reasons for the variance can be accurately detected.

In graphical management accounting, the trends arising from mix, price, and volume and any forecasts that may be guided by the trends are important factors that can have a significant impact on margins.

Mix and volume variances can be identified through the use of multiple charts (one for each income stream) where it will be evident how the ups and downs of each trend applies to each type of income and therefore what impact this has on the total. We have already seen in the earlier example of ties and socks an overall upward trend in total income but one of the products was on a decreasing trend.

Where sales discounts are offered the trends on discounts may also be monitored. Consider the chart Fig. 5.25.

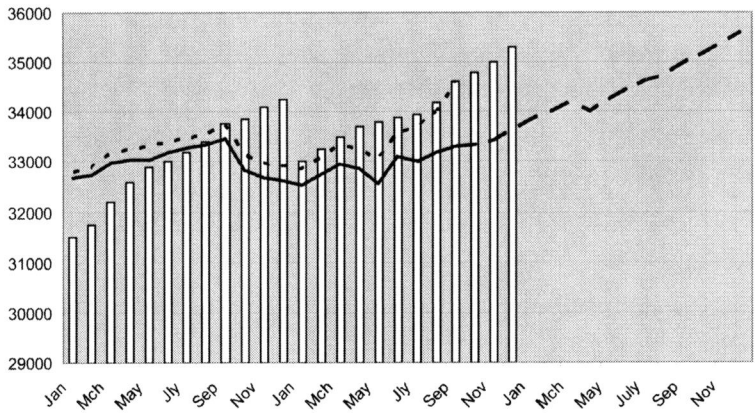

*Fig. 5.25*

This chart depicts a comparison between actual price achieved (solid line) compared to the list price (dotted line). The dashed line rolling forward indicates the twelve-month rolling total of *forecast* sales at actual price. The vertical bars are the budget. The gap between the solid and dotted lines displays a gradual increase in discount rates. Remember that both lines are twelve-month rolling totals, so the widening gap represents an increase in annual rate of discounts. The gap has widened by a value of about 1,000 and in discount percent terms this is an increase from 1 percent to 4 percent (approx.) In this case it is clear that had volume been retained at the budgeted full price then budget would have been achieved in the current month. Plotting these lines on individual charts for each salesman, product, or branch, etc. will reveal those that abuse discounts.

## Continuous improvement

All organizations want to improve, not just in the essential areas of customer service and quality, etc., but in sales/income levels, margins, cost levels, and of course net results too. Continuous improvement is a much wider subject than just the management accounts, although it is often the financial results, directly or indirectly, that measure the effect of other improvements in the business.

Non-financial measures play a significant role in measuring continuous improvement, and this is examined in the next chapter, but graphical management accounting can also play a significant part. It will be obvious from the previous chapters that financial twelve-month rolling trends indicate improvement or decline in financial performance and twelve-month rolling totals of cost-to-sales percentages show how each cost either improves or not in relation to sales and net profit. Conventional management accounts do not fulfill the function of showing continuous improvement because they fail to show trends.

It is repeated that financial measures for continuous improvement do not stand alone. It is possible to have an improving financial measure while a non-financial measure declines; e.g., extending credit periods may well increase sales, but at what cost to average credit periods, bad debts, and cash? Reduction of delivery lead times can be achieved by increasing stock levels, and this may increase sales but it is likely to be to the detriment of stock turn performance and may once again detrimentally affect cash.

It will become evident in the next chapter how non-financial and financial measures can be correlated to help manage actions taken to improve non-financial indicators.

## Not-for-profit organizations

In the above example we have looked at a retail business, a profit-making private or quoted business that has to satisfy its owners with a return on their investment. Many organizations do not fit this model; they may be public, private, or social, and the interpretation of the charts may require a different perspective. But although these organizations' objectives are not to make profits, they do have to balance the books, and for these purposes they are required to strike a net surplus or deficit. They also have income. This may be in the form of a grant, allocation, allowance, donation, rate, etc.

In essence there is no difference between any organizations as far as the graphical system is concerned. The percentage variations that may apply in cost-to-income represent shifts in financial resources.

There are other factors. For purposes of the charts it will probably be necessary to divide the total income and costs into accountable units of operation, a cost and income center that will measure each department's individual result. This will help to measure the efficiency of how each division uses the resource allocated to it and what trends may be applicable. The same budgetary controls as those used in commercial enterprises will usually apply to not-for-profit organizations, and the charts will measure the annual cumulative variances from budget in the same way. The use of forecasting techniques is just as valuable to managers of not-for-profit organizations and is especially important to their boards; the division of resources, trends, and forecasts, when expressed in graphical format, make accounts quick and easy to understand—an important factor for the cross-section of society that often comprise the boards, councilors or trustees of these organizations.

# CHAPTER 6

# Non-financial Performance Indicators (NFPIs)

In an article on October 16, 2000 in the *Financial Times'* "Mastering Management" series, Wharton School of Pennsylvania University accounting professors Christopher Ittner and David Larcker suggest that financial data has limitations as a measure of company performance. Of course many have said this over the two decades but Ittner and Larcker sum this up succinctly. Below is part of the text of their article.

> "Choosing performance measures is a challenge. Performance measurement systems play a key role in developing strategy, evaluating the achievement of organizational objectives, and compensating managers. Yet many managers feel traditional financially-oriented systems no longer work adequately. A recent survey of US financial services companies found most were not satisfied with their measurement systems. They believed there was too much emphasis on financial measures such as earnings and accounting returns and little emphasis on drivers of value such as customer and employee satisfaction, innovation,

and quality. In response, companies are implementing new performance measurement systems. A third of financial services companies, for example, made a major change in their performance measurement system during the past two years and 39 percent plan a major change within two years."

The growth in the use of NFPIs over the last twenty years has been notable and the criticism of financial measurement systems very significant. There have been passionate propositions to monitor other business factors such as the organization's value drivers and strategic development. These can't always be directly monitored using financial measures, so arrays of NFPIs have been developed. They claim, correctly, that the global markets, IT, and modern communication systems have dramatically changed the nature of competition and that financial measures alone are inadequate. All this is evident but some have claimed that if you take care of these other non-financial factors the profits will take care of themselves. This latter argument goes too far, the fine margins that most organizations now work to cannot be controlled and monitored using non-financial measures alone and good financial measures have a vital part to play.

We have seen in this book how financial measures can be developed to drive performance, speed decision-making, and encourage managers to look forward, but I do not imply that managers should take their foot off the NFPI pedal. There can be immense value in using NFPIs. They complement, not detract from, good financial measures. It is the combination of the two types of measures that provides the breadth of weapons in the armory that modern managements need in the dynamic and volatile environment that all organizations exist in today. I reject the thoughts of some that NFPIs are now of greater import than financial measures and it would be a mistake for managers to give priority to either. The fact is that a commercial organization is ultimately judged by its financial performance and an improvement in this is often the end result from an improvement in the NFPIs. The two types of measure go hand in hand, each has its function, but they do have to be effectual and presented in a clear and understandable way. This book has criticized the effectiveness of current-day management accounts on both these counts and proposed improvements that will make them a significant force and a worthy companion to an organization's NFPIs, but if these NFPIs are not also well designed and presented these too can let management down. It must be said that in public organizations the purpose of NFPIs is not always to improve financial performance, but this does not detract from the fact that the organization still has to work within set budgets, and directly or indirectly, changes in NFPIs can have serious implications on final results. In addition, financial reports are not just measures of the success of the NFPIs, they can also be valuable in their own right when they include forecasts and trends. No organization that produces management accounts, public, social, or private, can ignore the information they contain. All have limits on the cash they have available and management accounts are fundamental to good cash planning.

So what factors are necessary for us to consider before introducing a new NFPI? All will be familiar with the age-old axioms "What gets measured gets managed" or "You get what you measure," and the message behind these is largely true, based on human nature, those qualities of pride, fear, reward, praise-seeking, etc. It is true that most of us strive to progress, and if this is measured, then most of us would seek to improve against this measure. But staff can be driven to achieving the wrong outcome if the NFPI is thoughtlessly designed; it is not uncommon for a manager to single-mindedly set upon achieving a particular NFPI that inadvertently, if not knowingly, can damage the organization in a related but different area of its activities, an area that is often the responsibility of another manager.

Take a fairly simple example of this, the conflict between improving sales by shortening delivery lead times. The NFPI on average lead time may conflict with that of stock turnover because the lead time improvement could entail holding more stock. This could have a further impact on space and cash. Another, also to the detriment of cash, would be giving longer credit in an attempt to increase sales; this might increase bad debts too. There are many such similar examples.

The selection of performance indicators, therefore, must be a thorough and detailed process with all possible outcomes predicted and accounted for. Any detrimental effects elsewhere need to be assessed and if necessary new targets set. It is a process that can easily be underestimated; on the surface it appears to be very simple to construct a PI but in reality it can be complex, and the consequences of getting it wrong may have serious adverse effects.

This chapter is not a guide to the selection of performance indicators or their qualities, attributes, and efficacy, but the subject is included because of the potential correlations between your NFPIs and your graphical management accounts, more specifically the links between your financial and non-financial measures and the way they are presented. It examines what advantages there may be in using the principles of the method of presentation of management accounts as described in this book to your NFPIs too. It is just as important to present NFPIs to managers effectually as it is with management accounts.

There is a wealth of material available on the subject of non-financial performance indicators (NFPIs), sometimes known and divided by the terms key performance indicators (KPIs), performance indicators (PIs), key results indicators (KRIs, usually associated with the balanced scorecard), performance ratios/metrics, and business indicators. There are differences between these terms, although a definition that clearly differentiate them from each other is hard to find. This probably means there may be fuzzy lines between them and many put their own definitions on them. In essence, however, KRIs are distilled from or the result of a number of KPIs and are largely for top-level management consumption. KPIs are for middle management and PIs for lower management. It is clear from this that each addresses the responsibilities of each level of management.

The published material available on this subject, referred to above, covers the choice, range, type, design, and application of NFPIs to all types of organizations and from many viewpoints. It is a subject that has been well covered in the business press, and there are in excess of 26,000 publications revealed in an Amazon search for "performance indicators" should you want to study it further.

All we shall deal with here are some basics that are relevant to the objectives of this chapter.

The choice of NFPIs is critical to their success, and it is here that many initiatives fail even before they get started. It is essential that these vital decisions, taken at the start of the process, are driven and linked to an organization's strategy, value/business drivers, and objectives. It is important that managers drill down to the essential mechanics of the organization to what makes it tick. While it may be helpful to examine available models to obtain a guide, managers must understand that there is no standard approach. These indicators are bespoke to each organization; even organizations that operate in the same area of activity may have different value drivers.

Managers must also be aware that the choice of performance measures is not a once-and-for-all exercise, it is a dynamic process. Measures may be appropriate today, but the system needs to be continually reassessed as strategies and competitive environments evolve. There is also a tendency to overdo the number of measures; "less can often be more."

There is a good example of the selection of performance indicators that illustrates how powerful the selection of the right indicator can be:

As a result of dissatisfaction with the organization's NFPIs, a former chairman of British Airways, Lord King, employed consultants to help determine the key indicators that he should use to turn around his ailing business. The consultants reported that the only key element that he should focus on was meeting planned departure/arrival times of BA's aircraft. To begin with he felt he had been let down by this advice since it was common knowledge in the industry that this was an important factor. He was hoping for something new, something more complex and clever. However, the consultants insisted that this couldn't be bettered and told him to concentrate his attention on late flights, so he agreed to be notified whenever an aircraft was delayed by more than two hours at any airport in the world and that whenever this happened Lord King should personally telephone the controller at that location to find out why the delay had occurred. It wasn't long before BA aircraft had a reputation for leaving and arriving on time.

Some airlines' top management had tended to overcomplicate the issue by measuring associated factors such as costs of emergency accommodation for passengers due to aircraft delays, consequent airport surcharges, customer dissatisfaction, extra aircraft fuel usage because of circling the destination airport due to late arrival, or higher aircraft speeds to make up for the delay. BA's one recommended key measure for the top manager covered all these matters. The only really important factor for them was the final "outcome"; all other indicators, while useful to those local controllers and at lower levels of management, were not necessary at the top. In fact they would only have served to confuse top management. How were they to know how to prioritize these factors? Nor did they have the knowledge to suggest appropriate solutions. In fact, solving these various problems and using these NFPIs was the job of the local controller and his staff, top management would have been guilty of micromanagement had they attempted to do so. Although this seems an obvious senior-management error, it is surprising how often it happens. There is a tendency for senior managers to "wade in" without considering the consequences or thought for the motivation of the less senior manager whose responsibility it is to solve the problem.

Another example of how powerful indicators can be was within one of the companies formerly managed by me. In this case the company was attempting to persuade users of certain types of products that a central nationwide delivery could be more efficient than the customary practice of the product being sourced from a distributor local to the user. To begin with, a small discount was offered if the product was not delivered the following day, our investigations had established that modern distribution services could achieve a very reliable next-day delivery service. However, this discount offer had little effect on the habits of the user whose customary practice of buying local had been established for decades and who firmly believed that it was impossible to compete with a local distributor on delivery. The fact that a local distributor held limited stocks when a central warehouse could hold considerably more seemed to cut little ice with the customer.

Considerable research indicated that manufacturers selling direct had a bad reputation for service and delivery, not just in our industry but generally, and this was adding to the customer's belief. We formed a new company within the group with an entirely different customer service staff, with a new customer service director recruited from outside that introduced a new ethos; the company name did not immediately connect it with the manufacturing company but it did include the word "direct."

Much publicity took place for the wide range of stocked items and next-day delivery; working partnerships were formed with selected distribution services. But the crowning part of the offer was that the goods were free if goods did not arrive next day. A simple performance indicator was introduced that reported any instances of failure to the full board the morning following the event. Prior to the introduction of this new next-day-system delivery, failures were reported by reason: lack of stock, goods lost in transit, staff shortage, showed in the stock records but not on the shelf, couldn't locate the customer, weather, and so on. Our top management found that they did not have the knowledge or the time to examine each of these in detail and take the right corrective action; in fact, when they did they often got it wrong. This task was the responsibility of those staff dealing with the issues every day and all that was needed from top management was to empower them to deal with it.

On one occasion, during a winter and after all managers had departed for the night, the warehouse suffered a power failure at a critical time in the evening, just before all the packaging process had been completed and before the deadline arrival time of the delivery contractor. The warehouse was plunged into darkness. In these circumstances many staff would have thrown up their hands and given up; not in this instance. On their own initiative and without any management instruction they brought up a number of cars to the warehouse doors and completed the packaging and parcels in the lights of the car headlights. All deliveries that day went out and were delivered on time. Management had no knowledge of this initiative until the following day.

The system was a huge success; it gave the customer the confidence to deal with a remote supplier for urgent supplies. The success percent rate of delivery on time was in the upper nineties every month and sales grew rapidly. It was not long before the new subsidiary company was the leading distributor on a range of measures from customer service to delivery on time.

There is a common factor in these two examples: the adoption of a simple performance indicator, an outcome reported directly and promptly to top management.

As CEO I also chaired monthly meetings of middle managers comprising the "owners" of the KPIs within the company. Each KPI would be discussed at the meeting and ideas for improvement sought from all parties. Often a KPI in one department affected another and the meeting assisted in the coordination of actions to achieve optimum results. The objective was using the whole team to achieve continuous improvement, and this focus, led by a CEO, achieved considerable success. Such meetings do require careful management. It is vital that such meetings avoid demotivating any staff members;

the generation of team spirit and the avoidance of witch hunts is imperative.

## How NFPIs contribute to financial performance

We have discussed above why it is essential, when choosing NFPIs, for all organizations to be guided by drivers of value such as customer and employee satisfaction and loyalty, innovation, market standing, intellectual property, management development and training, quality, plus a host of other non-financial issues. These aspects of a business do not lend themselves directly to individual financial measurement but nevertheless they are critical to an organization's success and must be monitored and assessed accordingly. It is evident in today's commercial environment that the source of value in an organization has shifted from tangible to intangible assets, and these are not easy to measure in financial terms. Consider the flow chart in Fig. 6.1.

*Fig. 6.1*

This flow chart contains a number of non-financial processes contributing toward the financial values of sales revenue and lower cost. None of the processes are easily valued in financial terms but all are relevant to an improvement in sales revenue and cost efficiency. It is this correlation and balance between financial and non-financial measures that provides management with the full picture.

It is also important to understand that NFPIs are used increasingly in the setting of budgets. They are now commonly used to model resource requirements, and this leads to an evaluation of necessary costs to achieve NFPI targets.

*Linking non-financial and financial measures*

There are definite and critical comparisons to be made between individual NFPIs and financial measures and these should be sought out by every organization and reported upon regularly. It may also be more than a one-to-one comparison requiring visual examination of a number of measures together, financial and non-financial.

Research carried out by Mercer Consulting found that 50 percent of organizations do not use NFPIs to drive financial performance, and Wharton/PWC found that an astounding 79 percent have not attempted to validate the linkages between their NFPIs and future financial results. To link the two measures appears an obvious corollary to the production of an NFPI, and it is therefore a major omission by the majority of organizations. It might be speculated to what extent this is due to a failure of finding ways of *presenting* the two types of measures so that this linkage is better perceived or it may be that some just find it too difficult. This is not surprising; it is hard sometimes to find reliable links. These problems will be explored below.

*Comparing NFPIs with financial measures*

To enable effective and simple comparisons of NFPIs with management accounts, it is essential to present the data in similar ways. But how many actually do this? It is common to find NFPIs presented as tables, dashboards, balanced scorecards, histograms, graphs, and pie charts, all within one organization. Very often this is done for visual effect rather than from consideration of how best to present them as a tool for making better decisions. There may be occasions when it is appropriate to "dress up" indicators for a specific purpose, but this can be inappropriate when using them as a management tool. Many omit to consider that the essential reason for most NFPIs is to foster continuous improvement, and to achieve this the latest result must be put in context; it must consider past results, as well as assist in making decisions for the future, and in this respect it is no different from the needs of good management accounts.

NFPIs must show *trends*. Not only does this indicate improving or deteriorating performance, it also aids the essential comparison of related financial and non-financial information. For example, has extending credit (average credit period)-been of influence in sales income? If stocks are rising but sales are static or slowing does this indicate a failure to hold the right stocks? There are also many measurement relationships that are inversely related as well as those that move in sympathy; e.g. spending more on quality inspection to reduce warranty costs. It must also be recognized that there is often no immediate reaction from a financial measure following an improvement or deterioration in a NFPI; it is more common to find a delayed reaction, and this is far more visible in both magnitude and timing when each measure is presented in graphical trend from over a long period than when presented in purely numeric format. Of course it is not only the comparison between financial and non-financial measures that is important but between different NFPIs as well, so a common format is important for this exercise too. There are some definite comparisons to be made between financial and non-financial measures, ones that are directly related, but there are also tenuous ones too. For example, just because income is rising it does not mean that this is due solely to an improvement in delivery lead times or a recent advertising campaign; there are a host of reasons that may have contributed to such an improvement and no one can be sure what sales would have been if these other initiatives had not been taken. It is easy for management to jump to conclusions when such tenuous relationships exist and natural that they will want to believe their initiatives have made the improvement. In these circumstances judgments can be clouded. Such linkages will therefore need to be viewed with caution, careful judgment, and objectivity. Reliable forecasting within the management accounts may assist such comparisons; these may take account of the additional factors affecting sales before those resulting from the initiative are superimposed.

*Management account and NFPI trends are different from other systems*

It is easy to jump to the conclusion that this joint financial/non-financial approach is really just a balanced scorecard or dashboard in another guise, but there is a distinct difference between these two approaches. In the case of balanced scorecards the objective is to combine NFPIs and financial measures and targets, at one point in time, in one easily understood document that focuses on the achievement of predetermined strategy. The end result of the balanced scorecard or dashboard is not to replace management accounts and associated NFPIs or necessarily directly correlate the two types of measure; it is to provide a summary of recognized measures that are key to the achievement of the organization's strategic objectives. There is, therefore, no competition between the graphical presentation of trends in management accounts/NFPIs and balanced scorecards/dashboards; they are complementary. The graphical presentations proposed in this book show more detail: trends, budget variances, and forecasts, and so may provide explanations of the data contained in the scorecards. These three features of graphical management accounts are critical to prompting more informed and prompter management action. They tackle the long-held criticism that management accounts are too late and too historical for the current era.

*You can have too many performance indicators (PIs)*

The range of NFPIs is wide and the choice can be perplexing. Consider this list of topics. Within each heading there are scores of possible subjects

- Compliance, government and legal
- Customer service and loyalty
- Human resources
- Marketing
- Information technology
- Sustainability

- Health and safety
- Property and facilities
- Procurement
- Suppliers, outsourcing, and supply chain
- Quality improvement
- Innovation
- Inventory and logistics
- The Web, social media, and E-business

It is clear that the initial choice of NFPIs can be bewildering and it is easy to allow them to proliferate. This must be avoided. Focus must be maintained on the key drivers. It is not astute to swamp managers with too many NFPIs. There is no magic number, but clearly the more measures the less time there will be to devote to improving each one, and there is a good chance the important ones may slide down the list of priority.

Nor is the number of measures chosen at the outset a once-and-for-all exercise. It is an ongoing process, because as circumstances change PIs tend to be added rather than taken away. It is therefore important to re-evaluate the relevance and value of each indicator periodically and always consider the cost of producing the statistic; it is usually not cheap and the more things you measure the more it costs.

## Ownership of PIs

It is also essential that PIs can be tied down to an individual, usually the leader of the team concerned. Any NFPI that cannot be tied down in this way can lead to a blame culture. Ownership is critical but make sure that the "owner" has control and can influence the factors that make up the measure, ensure that factors outside their control are attended to, and strongly discourage a "throw the problem over the fence" attitude.

*Commonality of time scales*

We have establishes that if a NFPI is to be linked to a financial measure within graphical management accounts or another NFPI, then it should be presented in the same way. The horizontal time axis should follow the same timeframe. Since that recommended for management accounts is the current financial year, the previous year, and the following year, then this should be the timescale chosen. Not to do so will be to abandon the main advantage of adopting similar formats for each. This is not to say that all NFPIs will be correlated with sections of the management accounts, and therefore this time span will not always be applicable; however, this timescale does provide a reasonable historic trend and room to add forecasts that will be dealt with later.

Note that it may also be necessary to adapt the management account graphs to present the financial values relevant to the NFPIs chosen; i.e., to consider cost groupings and ensuring that certain types of cost as displayed in Fig. 2.1 in chapter 2 are segregated.

*Units of measure*

The vertical value axis, however, may be in value, volume, or percentage to suit the NFPI. For example, value of debtors over three months old will clearly be in value, while number of customer complaints may be in volume and product returns may be expressed in percentages. *The objective is the comparison of* trends *of the NFPI and financial value* and therefore to what extent the trends of the NFPI are influential on financial performance.

*How the trend for NFPIs is calculated*

When calculating a trend in an NFPI, the methods previously suggested for the management accounts—twelve-month rolling totals—may not be applicable. It may be necessary to use twelve-month rolling "averages" (as distinct from totals) or just the monthly figures themselves without any rolling totals being applied, or even shorter-period rolling totals. If percentages are used, then remember the rules in chapter 2 regarding averaging percentages.

The application of rolling totals or rolling averages would occur when seasonal factors or a frequent incidence of peaks and troughs affect the NFPI, because these virtually eliminate seasonal affects. However, if there are no seasonal factors, then the monthly (or other period chosen) value/numeric itself may be sufficient. The fact that an organization as a whole may be financially seasonal does not necessarily mean that all NFPIs are seasonal. This will require careful consideration when the NFPI is designed.

## The frequency of NFPIs

Some businesses operate a twenty-four-hour business cycle (e.g., bakeries) and a monthly indicator would be of limited value as a management tool. Where it is considered relevant to link such NFPIs with periodic management accounts, they may be averaged (weighted or not) or sometimes simply totaled for monthly graphical purposes so that format similarity is maintained with the management accounts.

## The incorporation of targets and forecasts into graphical presentations of NFPIs

Graphical representations of management accounts incorporate budgets and forecasts; these "titles" are not directly attributable to NFPIs, at least not in so many words. However, NFPIs often have targets and expected outcomes attached to them and it would therefore be valuable to incorporate targets and forecasts within graphs of the NFPIs. The three-year time span of the graphs used in management accounts will facilitate this.

As with all performance measures, NFPIs are prepared not just to monitor performance, but to drive improvement too. These often involve changing systems and methods or making further investment, and if time and money are being invested then some forecast of outcome, goal, or ambition should be displayed in the

NFPI graph together with progress toward achieving it. How can an investment be justified if a target has not been set? The projected goals effectively become the "budget" and the extended trends of expected performance become the "forecast," so mimicking the management accounts and adding to the value and comprehension of the measure and its comparisons with its sister financial measure; the performance gaps, present and future, will be starkly evident. It is also recommended that earlier forecasts are kept on the chart in the same way as depicted in the chapter 4. The accuracy of what was forecast three, six, or nine months before can be tested, and it leads to questions of why previous forecasts were either over ambitious or under estimates.

## NFPIs and better budgeting and forecasting

It will be found that NFPIs can often be of value in creating more accurate financial forecasts. In view of the delayed reaction of financial measures arising from movements in related NFPIs, the actual and forecast trend in the NFPI can be used to forecast the future financial result, often with more accuracy than other methods. NFPIs can be easier to predict than a simple financial forecast.

Forecasts should therefore not be produced in isolation when relevant NFPIs are available to assist the process.

In summary, there is much to be gained from consistency in the presentation of financial and non-financial measures, and the addition of targets and forecasts to NFPIs adds considerably to their value. It is essential to review the relevance, number, and effects of your performance indicators regularly. Ask yourself whether the balance between financial and non-financial is right and whether it facilitates comparisons; whether your measures help you to predict the future as well as see the past and whether your measures are assisting and encouraging your staff to do the things you want them to do.

*Balance sheets*

The first thing a trainee accountant is taught when his/her studies turn to the production of management/financial accounts is that a profit-and-loss account is for *a period of time,* and a balance sheet is struck *at a moment in time.* This factor, in itself, provides a clue to the application of twelve-month rolling totals to capital items on a balance sheet. It is possible to monitor trends in balance sheet entries but a twelve-month rolling total approach is not appropriate; a balance sheet item is stated at a "moment in time," it is not accumulated in the same way as that of a revenue item that appears in a profit-and-loss account, so totaling twelve months' values is inapplicable and plotted values would be meaningless. There may be some value in using rolling *averages* for certain lines on a balance sheet; this may apply to stock levels, for example, but even this has weaknesses. The rolling average calculated month on month will provide a trend, but unlike a twelve-month rolling total in a profit-and-loss account that will always provide an annual total comparable to the financial year, the twelve-month rolling average in a balance sheet provides a hybrid figure that will not provide a view of the current position.

If readers want to monitor trends in balance sheets it may be better to utilize graphs over the same timeframe but simply plot monthly values. The volatility of values is likely to be less than in those within a P&L account and any seasonality should be visible; e.g., stock build up in readiness for busy sales periods such as Christmas.

Other common methods for monitoring balance sheet performance may be more appropriate. Balance sheet or accounting ratios are commonly used and it is possible to monitor these graphically where it is felt necessary, but again it is likely that a simple monthly or quarterly plot would be adequate for the examination of trends.

The methods outlined in this book, therefore, are designed for use with revenue accounts like the profit-and-loss account or income and expenditure accounts.

# CHAPTER 7
# Final Thoughts

All the evidence indicates that the accountancy profession is slow to change; there are many aged practices still in general use: double-entry bookkeeping from the thirteenth century; job, order, and product costing with allocations of overhead costs; allowances for wastage and shrinkage and elements of rudimentary standard costing from the eighteenth century; costing methods introduced by engineers in the nineteenth century; budgeting from the 1920s; and a presentation format of management accounts that dates back about four decades.

All these are still thriving today.

There aren't many professions that are this slow to develop or introduce step changes, despite the fast pace, rapid shifting, instant communication, short business cycle and electronic world in which we live today that demands so much more from managers. Accountants have embraced IT to speed up accounting processes and make their life easier, and it's true to say that accounting reports are more prolific and much neater with the coming of spreadsheets and other software, but it still takes up to two weeks and more at the end of each month to produce the management accounts, two to three months to produce a budget and about three months to produce the end-of-year accounts, all of which are history by the time they are presented. Modern-day accounting still focuses on data that can't be changed, measuring what has already happened, and as we all know you can't change the past. This just isn't enough for today's world.

But as we have seen, you can use history to identify which way you are headed and at what rate, as well as helping to forecast the future, guiding managers toward prevention rather than cure. This moves the accountant toward financial control rather than financial reporting.

But hold on, I hear the accountants shout, "What about the balanced scorecard, lean accounting, dashboards, enterprise resource management, enterprise performance management, activity-based costing, and non-financial performance indicators? And that's just for starters. We've led the way with these changes." N.B.: I can't be sure whether all these were inspired by accountants. They are admittedly good advances, but have they really thrived? Have they led to significant, widespread change across the profession? The balanced scorecard was introduced over ten years ago and has probably received more exposure through the media than any other new management information technique. It was meant to be the answer to flawed budgeting, historic financial information, and monitoring strategic plans, but despite its publicity and all the accolades it has not been adopted on a widespread basis. Most organizations, by far, still stick to their age-old defective and inadequate budgeting processes, their outdated financial-reporting system, and a range of miscellaneous performance indicators not designed to address the achievement of the organization's strategy. Many consultants and software houses have probably made a living from these new techniques and many organizations are using them satisfactorily today, but why are they not commonplace?

Is it accountants that stand in the way of change or the lack of demand from senior management?

These days the life of many in-house accountants is taken up with new legislation, changing regulations, standard practices, new procedures, complex tax issues, and a host of other red tape that take their time away from their core function. And this may be a factor, but it surely goes further than this. If you really want or need to make a change then being busy doesn't usually stand in the way.

Accountancy is a profession that takes many years of study before a qualification is awarded. Like doctors and lawyers, but unlike a degree, this award can be removed if an individual is found to be bringing the profession into disrepute, and this effectively ends a career. While this is a rare event, it does loom in the background, like an axe over the head, and as an accountant myself I never really lost consciousness of it. It introduces a note of caution into an accountant's behavior. This shouldn't prevent accountants from introducing new ideas, but perhaps this foreboding does imbue something into an accountant's psyche, a natural caution. This can also be frustrating to an accountant's colleagues and lead to an attitudinal problem within a management team. Is an accountant sometimes seen to be holding back new ideas, always expounding the negative? Sometimes it must seem this way, but does this attitude among peers constrain an accountant's own inventiveness and innovation? Or worse, is such inventiveness from an accountant, on a subject outside his or her skill set, always taken seriously? Speaking from personal experience, this happened to me many times when engineers effectively dismissed my ideas about their subject: "He's just an accountant, what does he know about engineering?" It wasn't voiced in these terms but my ideas were mostly disregarded, and this did have a restraining influence on my enthusiasm for making suggestions. Perhaps this tells its own story, that accountants, usually intelligent, thoughtful individuals quite capable of innovation, have had their ideas quashed or discouraged. Is this why management accounts have not improved for forty years, failing to adapt to the modern age, falling short of the needs of today's managements?

I am not suggesting that an accountant should attempt a transformation of character. The qualities of integrity and independence instilled during an accountant's training are important elements of a management team, which must have balance across its members. Ideas that are challenged constructively usually makes them better and more sustainable. In addition, assessing risk, particularly to the cash balance, is very much an accountant's job, and this in itself can sometimes disappoint other team members; when risks are highlighted they don't always receive the welcome they deserve.

There is another factor to consider. An accountant has always had ownership of the historic results, this has been their domain, they have needed no input from outside their departments when it comes to historic accounting. Budgets and forecasts, however, have been partly in the hands of "others," accountants can't produce these by themselves. These "others" have an essential role in these functions, and without their cooperation and time it would be hard for an accountant to make changes that may lead to these "others" investing more time. While annual budgets are a necessary evil for most managers, updating them midstream, despite a clear necessity, is not something in their agendas, and revised forecasts every quarter may fill them with dread.

The ideas and the resulting system outlined in this book were introduced by me long after my days as a financial controller, but even as a CEO it was not easy to persuade my colleagues of the potential of the new system entailing significant changes to our management accounting systems. Interestingly it was middle management that received the ideas with most enthusiasm and it was only when they were asked their views that they too expressed deep dissatisfaction with the management accounts they were presented with; these opinions had never been voiced before. My later research found that the same dissatisfaction from middle managers was widespread.

I do wonder now whether if I had still been the CFO instead of the CEO the idea would have come to fruition. It was surprising that most of the lack of enthusiasm came from the most senior managers.

There are many reasons why a manager is driven to find new ways of doing things. In my case it was pure frustration and irritation with the time absorbed by discussing history at board meetings that caused my "thinking cap" to activate; this was time we were not devoting to the most important issues facing us. I thought it essential to find a better way. It was necessary for our organization to improve its planning processes, and as they say "necessity is the mother of invention." There is an apt opening to the stories of Winnie the Pooh that perhaps sums this up. If you remember the picture in the book, he was being dragged downstairs by his foot by his owner Christopher Robin.

"Here is Edward Bear, coming downstairs, going *bump, bump, bump* on the back of his head. But sometimes he feels that there must be another way, if only he could just stop bumping his head and think about it."

I had been in this "head bumping" situation for many years. There was just too much to do to stop and think.

The ideas in this book are not revolutionary. There is nothing contained here that required the arrival of a genius. The use of trends to monitor progress and the incorporation of forecasts into management accounts is hardly beyond the wit of most accountants. The balanced scorecard required far more ingenuity than this but its implementation is more difficult because it was promoted alongside a recommendation of abandoning the customary, familiar budget and introducing a range of new unfamiliar NFPIs. This was a revolutionary idea. The balanced scorecard also requires a degree of fashioning and adaptation to suit the target organization, and this, alongside a move away from "trusty" budgets, takes great courage. Remember, accountants are cautious individuals.

Sometimes the simple ideas are the best ones.

None of the downsides to the radical changes needed for the like of the balanced scorecard are attributable to the graphical presentation of trends in the management accounts. The system does not propose to renounce budgets or introduce culture change, it is merely a change in presentation with more regular forecasting, and this can be introduced by any organization that produces management accounts anywhere in world without any risk or disruption. And it is reiterated, this new mode of presentation does not replace any other performance measures, it complements them.

While it is accountants that should grasp the initiative on this matter because it is they who can coordinate and complete the "number crunching," the instigation of this system can equally come from the CEO or indeed any other senior manager. Frankly, it doesn't matter who it is, they just need to step out of their comfort zone and get a grip of the situation and reassess the critical functions of budgeting and forecasting if they are to make progress. They need to sell new ideas to their colleagues, find new ways of proving that better management information systems will help the team to perform more effectively, and they need to find champions to the cause. They need to persuade their colleagues that the use of trends displayed graphically not only improves the comprehension of this vital financial report, it also enables them to challenge inaccurate budgeting and forecasting and improve their accuracy.

The non-accounting colleagues of financial controllers need to take note, if you restrict your accountant to recording and reporting the power and influence of the accounting function will decline and your organization may suffer as a result. Instead, encourage ideas and innovation from your accountants. Get them more deeply involved.

It is my hope that a wide variety of managers are reading this book and are now persuaded that trends and forecasts will be of significant help to you in the day-to-day management of your departments. They will introduce a new discipline that ensures you are always looking forward. They will assist in the development of strategy as well as prompt earlier action and decisions. Yes, it will require a time investment from you but the dividend that accrues will be more than worth it.

It is essential to recognize that the introduction of regular forecasting is fundamental to gaining full value from this "graphical trends" approach. While its adoption would still constitute a major improvement in the value of management accounts, this would be significantly reduced without the adoption of a good forecasting system; without it there could be a tendency to simply extrapolate the existing trend in the graphs of actual performance, and that would be a bad mistake with potentially dangerous guesswork for all the reasons we went into in chapter 4. Nor should one fail to understand that the development of a forecasting system is the most difficult part of the transformation, it should not be underestimated. There is no need to repeat here the advice given earlier but the difficulty of the task is worth reiterating. It entails recruiting the enthusiasm and time of many managers. An accountant can change the management accounts to the new system without help from any manager but an accountant can't do the same with a forecasting system. Unless managers embrace the need for this and give it their time and support, any regular forecasting system is a nonstarter.

These thoughts may provide an explanation of why the accountancy profession shows reluctance to or is obstructed from making change, but it is difficult to draw a full conclusion over the issue. Accountants are individuals with a broad-based training in business and the needs of managers. Drawing together forecasts and budgets from time to time and the regular production of management accounts is second nature to an accountant, and given the acceptance of regular forecasting linking these processes through trends and their display graphically is not a huge exercise but the will and determination must be there. It is hoped that it is now crystal clear that accountants have to respond to present-day demands and address the criticisms outlined in the introduction to this book. *They must add more value* and it is vital for them to lead initiatives to more accurately predict what might happen in the future.

A step change in management accounting practice is overdue.

Don't, from this diatribe, run away with the view that I believe this new approach to presenting management accounts is the nirvana.

It isn't. It will assist in producing more accurate budgets, forecasts, more control over costs, better strategic decisions, and it will be the vehicle for management accountants to enhance their value. And this is not just good for accountants, it is also better value for money for an organization. You are not stepping into the unknown here. I need to emphasize that these ideas are not theory; they have been tested over many years and have a proven risk-free success. Implement the same ideas and you too will come to realize that it is *only trends that matter.*

Lightning Source UK Ltd.
Milton Keynes UK
UKOW051335060213

205922UK00001B/76/P

9 781466 972957